BAD MEN

BOLLYWOOD'S ICONIC VILLAINS

ROSHMILA BHATTACHARYA

RUPA

Published by
Rupa Publications India Pvt. Ltd 2024
7/16, Ansari Road, Daryaganj
New Delhi 110002

Sales centres:
Bengaluru Chennai Hyderabad
Jaipur Kathmandu Kolkata
Mumbai Prayagraj

P-ISBN: 978-93-6156-160-3
E-ISBN: 978-93-6156-496-3

First impression 2024

10 9 8 7 6 5 4 3 2 1

The moral right of the author has been asserted.

Printed in India

To my husband, Pallab, the good man
in my life who pretends to be bad.

❧

CONTENTS

INTRODUCTION

THE GALLERY OF ROGUES

'Nayak nahin, khalnayak hoon main.'

—*Khal Nayak* (1993)

A text no less than the Ramayana underscores the sheer undeniability of the villain—where there is a Rama, there is a Ravana too. It's a given that in any dramatic conflict, be it on stage or on screen, good is always pitted against evil. 'In Hindi films, this becomes a fight between the *nayak* [hero] and the *khalnayak* [villain]', Subhash Ghai points out to me. The producer-director, down the years, has given us many unforgettable khalnayaks, from Lion in *Kalicharan* (1976) and the chillingly mute Sir Judah in *Karz* (1980) to Dr Dang in *Karma* (1986), *Ram Lakhan*'s (1989) 'Bad Man', and Sanjay Dutt in and as *Khal Nayak* (1993).

Whether they come out of real life or a writer's imagination, the black deeds and blacker souls of these blackguards have made it difficult to banish them from memory. The dark-skinned *rakshasa*s (demons) of our mythology, who battled the devas (gods), mutated into the tyrannical *gora*s (white-skinned, a moniker for British officers), who made life hell for our fiery nationalists in pre-Independence India. Even after India attained Independence, these despots continued to rule on screen.

One actor who portrayed such despots is Robert John 'Bob' Christo. A civil engineer, Bob was on his way to Muscat when he turned up at a shoot near Bombay's (now Mumbai) Churchgate station to meet Parveen Babi, whose picture he had seen on the cover of a magazine back home in Australia. Reportedly, he was disappointed because without make-up, the Indian actress looked nothing like his glamorous dream girl; but Parveen and he quickly became buddies, and Bob stayed back in India to make a name for himself as a Bollywood villain. Debuting as a magician in Sanjay Khan's *Abdullah* (1980), Bob Christo worked in almost 200 films, including *Qurbani* (1980), *Kaalia* (1981), *Namak Halaal* (1982), *Mard* (1985) and *Mr. India* (1987). As Michael in *Kaalia*, he tells a crippled prisoner in jail, '*Hum jahan khade hote hain line vahin se shuru hoti hai* [The line starts from where I stand].' Even as the other prisoners scurry to queue up behind him, Amitabh Bachchan's Kaalia challenges the big man, mouthing the same line and turning it into a cult dialogue.

Another name that comes to mind is Brian Glover. The Yorkshireman, a professional wrestler, appeared on stage, in commercials, on television, and in films like *The First Great Train Robbery* (1978), *An American Werewolf in London* (1981) and Alien 3 (1992). India remembers him as the much-hated General Douglas in Vidhu Vinod Chopra's *1942: A Love Story* (1994).

Then, of course, there is Paul Blackthorne's Captain Andrew Russell who leads the English cricket team in Ashutosh Gowariker's *Lagaan: Once Upon a Time in India* (2001), eventually losing to Aamir Khan's bedraggled band. The British actor spent three months learning Hindi, along with cricket and horse riding.

After the goras, the 'haves' were the villains for the 'have-nots' in rural India. The *zamindar*s (landlords) and the *sahukaar*s (moneylenders), whose vaults were full and hearts empty, routinely tortured the peasants, whose debts put them at the mercy of these Shylocks. Kanhaiyalal Chaturvedi's loan shark in Mehboob Khan's *Aurat* (1940), who preys on a hapless widow (played by Sardar Akhtar), offering food and medicines for her starving, ailing children in return for his pound of flesh, is a perfect example. The actor earned the odium of the spectators, and over the next 18 years, appeared in over 60 films, playing the slimy sahukaar, the crafty *munim* (accountant) and the corrupt pandit (priest). For *Mother India* (1957), the colour remake of *Aurat*, producer-director Mehboob Khan went with an entirely new cast but retained Kanhaiyalal, immortalizing Sukhilala and setting the yardstick for similar roles that followed, including Paresh Rawal's Bhanu in *Ram Lakhan* (1989).

As India moved to the cities, urbanization brought along a new set of villains who crawled out of their underworld dens to loot and scoot. K.N. Singh, who had played the vengeful dacoit Jagga in *Awaara* (1951), metamorphosed into the smuggler Gonsalves in *Detective* (1958). The actor might have contested in the Berlin Olympics, studied law in London, or joined the army had Prithviraj Kapoor not drawn him into showbiz. He became the highest-paid villain of his time, and in the 250-odd films that he appeared, he was always immaculately dressed in a suit, an overcoat and a hat, puffing on a cigarette or a pipe.

K.N. Singh never raised his voice or got abusive. His brand of villainy—quiet, without heat—was carried forward by Pran, Ajit, Madan Puri and Iftekhar. In a career spanning five decades, Iftekhar was often seen as a cop in films like

Shree 420 (1955), *Teesri Manzil* (1966), *Ittefaq* (1969), *Zanjeer* (1973) and *Don* (1978). Sometimes, though, the lines got blurred, like when Inspector Bhupendra Singh turned out to be the venomous criminal Black Cobra in *Khel Khel Mein* (1975).

One of my favourite gangsters is Sir Judah, whose genesis dates back to the '70s. On the set of the Punjabi film *Sherni* (1973), a young actor, none other than Subhash Ghai, wooed Prem Nath with his singing and tabla playing. Three years later, when his 'Sonny', as he called Ghai, approached him for his debut directorial, the senior actor was quick to give his nod to the role of Inspector General P.N. Khanna in *Kalicharan* (1976). 'He even suggested we title the film after his character, even though it featured Shatrughan Sinha in a double role of the criminal Kalicharan who, on the behest of the Inspector General of Police, masquerades as his lookalike, the slain cop Prabhakar, to unmask the wily villain, Lion,' the filmmaker recounts.

Five years later, Subhash Ghai returned to his 'swami-ji' (which is how he addressed Prem Nath) to ask him to play a don, GNK, in his next film, *Vishwanath* (1978). Soon after followed *Karz* (1980), Ghai's first production under the Mukta Arts banner, which brought along a new godfather. The reincarnation drama revolves around a popstar, Monty, played by Rishi Kapoor, with Simi Garewal as Kamini, his murderous wife from a previous birth. Prem Nath had heard about the film from his nephew Rishi and called up the filmmaker to ask, 'Am I in it or not?' When Ghai admitted that he did not have a role for Prem Nath as the film had a female antagonist, the veteran actor warned, 'You are losing a big talent.'

A few weeks later, Subhash Ghai came to him with a character he had specially written for him, telling him that while Sir Judah was supposed to be an international gang lord, he had just three or four scenes and no dialogue. Prem Nath burst out laughing, amused that his Sonny wanted him to play a mute character when he was famous for his booming voice and his distinctive dialogue delivery. However, he accepted the film after making the filmmaker promise to take care of him. Determined not to betray his swami-ji's trust, the writer-director continued to flesh out the character, giving him a nameless henchman (Mac Mohan) who interprets the messages Sir Judah taps out on his whisky glass and conveys them. 'It was amazing how well the character worked despite the limited screen time. Sir Judah surpassed all our expectations!' the showman exults today.

After almost three decades, producer Bhushan Kumar decided to remake *Karz* with singer-composer Himesh Reshammiya playing a double role and Gulshan Grover as the iconic villain. While Prem Nath's Sir Judah wears a black wig, a genial smile and a bald pate with a fringe of white hair around it in the climax, Gulshan Grover's Sir Judah sports a shaved head and a white goatee. He taps out his messages on a musical synthesizer attached to a metallic left arm. The performance was appreciated for its novel flourish, but *Karzzzz* (2008) sank faster than the Titanic.

Gulshan Grover's Sir Judah reminds one of Joseph Wiseman's Dr Julius No in the first Bond film, *Dr. No* (1962). The latter, along with Ernst Stavro Blofeld, acted as the inspiration for Kulbhushan Kharbanda's first negative role, Shakaal, in Ramesh Sippy's *Shaan* (1980). Blofeld was a regular Bond villain in films like *Diamonds Are Forever* (1971), *For Your Eyes Only* (1981), *Spectre* (2015) and *No Time to Die* (2021). The master criminal favours jackets without lapels, inspired by Nehru jackets or Mao suits, just like Shakaal, who also inherits the

Bond villain's love for gadgets. He operates from a submarine with sharks swimming outside the window. With a touch of a button, he can open doors and panels on the floor, send chairs spinning and manacle henchmen to their seats while trying to pin the Judas amongst them. Once his suspicion is confirmed, Shakaal mercilessly tips the double-crossing goon straight into a bloodthirsty crocodile's mouth.

Kulbhushan Kharbanda landed his big break after he was spotted in Shyam Benegal's *Manthan* (1976) as an upper-caste sarpanch. At screenwriter Salim Khan's residence, the actor was introduced to director Ramesh Sippy and was signed that very afternoon to play the gangster K.D. Narang in Mushir–Riaz's crime drama *Shakti* (1982). Following this, Ramesh Sippy offered him *Shaan*, leading to the birth of arguably the most famous villain of the time after *Sholay*'s (1975) Gabbar Singh. *Shaan* itself was like a Bond film, with car chases, gadgets, special effects and its techno-whiz villain. However, despite the sky-high expectations, the film sank. But Shakaal lives on, and his words '*Main unko yunhi nahi maar daloonga, bahut khel khel ke maaronga, jaise billi chuhon ko maarti hai* [I won't kill him just like that, I will toy with his life, just like a cat does with a mouse]' remind us of him, *shaan se* (majestically)!

Kader Khan's Supremo in *Parvarish* (1977) is another cool techno villain, dressed in dapper suits, sporting a goatee and sunglasses, and also operating from a submarine. The same year, the actor took on Amitabh Bachchan and Vinod Khanna in another villainous turn in *Khoon Pasina* (1977), this time in a pathani suit, as Thakur Zaalim Singh, the inciter of communal riots. Dialogues like '*Log hamein gunda kehtey hain. Gundon ka mazhab gundagardi hota hai, aur gundagardi mein paap aur punya ki koi jagah nahin hoti*

[People call me a thug, and thuggery is a religion unto itself, one where there's no place for vice and virtue],' flowed from Kader Khan's own pen.

Formerly a professor of civil engineering at a Bombay college, Kader Khan acted in over 300 films, playing characters ranging from Zafar Khan, the obsessive lover of Waheeda Rehman's Salma in *Coolie* (1983), to a diabolical triple role in *Khoon Ka Karz* (1991)—Champaklal, Hitler Champaklal and Ravana Champaklal. He is also memorable as the wily politician in *Insaaf Ki Awaaz* (1986), whose name—Chaurangilal Domukhia—underlines his double-faced nature.

Unscrupulous netas (politicians) have often crossed swords with righteous nayaks. Twenty years after Ram Gopal Varma's cult film *Satya* (1998), Saurabh Shukla's gun-toting Kallu Mama turned into the psychotic, power-hungry Member of Parliament Rameshwar Singh, the don of Sitagarh, in *Raid* (2018). Since he doesn't have the height or physique to intimidate, the actor had got a wig designed for the character. But to his surprise, director Raj Kumar Gupta told him on the first day of shooting that he didn't want him to resort to any artifice that could strike a false note. The actor faced the camera looking the way he does in real life and still managed to make his Tauji a formidable foe.

Talking about appearances, Subhash Ghai recounts how in the late '80s, he was going home at around 2.00 a.m. after a party and was on his way to his car, when Anupam Kher entered the lobby of the five-star hotel. Spotting the filmmaker, the actor started walking towards him purposefully. Having made an applause-worthy debut in *Saaransh* (1984) and bagged the coveted role of Amitabh Bachchan's friend Mahesh Shandilya in *Aakhree Raasta* (1986), he told the filmmaker that he was looking forward to working with him. 'I was intrigued by Anupam's appearance. The soft, handsome face and the confident yet somewhat effeminate gait—I thought he looked perfect for Dr Dang, a somewhat foppish professor and the mastermind of a terrorist organization,' he recalls. The actor was asked to drop by the filmmaker's office at around two in the afternoon the next day. There he was informed, to his delightful surprise, that he would be cast against Dilip Kumar in *Karma* (1986), one of the most-talked-about films of the time. The filmmaker admits that he had not seen *Saaransh*, but he was aware that Anupam Kher was a trained actor from the National School of Drama (NSD) and was confident that he would hold his own against the much-revered older actor. On the set, though, looking at him gazing with wide-eyed awe at the thespian, Ghai wondered momentarily if he had made a mistake. His doubts vanished as Kher sailed through the first 100 feet shot, doing it in one take despite pages of monologue. Even Dilip Kumar, whose slap in the film still resonates in our collective memory, described Anupam Kher as a dangerous actor who would go far. Today, 'Dr Dang' has moved beyond the 'bad man' tag to excel as a comedian, is convincing in strong supporting roles, and has even played the lead in films like *Maine Gandhi Ko Nahin Mara* (2005) and *The Kashmir Files* (2022).

Similar is the story of Raj Babbar, who even today remains unforgettable for his villainous turn as Ramesh Gupta from *Insaf Ka Tarazu* (1980). The scene in his office, in which he compels Padmini Kolhapure's Neeta to strip down to her undergarments and has his way with the terrified teenager after having brutally ravished her sister, Zeenat Aman's Bharti, as revenge for turning him down, is one of the most chilling rape scenes in Hindi cinema. Not surprisingly, the role had been turned down by several top actors when B.R.

Chopra approached Raj Babbar. As an NSD student with a background in theatre, he was not overly concerned about his image. Speaking to Rajat Sharma on his television show *Aap Ki Adalat* in 2016, the actor shared how he had taken his mother to the film's premiere. Since he was fairly new, Babbar went unrecognized, and during the interval, they heard all the abuses being hurled at his character, most of them from women. On their way home, his mother broke down in the cab. Initially, he thought they were tears of joy, till she sobbed, '*Hum kam kha lenge* [We will cut down on food], but *beta* [son], don't do such roles again.' His mother's reaction was validation for the actor, undeniable proof that he had lived the character to perfection. But Raj Babbar quickly moved to playing the hero, only later graduating to character roles with shades of grey.

An actor has many different faces, and five-time National Award-winning actor Prakash Raj has played just about every character conceived for the screen—from a madman who is obsessed with his sister-in-law (*Aasai*, 1995) to the transgender madam of a brothel (*Appu*, 2000), and from God (*Arai En 305-il Kadavul*, 2008) to a cosmic destroyer (*Little John*, 2001). He plays a don, Ghani Bhai, in *Wanted* (2009) and the evil incarnate Jaykant Shikre in *Singham* (2011). In *Dabangg 2* (2012), his gangster-politician Thakur Bachchalal Singh mocks Salman Khan's Robin Hood cop, Chulbul Pandey, '*Bada khiladi hai na tu, toh khel bhi bada hi hoga tere saath* [You are a big player, huh? We will play a big game with you, then].'

The third instalment of the series, *Dabangg 3* (2019), acts like a prequel. In the film, Chulbul, whose real name turns out to be Dhaakad Chand Pandey, goes into a violent flashback to trace the genesis of his enmity with neighbourhood goon

Bali Singh, who had thrown his lover off a cliff, framed him for the murder of her uncle and aunt, and put him behind bars. Telugu superstar Sudeep was brilliant as Bali, but the most remembered antagonist of the franchise is undoubtedly Chedi Singh from the original *Dabangg* (2010). Surprisingly, Sonu Sood had initially turned the role down, dismissing it as one-dimensional, and only came on board after the makers agreed to give Chedi a few laughs.

Chedi Singh is accompanied by a photographer who frequently turns his lens on him and cajoles, '*Bhaiyya-ji, esmile!*' The actor shares that when he moved to Bombay to study electrical engineering, his hostel roommates, who were from Bihar, loved getting themselves clicked. Since the age of selfies was yet to arrive, they hired a photographer to follow them around. Even though the final confrontation between Chulbul and Chedi is brutal, for years Sonu Sood has had strangers coming up to him and saying, '*Bhaiya-ji, esmile!*'

Down the decades, khalnayaks have sprouted with every new film and evolved with the times. Going from symbolizing inequalities in region, religion, caste and class, to trying every trick in the book to keep Romeo and Juliet apart, they have become ruthless in their quest for money, women and power, taking on the law fearlessly. To quote Prem Nath in *Dharmatma* (1975), '*Kanoon... Kanoon... Kanoon... Kaun sa kanoon? Main apne liye khud kanoon hoon* [Law... Law... Law... What law are you talking about? I am the law unto myself]!'

Interestingly, the legacy of villainy often becomes the inheritance of heroes too. The almost triumphant war cry of Sanjay Dutt's Balram Prasad, aka Ballu, '*Nayak nahin, khalnayak hoon main,*' in *Khal Nayak* (1993), has given a fascinating subtext to this section. From the Shahenshah

(Amitabh Bachchan) to the Badshah (Shah Rukh Khan), almost all our leading men have strayed down the wrong path at least once.

The 'good is bad' trend is not new to Hindi cinema. It dates back to the early '40s, with Ashok Kumar bringing the anti-hero into mainstream Hindi cinema with *Kismet* (1943). Interestingly, his desi Robin Hood, Shekhar, a small-time thief who commits one last robbery to finance the surgery that will put his crippled lady love back on her feet, had a role model in the actor's own *parnanu* (maternal great-grandfather). As Ashok Kumar's daughter, the late Bharti, shared, their ancestor Raghu Thakur would boldly ride into wedding *mandap*s and rescue brides from grooms demanding large dowries, finding them better matches.

This, however, didn't appease the guardians of morality in the '40s. 'Which young man would not like to be a criminal and a pickpocket after seeing Ashok Kumar get all this glory and popularity in *Kismet*?' stated a scathing review in the popular magazine *filmindia*.[*] However, despite the criticism, the film enjoyed an uninterrupted run of 192 weeks in Calcutta's (now Kolkata) Roxy Cinema, setting a new box office record. It was one of the top grossers of Hindi cinema and its emboldened leading man turned bad with a vengeance in another Gyan Mukherjee directorial, *Sangram* (1950), playing the wayward son of a cop who is eventually gunned down by his own father after a bloody shoot-out.

Sangram was another blockbuster, but it was pulled out of the theatres in its sixteenth week of playing to a full house. Morarji Desai, the then chief minister of Maharashtra, even

---

*Bhattacharya, Roshmila, 'Kismet: The Biggest Blockbuster before "Sholay"', *Times Entertainment*, 7 October 2014, https://tinyurl.com/4pxntjym. Accessed on 10 June 2024.

sent the police commissioner of Bombay across to Ashok's home to counsel him. He was told that as a youth icon, he should not play a profligate. After that, the actor stayed true to the insipid role of the hero, but bored with the same old beats of the good side, he would stray occasionally.

He gambled with the intriguing courtroom drama *Kanoon* (1960), in which he plays the presiding judge who turns out to be the real murderer in a murder trial. In *Bhai-Bhai* (1956), he plays the virtuous older brother who suddenly abandons his wife and child for another woman. His tour de force, though, was undoubtedly the invisible intellectual villain of *Jewel Thief* (1967). By then, however, memories of *Kismet*'s thief had faded and, as director Vijay Anand had known, when Ashok Kumar was unmasked in the last reel, it was a huge surprise for the audience, even though the credits themselves stated, 'Ashok Kumar in and as Jewel Thief.'

Dev Anand, the producer and leading man of *Jewel Thief*, had watched *Kismet* four times at Bombay's Roxy Cinema. He himself had gambled in *Baazi* (1951), and played a smuggler in *Jaal* (1952), a pickpocket in *Pocket Maar* (1956), and a black marketeer in *Kala Bazar* (1960). However, the real challenge was the Hindi-English bilingual *Guide* (1965) and its tourist guide Raju, who lures away Rosie, the young wife of an archaeologist, with promises of stardom, lives off her earnings, is thrown in jail for forgery, battles penury, then tries to pass off as a holy man before finally finding redemption and salvation. 'People called me mad. They said the Indian masses would never accept a film like *Guide*. It had sex. It had adultery. But one has to have an element of madness to do something out of the ordinary,' Dev Anand admitted later.

It takes conviction to walk a different path. According to the producer of *Baazigar* (1993), Ratan Jain, Shah Rukh Khan showed it early in his career by immediately agreeing to play Ajay Sharma, aka Vicky Malhotra, in the film—a role turned down by both Salman Khan and Anil Kapoor, who did not want to go against their image as heroes. Like Ashok Kumar, Shah Rukh Khan is credited with bringing the anti-hero back into mainstream Bollywood in the '90s with this Indianized adaptation of the Hollywood thriller *A Kiss Before Dying* (1956). The film was a surprise blockbuster and put him on the path to superstardom.

However, Shah Rukh himself didn't think of Ajay/Vicky as the villain despite him scheming, swindling and even killing three innocent people. For him, it was revenge for the deaths of his father and sister, and the suffering his mother had endured—a personal angst that benefitted no one in the end. I still remember his parting words to me during a 1998 interview for *Zee Premiere* on the subject, that Vicky could be sitting next to me in a bus and I wouldn't even suspect he was planning to make this our last ride. They still send a shiver down my spine. The performance fetched Shah Rukh the Filmfare Award for Best Actor. He was also nominated for another Black Lady that evening, this one for Best Performance in a Negative Role for Yash Chopra's *Darr* (1993). The role of Rahul, an obsessive, vicious man in love, is another one that came to him after it was turned down by Ajay Devgn and Sanjay Dutt, and Aamir Khan opted out of the film.

The next year, he played another obsessive psychopath in *Anjaam* (1994), originally titled *Maznoon—Majnu Ka Junoon*. The Rahul Rawail-directed psychological thriller was the first negative role Shah Rukh had signed, even before *Baazigar* or *Darr*, and it completed a terrifying trilogy for him, bagging him the Filmfare Award for Best Performance in a Negative Role. It also started a trend of newcomers being launched as

villains—case in point, Arbaaz Khan in *Daraar* (1996), which
was inspired by the Hollywood hit *Sleeping with the Enemy*
(1991). Shah Rukh had once pointed out to me during an
interview that one wouldn't call Anthony Hopkins the villain
of *The Silence of the Lambs* (1991) or Robert De Niro the
antagonist of *Cape Fear* (1991). He had a point. The lines
between the nayak and the khalnayak were getting so blurred
it was getting difficult to distinguish the hero from the villain.

In the climax of *Baazigar*, Shah Rukh Khan's fatally
wounded Vicky lies with his head cradled in his mother's
lap and says, '*Maa mujhe apni bahon mein samet le, apne
anchal mein chupa le maa, main bachpan se tere pyar ke
liye taras raha hoon maa, ab main jee bhar ke sona chahta
hoon...* [Mother, envelop me in your arms, hide me in the
folds of your sari, I have been craving for your love ever since
childhood, now let me sleep peacefully]'. The scene feels like it
has been taken straight out of *Deewaar*'s (1975) finale, where
Amitabh Bachchan's fatally wounded Vijay gasps, '*Main thak
gaya hoon maa, zindagi se ladte ladte thak gaya hoon, ek
baar mujhe sula de maa, sab theek ho jayega maa...* [I am
tired, mother, tired of fighting life, put me to sleep one last
time, mother, everything will be all right then]'.

It also brings back memories of Jyoti Swaroop's *Parwana*
(1971). In the film, Amitabh Bachchan played the murderer
Kumar Sen and was told that he was a perfect villain. He went
on to become the 'angry young man' of Hindi cinema who
voiced the collective anger and resentment simmering in
the '70s and the '80s with films like *Zanjeer* (1973), *Deewaar*
(1975), *Sholay* (1975), *Trishul* (1978), *Laawaris* (1981), *Shakti*
(1982) and *Inquilaab* (1984). But he was never considered a
villain, not even when he turned into a don to masquerade
as the gang lord in *Don* (1978). He was not even referred to

as the anti-hero. He was the hero. Period.

Amitabh Bachchan's experiments with good and evil continued even after he returned to the silver screen from a self-imposed exile in the autumn of his life. Having shed the baggage of the conventional hero, he could play a disgruntled employee who trains three blind men to rob the bank he once worked for, in *Aankhen* (2002), or a cop who is possessed by the spirit of a killer, in *Aks* (2001), under whose influence he commits marital rape and murder. Over the years, the Shahenshah has undoubtedly established his own 'Sarkar Raj'. With roles ranging from a demigod to a godfather, he paved the way for a rosy-cheeked Rishi Kapoor to play the diabolical Rauf Lala, the butcher-cum-trafficker who auctions young girls in *Agneepath* (2012), as well as the most-wanted terrorist Iqbal Seth, aka Goldman, modelled on Dawood Ibrahim, in *D-Day* (2013). The actor admitted that it was a 'bloody high' to finally play characters and not just be Rishi Kapoor.

Of course, the transition is never easy. Manoj Kumar once confided to me that after being idolized in films like *Shaheed* (1965), *Upkar* (1967) and *Purab Aur Pachhim* (1970), it miffed many of his fans when he accepted *Be-Imaan* (1972), in which his character, ditched on the day of his engagement, turns into a thief. Even though he bagged the Filmfare Award for Best Actor for the performance, while travelling by the Rajdhani Express to Delhi, he was pulled up by the train's canteen staff for being *beimaan* (dishonest) to his 'Mr Bharat' image.

Sunil Dutt was another actor who was not averse to taking on villainous roles, having played the rebellious Birju who forces his mother to pick up the gun in *Mother India* (1957). However, even Nargis, who played the character of the mother and later became his real-life wife, was appalled when he accepted the role of Rajendra, a singer-artist who starts an affair with his now-married former girlfriend, enacted by Mala Sinha, in *Gumrah* (1963). A fearless, formula-breaking actor, Sunil Dutt produced and acted in two other path-breaking films in the same year. In *Mujhe Jeene Do* (1963), a dacoit drama inspired by real incidents, he stars as Thakur Jarnail Singh, who kills without remorse; the performance won him the Filmfare Award for Best Actor. The other home production, *Yeh Rastey Hain Pyar Ke* (1963), had its muse in the sensational K.M. Nanavati case, and is about a decorated naval officer who finds himself in the dock for murder after having gunned down his wife's lover. A decade later, Vinod Khanna, who started his career as a villain in Sunil Dutt's *Man Ka Meet* (1969), portrayed a similar character, Major Ranjeet Khanna, a man who is hanged for the crime of killing his adulterous wife and her lover in Gulzar's *Achanak* (1973).

One remembered the Nanavati case again after watching Akshay Kumar as Rustom Pavri, a Parsi naval officer, whose wife Cynthia is drawn into an affair with his friend whom he shoots dead for this act of betrayal. His performance in *Rustom* (2016) bagged him the National Film Award for Best Actor.

Rajesh Khanna, Akshay's father-in-law (also known as the Phenomenon of the '70s), waited till the '80s to play a psychopath who preys on nubile girls, seducing and killing them, and videotaping the murders for his father, who is as deranged as him. Not many remember *Red Rose* (1980) because it wilted far before its twisted fragrance could leave much of an impact.

A performance as a villain that cannot be forgotten, however, is Saif Ali Khan's portrayal of an Indianized Iago, Langda Tyagi, in Vishal Bhardwaj's adaptation of Shakespeare's *Othello*. After experimenting with cool, noir villains in *Ek*

Haseena Thi (2004) and *Being Cyrus* (2005), *Omkara* (2006) was the beginning of Saif's coming-of-age journey in mainstream Bollywood. Hair buzzed, teeth yellowed and speaking like a rustic Jat, the Prince Charming limped away with all the Best Performance in a Negative Role awards.

Eleven years later, he exploded in jealous rage as the one-armed megalomaniac studio boss Rustom Billimoria, aka Rusi, in another Vishal Bhardwaj directorial, *Rangoon* (2017). The Casablanca-like romance unfolds against the backdrop of World War II, with the cherubic Shahid Kapoor starring as the hero, Jamadar Nawab Malik. Two years later, Shahid did a complete U-turn from his boy-next-door image in and as *Kabir Singh* (2019), an obsessive, self-destructive lover. He was run down by the critics for promoting toxic masculinity and glamourizing misogyny, but the film, directed by Sandeep Reddy Vanga, was a commercial success and gave Shahid the impetus to keep breaking out of the mould with the OTT crime thriller series *Farzi* (2023) and the film *Bloody Daddy* (2023). In another Sandeep Reddy Vanga directorial, *Animal* (2023), Ranbir Kapoor metamorphosed into a bearded brute with daddy issues, spilling blood and gore. The film was a monster hit and a sequel, *Animal Park*, was immediately announced, which will undoubtedly be meaner and bloodier.

Meanwhile, Saif Ali Khan continued to strike terror with characters such as Emperor Aurangzeb's vicious general Udaybhan Singh Rathore in *Tanhaji: The Unsung Warrior* (2020). In *Vikram Vedha* (2022), his character, a tough cop who sees the world in black and white, gets a lesson in morality from Hrithik Roshan, who plays a criminal. And in *Adipurush* (2023), he plays the ultimate antagonist, Ravana. 'I would love to be like Tom Hardy, who played the villain in *The Dark Knight Rises* [2012] and the hero in *Mad Max:*

Fury Road [2015],' Saif had admitted to me in an interview for *Mumbai Mirror* in January 2020. It's no longer an impossible dream for a mainstream Bollywood actor to essay roles that span the entire spectrum of morality.

Hindi cinema's gallery of rogues has always been crowded, showcasing different hues of villainy. But now, with mainstream actors experimenting with negative roles, their evil omnipotence has been diluted, leaving many of the branded bad men sitting at home. However, irrespective of how often we see them on the screen nowadays, some of these villains are iconic, and have been an integral part of my Bollywood journey.

This book is dedicated to 13 of them—stereotypical villains who have ruined and ended lives, but without whom stories like the Ramayana wouldn't exist. Men without whose rolls of dice so many Kurukshetras would not have been fought. Men without whom none of the heroes that we love and idolize would have appeared heroic.

PRAN

THE GENTLEMAN VILLAIN

'Sher Khan ko kaun nahin jaanta?'

—*Zanjeer* (1973)

He almost got thrown out of his first film. Before that, he had almost walked away from a lucky break. To understand how he still went on to become the most hated man in the country, let's start at the very beginning.

Having quit studying after passing his matriculation exam, Pran Krishan Sikand, the son of a civil engineer and contractor working for the government, signed up as an apprentice with a photography studio in Delhi. When Das & Co. opened a new branch in Simla (now Shimla), he moved there. A year later, they expanded to Lahore and he was packed off again. This was before Partition, and Lahore, with its buzzing nightlife, was the place to be for the dashing 19-year-old Pran.

One night, while waiting with his friends at a roadside stall for his after-dinner paan, he was disconcerted by a man staring at him fixedly. A complete stranger, he even had the audacity to ask him his name! 'It was only when I angrily asked him why he was so interested in me that he introduced himself as Wali Mohammad Wali,' Pran reminisced, four decades later, when we met at his Bandra residence in 1998 for an interview for *Screen* magazine.

Back then, Wali Mohammad Wali was a well-known scriptwriter and lyricist, a big name in show business. Pran was unimpressed. He glared as Wali continued to stare unashamedly at him, finally asking, 'Would you be interested in acting in a Punjabi film? You look perfect to play one of the characters.' 'No, I'm not interested,' Pran told him curtly, turning sharply on his heels. But the screenwriter wasn't going to let him get away so easily. He insisted Pran drop by the next morning and meet his boss, the studio owner and film producer Dalsukh M. Pancholi. He scribbled the address down for the young man, who pocketed the chit, promising to be at the studio the following day, and disappeared into the night.

The next morning, Pran glanced at the chit disinterestedly, convinced the man he had met the previous night had been inebriated and would not recognize him in the light of day. He went to his photography studio as usual, the encounter wiped from his memory. However, the following Saturday, he bumped into Wali Mohammad Wali again, this time in the foyer of Plaza Cinema. To his surprise, the screenwriter instantly spotted him in the crowd and started cursing Pran loudly, using the choicest expletives to berate him for not showing up at the studio as promised. He groused that he had persuaded his boss not to sign another actor for the role, only to lose face when Pran, whom he had recommended so highly, did not turn up. By then, they were beginning to draw curious stares. Squirming awkwardly, an embarrassed Pran assured Wali that he would drop by the studio the next morning, promising him that this time, he would not go back on his word. Before they parted ways, Wali asked for Pran's address, and the next morning, he turned up at his doorstep to personally escort him.

In the studio, he was introduced to Pancholi. After a short interview and a quick photo session, Pran landed his first film at a monthly remuneration of ₹50. In *Yamla Jat* (1940), directed by Moti B. Gidwani, he plays a debonair trickster who deserts his wife and child, seduces Anjana's character, a simple village girl who has inherited a fortune, and alienates her from her adopted father and younger sister. The film's music was composed by Ghulam Haider and is still remembered for Noor Jehan's 'Kachiyaan Ve Kaliyaan Tu Na Toor' and Shamshad Begum's 'Kankaan Diyaan Faslaan Pakiyaan Ne'. Both songs were penned by Wali.

'When I accepted the offer, I had insisted that I be allowed to work at the photography studio when I was not needed for shoots. To my relief, the producer agreed,' Pran recounted during that interview. He admitted that despite Wali Mohammad Wali's conviction that he was perfect, he was not convinced he could make a career in front of the camera. He wanted a secure job to fall back on if the gamble didn't pay off. He was also worried that his father might be upset if he learnt that his son was acting in films and swore his three sisters to secrecy when the news of his being signed appeared in the newspaper. However, when Kewal Krishan Sikand finally discovered his son's secret, he was far from angry.

Yamla Jat was a huge hit. After that, Pran landed another Punjabi film, *Chaudhry* (1941), again produced by Pancholi and featuring Noor Jehan.

With *Khandaan* (1942), the actor graduated to becoming a hero. Noor Jehan, who had played Anjana's 11-year-old sister in *Yamla Jat*, was cast as his fiancée in this film. The young actress who had just entered her teens had to stand on a pile of bricks to look into his eyes. Surprisingly, for someone who went on to become infamous for luring young women to their doom, Pran was distinctly uncomfortable running around the trees and romancing the coy heroine. Every time he was called upon to do so, he would run away from the set.

He acted in 22 films between 1942 and 1946, including *Dasi* (1944), *Pardesi Balam* (1945), *Badnami* (1946), *Khamosh Nigahen* (1946), *Mohini* (1947) and *Do Saudagar* (1947), playing the leading man with aplomb.

Life was cruising along smoothly until 1947 when, as communal tensions ran high in Lahore, an anxious Pran packed off his wife Shukla and 11-month-old son Arvind to his sister-in-law's home in Indore. He himself stayed back and continued shooting. But eventually, giving in to Shukla's threat that unless he came for their firstborn's first birthday she wouldn't celebrate it, he left Lahore. 'I reached Indore on 11 August, on the day of my son's birthday. I had planned to stay for just a week and had packed only a couple of suits. The next day, the Hindu–Muslim riots began; after that, I never returned to Lahore despite several invitations in later years,' he reminisced.

Back then, Bombay, alongside Lahore and Calcutta, was thriving as a prominent film centre. With his wife and son, Pran moved to the 'city of dreams' on the eve of India's Independence. Over the next six months, they moved from the plush Taj Mahal Hotel to smaller hotels and finally a paying guest accommodation as money quickly ran out, while the promised roles didn't materialize. He even worked in a hotel on Marine Drive and was forced to sell his wife's gold bangles to survive.

Then, what can only be described as a miracle happened

to the hard-up Pran. In three days, he landed four films!

The first was Bombay Talkies' *Ziddi* (1948), based on a story by Ismat Chughtai and directed by Shaheed Latif. *Ziddi* starred Dev Anand in the lead opposite Kamini Kaushal. Pran, on the recommendation of the late actor Shyam, as well as author-playwright Saadat Hasan Manto (a close friend of studio head Ashok Kumar), was roped in to play the villain for a remuneration of ₹500.

Soon after he signed *Ziddi*, Pran drove down to Pune, where he was offered *Aparadhi* (1949), which Yeshwant Pethkar was directing for Prabhat Film Company. He plays a freedom fighter on the run, whose presence creates problems for Madhubala's character as her husband, played by Ram Singh, suspects her of infidelity. 'I almost turned down the offer because the studio would not pay me more than ₹500 and I was determined that with every new film I signed, my price would go up. I was eventually paid ₹600, but told to keep this a secret from the film's hero who had been signed for ₹500,' Pran shared.

By then, his mentor Wali Mohammad Wali had also moved to Bombay. Pran was cast in *Putli* (1949), Wali's own production, also featuring Lala Yaqoob and Mumtaz Shanti. The fourth film he snapped up was S.M. Yusuf's *Grahasti* (1948), which went on to celebrate a diamond jubilee.

After that, there was no looking back as Pran's characters grew more devious with every film. In D.D. Kashyap and Ram Daryani's *Bari Behen* (1949), he seduces and abandons Kiran (Geeta Bali) after she gets pregnant, forcing her sister Shyama (Suraiya) to rush to her rescue. This was the first time we saw him blow smoke rings on screen, a character detail that would go on to become his trademark. His son, Sunil Sikand, later recalled his father smoking over 100 cigarettes a day until he was 57. Then somehow, overnight, he kicked the habit.

After *Bari Behen* came Sohrab Modi's *Sheesh Mahal* (1950), with Pran playing Naseem Banu's fiancé who breaks off their engagement when her father, a feudal aristocrat, loses his fortune. However, he returns to fan the old man's ire to stop her from moving on with another man. The following year, in *Bahar* (1951), he plays a spurned lover blinded by jealousy. The film, a remake of the Tamil blockbuster *Vazhkai* (1949), introduced South Indian actress Vyjayanthimala to Bollywood in AVM Productions' first Hindi film. Pran drove his wife to the film's premiere in a new Chrysler as their old car had been totalled in a crash. Relieved that Shukla, who had been driving, was not hurt, he had told her, 'Maybe God wants us to buy a bigger car.'

During the next decade, Pran worked with several debutant directors, including Subodh Mukherji (*Munimji*, 1955), Shakti Samanta (*Inspector*, 1956) and Nasir Hussain (*Tumsa Nahin Dekha*, 1957). Suave and sophisticated, he always managed to woo the heroine till his darker side revealed itself. Then she would look to the hero to extricate her from his clutches. One of his most memorable performances was in Raj Kapoor's production *Jis Desh Men Ganga Behti Hai* (1960). He plays the dreaded dacoit Raka who, when asked his name, growls, '*Tera baap* Raka [Your father Raka].' He is a man without morals or scruples who, to get the girl he loves, kills her father, the *sardar* of their gang. Raka's tic of running a finger around his collar while conversing makes the character unforgettable.

'Do you know why Raka is so preoccupied with his neck?' he is reported to have once asked a journalist after the film's release. She didn't have an answer and he explained that being an outlaw, the dacoit knows that either the law will catch up with him and he will hang from the gallows, or his throat will be cut by rivals or even his own gang members.

Pran struck such terror across the country that in a survey conducted in the '50s, it was discovered that not a single child born in Bombay, Delhi, Punjab and Uttar Pradesh during the time had been named Pran. That was how much he was hated and dreaded, with young girls running away from him at parties and little children hiding their faces in their mothers' laps every time he appeared on screen.

Kamal Amrohi's son Tajdar recalls many visits to Pran's house as a boy of eight, along with his friends, N. Sadiq, and Ghulam Mohammed's sons. 'Pran uncle had several dogs and had built a fort-like kennel for them in his garden. Before leaving for shooting, he would inform his staff to call the *kathputliwala* [puppeteer] home. We loved those puppet shows and it was kind of him to organize them. But Pran uncle himself was so intimidating on screen that for a long time we believed he was really a bad man. It was only as I grew older that I realized that the eyes that gleamed with menace on screen shone with love off it,' the filmmaker narrates fondly.

Pran enjoyed playing the *khalnayak*, pointing out that one is interested in a film only till the antagonist is around. 'Once the villain is hauled off by the cops or killed, the film is over, and you leave the auditorium,' he would say. However, his young daughter Pinky was not convinced by this logic and urged her father to play some decent roles for a change after being ragged mercilessly by her classmates. Pran understood what she was going through in school and decided to accept more good-guy roles.

Earlier, in Raj Kapoor's romantic drama *Aah* (1953), he had played the doctor-friend of the hero who is diagnosed with tuberculosis, an ailment that was almost incurable back then. The original film ended with Nargis's Reshma, on the insistence of Raj Kapoor's Raj, agreeing to marry Pran's Dr Prakash. The man she really loves dies melodramatically as her wedding procession passes by his house. However, alarmed by the string of negative reactions at *Aah*'s premiere, the actor-filmmaker reworked the tragic ending. The hero is cured by Dr Prakash and the lovers reunite. The change couldn't save the film as the audience had by then grown used to seeing Pran as someone who looted, molested and murdered. They couldn't accept him as a good man who willingly sacrifices his love.

With his growing daughter in mind, Pran knew it was time for a change of image. Salvation came in the form of Manoj Kumar, who coaxed him to accept the role of Kehar Singh in *Shaheed* (1965), which he had written with the senior actor in mind. Pran, however, turned down the six-scene appearance after the film's producer, Kewal Kashyap, admitted he wouldn't be able to pay him his market price since they were working on a shoestring budget of just ₹10 lakh. 'A few days later, I ran into Manoj Kumar on another set. He told me that he would edit out the death-row prisoner from his script, even though he was integral to the narrative, if I didn't play the role. He reiterated that if I played Kehar Singh, he was confident the character would leave a lasting impact,' he shared.

Moved by his words, Pran asked Manoj Kumar to send his producer across again. Kewal Kashyap went over reluctantly, not entirely convinced that one of the highest-paid villains in the industry would reduce his price for their film. Half an hour later, he returned jubilant. Pran had agreed to do the film for just ₹7,000.

His last scene in *Shaheed* left many in tears. On his way to the gallows, Kehar Singh stops to shake hands with

Bhagat Singh, telling him that when he meets the maker, he will ask God why a common dacoit and Bharat Mata's brave son should meet the same end. Manoj Kumar himself has admitted that this is his favourite scene in the film, even though as Bhagat Singh he has his back to the camera in it.

Two years later, Manoj Kumar signed Pran to play a one-legged soldier, Malang Chacha, in *Upkar* (1967), his first film as a director. This time, the veteran actor didn't need much convincing. Many, including Raj Kapoor, tried to dissuade 'Mr Bharat' from casting a bad man in a strong supporting role, but he stuck to his guns, arguing that Pran was India's Anthony Quinn. And if a hero could play the villain, why couldn't a villain play a good man? To this day, that performance in *Upkar* and his iconic one-line dialogue, '*Ration par bhashan bahut hai, lekin bhashan par ration koi nahin* [There are a lot of speeches given on ration, but no one rations speeches],' remains memorable.

Manoj Kumar even shot one of the film's best songs, 'Kasme Wade Pyar Wafa', with the veteran actor, upsetting the composer duo Kalyanji–Anandji in the process. However, after seeing the first print, Kalyanji was the first to acknowledge that while other actors only lip-synced to their songs, Pran had sung it from the heart. The actor would request that the song be played at full volume on the set and would sing along, '*zor shor se* [loudly and enthusiastically].'

Before *Upkar*, Pran had sparked anger, fear and revulsion wherever he went. On the streets, people would address him as '*luchchey*', '*lafangey*', '*badmaash*', '*daku*' and '420'—all disparaging and callous terms that mean everything from 'streetside lecher' to 'robber'. After the film's release, he attended the wedding of actor Om Prakash's daughter, and while other stars were being mobbed, the minute Pran stepped out of his car, someone muttered, '*Malang Chacha aa rahe hain* [Malang Chacha is coming], make way for him.' And silently, almost respectfully, the crowd parted. The patriotic drama had turned the bad man into a good one, and films like *Nannha Farishta* (1969), in which Pran, along with Ajit and Anwar Hussain, gives up a life of crime for the love of a child, further cemented this metamorphosis on screen.

Biswajit Chatterjee, the guitar-strumming star of the '60s who has worked with Pran in the musical romance *Mere Sanam* (1965) and the costume drama *Do Dil* (1965), reveals the actor to be a gentleman even away from the camera. 'He was always courteous and chivalrous. During *Do Dil*, when someone on the set disparagingly told Durga Khote-ji, "*Pata hai umar ho gayi hai, par theek se to chal* [We know you are old, but at least walk properly]," Pran-sahab was instantly on his feet. Grabbing the culprit by the collar, he dragged him over to Durga-ji, telling him to apologize to her immediately,' the actor recounts.

While Pran made his life hell on screen, he was someone Biswajit enjoyed socializing with on the set. 'No one could beat Pran-sahab in the card game Flash,' he shares, recalling how while on an outdoor shoot in Jaipur, they had once partied till 4.00 a.m. 'I wasn't required to shoot the next day, but Pran-sahab had a 7.00 a.m. shift and I was worried he would not be able to report on time. But every time I told him he should call it a night, he would say, "*Chhod* beta, let's enjoy ourselves".'

The next day, Biswajit learnt that despite getting almost no sleep, Pran had arrived for the 7.00 a.m. shoot on the dot, dressed in his costume, his make-up done. 'He was a committed professional who would always say that since we were getting paid to act, we should never let our producer down,' the actor remembers.

Pran was extremely fit and agile, a natural sportsman. So was Biswajit. There is a sword fight in the climax of *Do Dil* and he had been warned by the action director Azam that many top actors, years younger than him, who had challenged Pran in a fight, had not been able to stand up to the master fencer. Determined to win their on-screen duel convincingly, Biswajit practised industriously and quietly for a few months. 'Every day, for two hours in the morning, a couple of Azam's assistants would train with me at home,' he narrates. His efforts paid off when during their face-off, Pran was wowed by the other actor's dexterous sword play. 'So too were the critics, who made a favourable mention of that last duel in their reviews,' he beams.

Speaking of film climaxes, director Chandra Barot shared that during a three-week schedule for the finale of *Don* (1978) at Bombay's Chandivali Studio, Pran did not arrive late even once. 'In fact, he would reach 10 minutes before his call time, which was 9.00 a.m., dressed in his costume and with make-up on, making the rest of us hurry,' he laughed.

For the debutant director, Pran was like a father figure. When he noticed that Chandra Barot was drinking at least a dozen glasses of tea every day, he called his man Friday, Kader, and instructed him to serve his boss only half a glass every time he called for chai. 'The tongue tastes only for the first 30 seconds and the taste lingers for a minute. After that, the tea is nothing but hot water, so it's best to cut your intake by half,' he explained.

The script of *Don*, written by the famous writer duo Salim Khan–Javed Akhtar, had been rejected by Dev Anand, Dharmendra and Jeetendra. With Amitabh Bachchan, Zeenat

Aman and Pran jumping on board, Chandra Barot went on to direct the film for their common friend, cinematographer Nariman Irani, whose last film as a producer, *Zindagi Zindagi* (1972), had tanked. Since their producer was in the red and had ran up huge debts, all four of them forfeited a part of their remuneration. Even Pran, it is said, forfeited his ₹5-lakh fee; but unfortunately, Nariman Irani died six months before *Don*'s box-office breaking run.

By the time they collaborated in *Don*, the Amitabh Bachchan–Pran duo had become a crowd-puller, after superhits like *Zanjeer* (1973), *Majboor* (1974) and *Amar Akbar Anthony* (1977). *Zanjeer* was Amitabh Bachchan's (popularly referred to as Big B) first film as the 'angry young man'. It was Pran who had recommended his son's friend to director Prakash Mehra. The actor, reeling after having faced a dozen debacles in his career, was so in awe of Pran that during their first shot together, he couldn't bring himself to kick the chair from under him and holler at him. The senior actor had to remind him that he was Inspector Vijay Khanna while Pran was Sher Khan, a pathan who ran gambling dens in the cop's jurisdiction.

Interestingly, when Prakash Mehra informed the veteran actor that his first shoot would be for the superhit *qawwali* 'Yari Hai Imaan Mera', which they would be filming the next day, he threw a royal fit. A dedicated actor, Pran liked to listen to a song several times and know the words by heart before landing on the set. 'You haven't even sent me my lines or a recording of the song, no way am I going to shoot for it tomorrow', he roared. The filmmaker eventually convinced him to show up for the shoot, promising that the rush print would be screened for him immediately after it was edited. 'If you don't like it, we will drop the song', he assured Pran.

A few days later, the filmmaker called Pran to arrange for a screening. To his surprise, the actor told him that he had watched the song already, through the eyes of friends and colleagues who had seen glimpses of it while it was being edited. 'They have raved about it to me, so you can retain it. I know "Yari Hai Imaan Mera" will be a hit,' he stated confidently. The song was a chartbuster, and *Zanjeer*, a surprise blockbuster. At the film's premiere in Calcutta, the fans were upset because their 'hero' Pran had not turned up. Amitabh Bachchan was a poor replacement for them till they watched the film; then, they had a new hero in Vijay. Pran himself only saw the complete film 20 years after its release, stumbling upon *Zanjeer* one afternoon while surfing television channels. After watching the film, he immediately called Amitabh Bachchan to tell him he had really enjoyed his performance.

Pran was not just a prolific actor, but a versatile one too. He started the trend of comic villains, taken forward in later years by Kader Khan, Shakti Kapoor, Prem Chopra and Anupam Kher. In Shakti Samanta's *Kashmir Ki Kali* (1964), his character Mohan's sole purpose is to wrest Sharmila Tagore away from Shammi Kapoor and marry her himself. His character's lisp, converting his 's' to 'sh', was what drew laughter—an arguably problematic tic in today's time, to be sure.

Victoria No. 203 (1972) was another laugh riot, with Pran and Ashok Kumar playing the golden-hearted crooks Rana and Raja. The two actors were the best of friends and did 27 films together between 1951 and 1987, many of them superhits. They were always in tune with each other, and many of their gags and one-liners came not out of dialogue sheets, but were improvised on set.

Pran had an innate sense of humour. When his brother got married, he draped himself in a sari and tried to create trouble between him and his new bride by pretending to be his scorned lover. In later years, he would play such pranks on his co-stars too. Actor-filmmaker Ananth Narayan Mahadevan remembers that while they were shooting together, he had nodded off during an extended lunch break. He woke up from his siesta to find Pran shaking him gently. As his eyes fluttered open, the veteran actor's eyes twinkled mischievously at him and he asked innocently, '*So rahe the kya* [Oh, were you sleeping]?' For a moment, his younger colleague just gaped at him, then burst out laughing at the impish Peter Pan standing in front of him. He learnt later that it was one of Pran's favourite pranks.

Pran acted in over 350 films, doing double roles in movies like *Jangal Mein Mangal* (1972), *Insaaf* (1973) and *Khoon Ka Rishta* (1981). He co-produced *Lakshmanrekha* (1991) with Satyendra Pal, playing Naseeruddin Shah's father in the film, which was directed by his own son, Sunil Sikand.

In 1998, Pran was recuperating from a recent heart attack. One of the valves in his heart had failed and he'd had to undergo an emergency surgery that had left him frail and often short of breath. 'This was the first time in 78 years that I had landed up in a hospital, believing I was suffering from a bout of indigestion,' he revealed, admitting that after being mobbed by enthusiastic fans for years, he was now terrified of large crowds. He was also struggling to memorize pages of dialogue and his health had forced him to cut down on his work, which was upsetting because he had committed to doing a film with Priyadarshan. 'There is also Chintu's [Rishi Kapoor] *Aa Ab Laut Chalen* [1999], his first film as a director, that I have given dates for. This heart attack has put me out of action for the first time in 60 years,' he complained. He was quick to add that he had promised Priyadarshan he would not leave the world without doing at least one film with him. He had not even met the director until then. But that was Pran! A man of principles and integrity.

Such was his popularity that it is said that readers wrote to Filmfare asking for a Best Villain award to be instituted to felicitate him. He took the coveted Black Lady home twice— winning the Best Supporting Actor award for his portrayal of Malang Chacha in *Upkar* (1967) and of Shambhu Mahadev Rao in Satyen Bose's *Aansoo Ban Gaye Phool* (1969). In 1997, he was honoured with the Filmfare Lifetime Achievement Award. There would have been another Filmfare Best Supporting Actor trophy in his showcase for the Manoj Kumar-starrer *Be-Imaan* (1972), which got seven nominations and won six awards, but Pran turned down the honour as a mark of protest after the jury voted for the film's composers Shankar–Jaikishan over Ghulam Mohammed and *Pakeezah* (1972) for the Best Music Director award.

'Would you believe *Pakeezah* did not bag a single award? Not for Best Film, Best Director or Best Music; even my *chhoti ammi* [Meena Kumar] did not win the Best Actress statuette! Baba [filmmaker Kamal Amrohi] and he were not the best of friends, but Pran uncle refused to go on stage and accept a trophy when other deserving recipients had been left empty-handed,' says Tajdar Amrohi. He ranks Pran's performance as Gajendra, the tyrannical brother-in-law who abuses Dilip Kumar's Ram in *Ram Aur Shyam* (1967), as one of his best—another performance that went unheralded.

I enjoyed the costume drama *Halaku* (1956), in which he plays the titular role of the Mongol emperor Halaku Khan, the grandson of Genghis Khan, who invades Persia, where a local girl Niloufer (Meena Kumari) becomes the object of his desire even though she is in love with Ajit's Parvez. Halaku's queen, Dokuz Khatun, stands in the way of his second marriage. With an eye-catching get-up and great lines, this well-researched role was one of Pran's favourite characters as well.

He was also brilliant as the scheming Raja Ugra Narayan in Bimal Roy's paranormal romance *Madhumati* (1958). The film's hero Dilip Kumar was one of Pran's friends, and along with Raj Kapoor and Manoj Kumar, would often drop by his residence and play dumb charades with the Sikand family.

In 2001, Pran was honoured with the third-highest civilian award in the country, the Padma Bhushan. Twelve years later, I watched him being presented with the Lifetime Achievement Award at the Zee Cine Awards in Mumbai. In his moment of glory, the veteran actor bent down and touched his forehead to the ground in a mark of respect to all those who had helped him reach the pinnacle of success. In response, an audience of around 5,000 rose to its feet to give him a standing ovation. He kept his acceptance speech short and sweet. '*Hum bolega to bologe ki bolta hai* [If I say something, you will say he speaks too much],' he quipped, borrowing a line from the Kishore Kumar chartbuster from *Kasauti* (1974). He was greeted with a roar of approval. Returning to his seat, Pran passed Rekha, who stood up and reverently touched his feet.

In 2013, he was felicitated with the prestigious Dadasaheb Phalke Award, the highest honour in the Indian film industry, awarded for outstanding contribution to the growth and development of Indian cinema. By then he was so unwell that he could not attend the award ceremony in Delhi. Manish Tewari, the then minister of information and broadcasting, brought the Swarna Kamal home to him in Mumbai.

Soon after, on 12 July 2013, Pran Krishan Sikand, at the age of 93, took his final curtain call. But even today, his crackling one-line from *Zanjeer*, '*Sher Khan kale ka dhanda karta hai, lekin imandari se* [Sher Khan may dabble in illegal business, but he is honest],' keeps the memory of this gentleman villain alive.

AJIT

THE ROARING 'LOIN'

Ajit, thoroughly disgusted with Mona's typing skills,
tells his henchman, 'Raabert, iske donon haath kaat do.'
'Magar kyun Baas?'
'Typing to nahin aati, kam se kam sharthand
to seekh jayegi.'

This is one of those nonsensical Ajit jokes, with certain words pronounced in his distinctive style, that always make me laugh, even as I hear the bad man chiding in my ear, 'Lily, don't be silly.'

I was smiling as the autorickshaw wound its way up Bombay's Pali Hill towards Florida Apartments for a meeting with the man himself, wondering if the 'Lion' would roar. Rather, he purred.

This was back in 1992 and by then, Ajit Khan was a distinguished gentleman of 70. The door opened and he stood before me, tall, straight and stately, his mane and flourishing moustache snow-white, his smile benign, his greeting that of a fond grandfather. Over the phone, while setting up our appointment for our interview for *Filmfare*, I had hesitatingly told him that I wanted to meet him for a feature on Madhubala, having recently learnt from one of his industry colleagues that the star villain had been the late actress's *mooh bola bhai* (de facto brother). I wanted to hear some stories about the 'Venus of Indian Cinema' that had yet to find their way into print. To my surprise, he readily agreed. I arrived to find three thick albums waiting for me.

For the next couple of hours, we went through these photographic memories of Ajit with various co-stars. They were monochromatic clicks, frozen in time. He remembered dates and locations with amazing precision, his memory leaving me open-mouthed in amazement. The stage set, we moved to Madhubala, whom he remembered as a simple, homely girl, almost unrecognizable without the pancake and paints. She had been just 16, sitting in a corner and giggling with her sisters, when he accompanied M.R. Navalkar, the producer of *Beqasoor* (1950), to her Peddar Road residence. The smothered giggles turned into peals of loud, uncontrollable laughter on the set of their first film together.

There was a scene where his jobless Brij and her mysterious Usha are travelling in a train, sharing the compartment with a slumbering pathan. 'Every few minutes, the pathan would loudly snort in his sleep, and Madhu would turn hysterical,' Ajit guffawed at the memory, recalling that she was laughing so hard that she had to excuse herself frequently from the set to compose herself, much to the annoyed exasperation of their director, K. Amarnath.

He quickly discovered that behind the fits of laughter was a shy, introverted girl brought up by a strict, conservative, disciplinarian father, Ataullah Khan. She was not even allowed to attend film parties or premieres. Madhubala would report for work at nine in the morning, and as soon as shooting was over, would come straight back home. Since she loved her work, there were no complaints and few friends. Her only indulgence was watching movies in the theatres, where she always went incognito.

'One day, when I was driving down Bandra, I was surprised by a woman in a burqa frantically calling out to me to stop. Intrigued, I braked to a halt beside her and leaning in through the open car window, she lifted her veil. It was Madhu, and she wanted a lift to Churchgate so she could catch a film she wanted to see at Eros theatre,' Ajit informed.

Once they reached their destination, the actor got out to open the door for her and was recognized by urchins loitering outside the cinema hall. As they crowded around him, Ajit pointed to the lady in the burqa who was hurrying inside. '*Woh dekho Madhubala* [See, that's Madhubala],' he whispered to them. By then, she was already a known name. As Ajit had correctly surmised, they immediately forgot him and ran after her. She shot him a dirty look. Chuckling, he got into his car and drove away, knowing she would be safe from her fans inside the theatre.

The laughter died away by the time they started shooting for K. Asif's *Mughal-E-Azam* (1960). By then, Madhubala had been diagnosed with a hole in her heart. She was also reeling from a real-life heartbreak, and the epic extravaganza, which immortalized her as Anarkali, only brought her never-ending pain every day. There is the iconic scene where Anarkali runs towards her prince, weighed down by the heavy iron chains that had kept her shackled in the dungeon on Emperor Akbar's orders. After the shot was taken, a frail Madhubala fainted. When she was revived, Ajit reminded her that the doctors had warned her that any kind of physical exertion could prove fatal. 'She smiled away my concern, insisting that she had to give this film her 100 per cent and prove to the world that she was the best Anarkali Hindi cinema would

ever see,' he sighed, marvelling at how despite her failing
health, Madhubala's steely determination and dedication to
her craft kept her in the race.

Ajit, who plays Prince Salim's friend and trusted
lieutenant Durjan Singh, specifically mentioned a scene in
Mughal-E-Azam in which, soon after 'Pyar Kiya To Darna
Kya', an imperious Prithviraj Kapoor as Akbar comes to the
battlefield and walks into his son's tent to find Salim and
Anarkali together. He fixes a contemptuous gaze on the
dancing girl, which makes her shrivel up visibly. 'I don't
think any other actress could have done the scene better,
such was the conviction Madhu brought to her performance,'
he applauded, acknowledging that after the film's release,
as she had so fervently wished, Anarkali indeed became
synonymous with Madhubala.

Listening to him, I was reminded of another scene in the
battlefield that had left a lasting impression. Spotting Anarkali
falling to the ground, Durjan Singh takes Salim's permission
to carry her off to safety. Riding with her clinging to his
back, he fights off almost the entire army. His words, '*Mera
jism zaroor zakhmi hai, lekin meri himmat zakhmi nahi* [My
body may be wounded but not my courage]' and '*Rajput jaan
harta hai, vachan nahin harta* [A Rajput may lose his life, but
he will never go back on his promise],' spoken in that deep
baritone, still echo in my ears.

I later heard an interesting story about Ajit's casting.
The shooting for *Mughal-E-Azam* had started sometime in
1945–46, with Nargis as Anarkali and D.K. Sapru as Salim,
at Minerva Movietone studio; Himalaywala, known for his
impressive dialogue delivery, had been signed to play Durjan
Singh. But after the Partition in 1947, the actor was one of the
first to cross the border and settle down in the newly formed

Pakistan, along with the film's producer Shiraz Ali Hakim. As a result, K. Asif's Mughal dream came to an abrupt halt and he had to wait till 1950 to resume shooting with a new financier. To everyone's surprise, the director roped in Ajit, known till then as an action hero, to fill Himalaywala's shoes. 'I guess it was my excellent command over Urdu that spoke in my favour,' Ajit pointed out when I brought up the subject, not bothering to hide the note of pride in his voice.

After bagging *Mughal-E-Azam*, the actor approached Sashadhar Mukherjee, whose *Anarkali* (1953) was being shot at Bombay's Filmistan Studio. He also met Kamal Amrohi, who was busy with another *Anarkali*, featuring Meena Kumari in the lead, at Dadar's Central Studio. 'I was hoping to bag roles in both films so I could boast to my grandchildren that I had featured in all three *Anarkali*s,' he admitted with a grin.

But Sashadhar Mukherjee, with whom he later went on to do *Samrat* (1954) and *Nastik* (1954), turned Ajit away for the same reason that K. Asif had cast him—his impeccable diction and command over Urdu. He didn't want his hero (Pradeep Kumar), who was from Bengal, and his Punjabi heroine (Bina Rai) to be overshadowed by a man who spoke Urdu like a royal. Kamal Amrohi signed him to play Salim in his *Anarkali*, but the film was shelved, and Ajit had to be content with just *Mughal-E-Azam*.

However, he did get to work with Kamal Amrohi in *Razia Sultan* (1983), with Hema Malini in the titular role. Ajit played the role of Amil Balban. Tajdar Amrohi recalls how his father was very fond of the actor, who was also their neighbour, while Ajit regarded the writer-filmmaker as his diction guru. 'Even though he was well-versed in Urdu and known for his impeccable dialogue delivery, he would always ask Baba to advise him on how he should speak a particular line during the *Mughal-E-Azam* shoot. My father would say, "Ajit-sahab, *aap apni tarah se boliye* [Ajit-sahab, you say it the way you think best]," but he would still insist on taking his cues from Baba,' shares Tajdar, adding that the actor's gentle demeanor and genteel ways endeared him to the entire Amrohi clan.

In Rajkumar Santoshi's cult comedy *Andaz Apna Apna* (1994), Paresh Rawal's Teja brings to mind Ajit's gangster character, Seth Dharam Dayal Teja, in *Zanjeer* (1973). In a further tribute to the iconic villain, Rajkumar Santoshi and his co-writer Dilip Shukla also gave their Teja two henchmen by the names of Robert and Bhalla, played by Viju Khote and Shehzad Khan, Ajit's son. In a hat-tip to his father, Shehzad apes Ajit's mannerisms and even his distinctive accent.

When we met, Ajit had just returned from a nine-year sabbatical in the city of his birth, Hyderabad, lured back by his love for the movies to flag off a third innings in Bollywood. He was delighted to be working with Karisma Kapoor, the fourth generation of Kapoors, in the Salim Akhtar production *Police Officer* (1992). He later recounted how the first day of shooting at Kamalistan Studio was memorable because almost half a century earlier, he had faced the camera there with the actress's great-grandfather Prithviraj Kapoor for *Anand Math* (1952).

In Hemen Gupta's patriotic drama based on Bankim Chandra Chatterjee's famous Bengali novel by the same name, Prithviraj Kapoor plays Satyananda, the leader of a *math*, who yearns to set his motherland free from British despots. Pradeep Kumar and Ajit are his disciples, Jivanand and Bhavanand. *Anand Math* was dubbed in Tamil as *Ananda Madam* (1953), and Ajit recalled how Prithviraj Kapoor, along with the rest of the cast, had to not only speak long pages of dialogue in Hindi, but also repeat the same in

Tamil. 'Papaji [Prithviraj Kapoor], under the cover of his long, flowing beard, would mutter a string of good-natured *gaali*s. Only Pradeep Kumar and I knew what he was saying and had to fight not to laugh on camera,' he recounted.

Ajit went on to work with Prithviraj Kapoor's sons, Raj and Shammi, in K.A. Abbas's *Char Dil Char Rahen* (1959). The film brought Captain, aka Raj Kapoor, into Ajit's life. He led the Bollywood cricket team Ajit played for while his buddy, Dilip Kumar, captained the rival team. 'If I floored a catch or got out cheaply, I would get an earful from Captain,' he pointed to pictures of them together at charity cricket matches.

Raj Kapoor's granddaughter Karisma, who had inherited his blue eyes, brought back memories of Captain. In *Police Officer*, a *Zanjeer*-esque revenge drama, Ajit plays a Teja-like smuggler, Dindayal, aka DD. He also collaborated with the actress in *Jigar* (1992) and *Shaktiman* (1993). In the latter, he plays Shamsher 'Tiger' Singh, a tongue-in-cheek reference to Lion of *Kalicharan* (1976).

Subhash Ghai's crime drama *Kalicharan* is Shatrughan Sinha's first film as a hero. He plays a double role—fearless cop DSP Prabhakar Srivastava and fearsome criminal Kalicharan, who has been jailed for murder. Ajit is unforgettable as the cultured mafia don Lion, who masquerades as Din Dayal, an honest businessman. Suave in a sherwani, with a string of pearls around his neck, he is the epitome of understated arrogance as he tells Prabhakar, '*Lekin ek baat mat bhuliye DSP-sahab, ki sara shehar mujhe Lion ke naam se jaanta hai, aur iss shehar mein meri haisiyat wohi hai jo jungle mein sher ki hai* [Don't forget, DSP Sir, the whole city knows me as Lion and my standing here is that of a lion].'

Subhash Ghai had written this shadowy figure

who orchestrates murders, thefts and blackmails while masquerading as a philanthropist tycoon with Ajit in mind, having seen him in films like *Mughal-E-Azam* and *Zanjeer*. That was why when narrating the script to producer N.N. Sippy, he had unconsciously aped the actor's voice, right down to the nasal twang. In fact, while sketching out Ajit's introduction scene in the bedroom, which begins with a cacophony of phones ringing and a languid arm reaching out for the one closest to him, he had told Sippy, 'This man is Lion, and he will be played by Ajit-sahab.'

The producer agreed with him that Ajit was the perfect choice to play the larger-than-life villain, and Subhash Ghai set up a meeting with the veteran actor. 'Forty minutes into the narration, Ajit-sahab assured me that he would do my film on the condition that as a new-age director and an actor myself, I would ensure that he did not slip into exaggerated histrionics. "*Mujhe sambhal lena* [Make sure I don't overact]," he told me, and I retorted tongue-in-cheek, "But sir, this character is theatrical!" My cheeky humour brought on an appreciative guffaw, but on the set, he behaved like an obedient student, following my cues on everything, from his performance to his dialogue delivery,' the filmmaker shared in an interview published on *Rediff.com* in 2022, Ajit's centenary year.

Kalicharan is remembered for its punchlines, and its writer-director is quick to acknowledge that what makes them unforgettable is the Ajit touch. When asked if he had deliberately got the actor to mispronounce the word 'lion' as 'loin', Subhash Ghai revealed that he had actually corrected him the first time. But when it happened a second time, even a third, he quickly realized that this was Ajit's way of speaking and decided to let it be. It was a wise decision because it not only made the dialogue iconic, but also turned 'Loin' into a cult figure. Other phrases, like 'smart guy' and 'bloody bostard' also became popular because of the way he pronounced the words, spurring a cottage industry of Ajit jokes that has kept 'Bass' (Boss) alive in our collective consciousness.

∞

Ajit was born as Hamid Ali Khan on 27 January 1922 in Hyderabad. He was a fine athlete who played football like a pro and continued playing the sport even after he became an actor, forming a football club with fellow actors Karan Dewan and Motilal. In later years, actress Tabassum recounted on her famous chat show *Phool Khile Hain Gulshan Gulshan* that during *Moti Mahal* (1952), starring Ajit and Suraiya in the lead and her as a child artiste, they would play football during breaks in shooting.

Ajit's father Bashir Ali Khan was in the army of the Nizam of Hyderabad and had wanted him to pursue a career in law or medicine. But the boy was never academically inclined and after clearing his matriculation exams, encouraged by an English professor who believed he was more suited for a career in the army or films, he dropped out of college in the middle of the term, sold his textbooks and bought a train ticket to Bombay to become the star he believed he was destined to be.

He started at the bottom of the ladder. For three years, he worked as an 'extra', as junior artistes were disparagingly called then. He was paid just ₹3 at the end of a long day. However, with his impressive build, deep baritone and impeccable dialogue delivery, Ajit stood out in the crowd and was signed as the leading man of *Shah-e-Misar* (1946) opposite Geeta Bose and Meghmala. He could finally move out of the Mahim shanty where he had been living.

Subsequently, he was seen in films like *Hatimtai* (1947),

Sone Ke Chidiya (1948), *Aap Beeti* (1948), *Patanga* (1949) and *Jeevan Saathi* (1949), to name a few. There was also *Beqasoor* (1950), opposite Madhubala, which went on to become one of the top grossers of that year.

Over the next decade, Ajit continued to play the hero, serenading actresses like Madhubala (*Saiyan*, 1951), Nigar Sultana (*Daman*, 1951), Nalini Jaywant (*Nastik*, 1954, and *Milan*, 1958), Bina Rai (*Marine Drive*, 1955), Geeta Bali (*Bara-Dari*, 1955), Meena Kumari (*Halaku*, 1956), Kamini Kaushal (*Bada Bhai*, 1957), Jayashree (*Mehndi*, 1958) and Shakila (*Guest House*, 1959). With the exception of Nargis, he wooed all the top leading ladies of the time. In the '50s, following the success of *Nastik*, he was frequently cast opposite Nalini Jaywant. The duo went on to do over 10 films together, including *Insaaf* (1956), *26 January* (1956), *Durgesh Nandini* (1956) and *Kitna Badal Gaya Insaan* (1957).

A memorable film from the '50s was B.R. Chopra's *Naya Daur* (1957), which bagged Dilip Kumar the Filmfare Award for Best Actor for his performance as the *tongawalla* (horse-carriage driver) Shankar, whose livelihood is threatened when the landlord's son starts a bus service in their village. When he protests, Jeevan's character, Kundan, challenges him to a race between his bus and the *tonga*. Ajit plays Krishna, Shankar's woodcutter friend who, following a misunderstanding over a girl, becomes his sworn enemy and hacks a wooden bridge in a fit of jealous rage, almost destroying Shankar's chances of winning. However, in the end, he redeems himself, paving the way for Shankar's incredible win.

The filmmaker admitted that there were serious misgivings within his unit over the casting of Ajit because of his Samson-esque image. The actor himself was uncertain about taking on a role which had shades of grey when he was still a saleable hero. B.R. Chopra assured him that he was the right choice for Krishna, pointing out that his muscular build made him perfect for the show of brute strength in the climax. Writer-producer-director Ramanand Sagar's filmmaker son Prem Sagar remembers watching *Naya Daur* in the theatre. 'When the all-important scene played, with Krishna, a la Hercules, single-handedly holding up the wooden bridge he had sawed through earlier even as Dilip Kumar gallops along on his tonga, the assembled audience broke into spontaneous applause,' he narrates.

Almost 20 years later, the actor played Kalicharan in Ramanand Sagar's *Charas* (1976), a sly caretaker-turned-mafia-don. 'We opted for Ajit-sahab because he had an "international" look, on the lines of a Bond villain,' Prem Sagar says, pointing out that even after he turned villain, the actor retained all the qualities of a hero. 'On the set, he was a pro—no *nakhra*s or problems over co-stars,' the filmmaker remembers appreciatively.

A bond was cemented between Ajit and Dilip Kumar during the long outdoor shoots for *Naya Daur* in Gwalior. The two actors went on to do *Mughal-E-Azam* together. Dilip Kumar had recommended his swashbuckling co-star from *Aan* (1952), Prem Nath, for the role of Durjan Singh, but eventually came to agree with K. Asif that Ajit was the better choice. The duo would hang out together at Mohan Studio as they waited for the lights and camera to be set up. They were called to the set only around two in the afternoon. It took at least six hours for all the actors to get into costume and make-up. Long hours of rehearsals were followed by an extended dinner break. The actual shooting only started after that, by which time Ajit and Dilip Kumar used to be exhausted. 'Sometimes we would step out of the studio after midnight, saying that we were going out for a stroll,' he recounted.

Once out of sight, the two actors would push Dilip Kumar's car out of the studio gate, jump in, and drive away. 'When Asif-sahab hollered for us, his assistants would start searching, returning to tell him that "characters *bhaag gaye hain*", Ajit shared. The director would laugh indulgently and move to the next shot, remembering how the boys had battled the desert sun for long hours in their stifling leather suits, heavy quilts and metallic armour when shooting the battle scenes outdoors in Rajasthan.

Despite Ajit showcasing his histrionics in film after film, the roles began to dry up. For around six to seven years, he spent his days playing cards at Mumbai's Sea Rock hotel. One of his card partners was Rajendra Kumar. The jubilee star pointed out to him that times had changed, and hero roles might be hard to come by. 'But there is the role of a villain in my film *Suraj* (1966), which is being shot in a Madras [now Chennai] studio. You would be perfect as Rajkumar Pratap Singh,' he suggested.

Suraj revolves around the prince's fiancée, Vyjayanthimala's Princess Anuradha, who is kidnapped by Rajendra Kumar's bandit, Suraj Singh, while on her way to his coronation. She loses her heart to her abductor, triggering a violent confrontation between the two men. The film had several sword fights and the swashbuckling Ajit was welcomed back with open arms by not just the audience, but the film fraternity as well.

He continued with his villainous turns, *Zanjeer* giving birth to a new khalnayak reportedly modelled on a real aristocrat—some say he was a gangster—who wore sherwanis and spoke in a low, refined voice. Teja's luxurious mane, aristocratic *tehzeeb* (gentility) and cool swagger in an array of bathrobes was the perfect foil to Amitabh's fiery Inspector Vijay Khanna, who often spoke with his fists.

Lines like '*Aao Vijay, baitho aur hamare saath ek Scotch piyo, hum tumhe kha thode hi jaayenge, vaise bhi hum vegetarian hai* [Come sit down and have a drink with me, Vijay, don't worry, I won't eat you. After all, I am a vegetarian]' had a sly humour that appealed to the audience of the '70s.

Zanjeer arrived in the same year as Nasir Hussain's *Yaadon Ki Baaraat* (1973), a lost-and-found tale of three brothers, with Ajit as the bad man, Shakhaal, who wears a size-8 shoe on one foot and a size-9 one on the other, a discrepancy in sizes that eventually gives him away. The film was another blockbuster. He also starred in Arjun Hingorani's *Kahani Kismat Ki* (1973), which was a superhit. After this, there was no looking back.

Suited, booted and puffing on a cigar or a pipe, Ajit roared through the decade, with films like *Shareef Budmaash* (1973) with Dev Anand, *Khote Sikkay* (1974) with Feroz Khan, *Pratiggya* (1975) with Dharmendra and, of course, *Kalicharan* (1976) with Shatrughan Sinha. What set him apart from other villains was that even when he had a moll on his arm, he did not make you squirm with his on-screen intimacy. Ajit was always careful with language, speaking in a soft, measured tone no matter what the provocation.

Producer-director Dharmesh Darshan remembers going with his filmmaker father, Darshan Sabharwal, for the mahurat of Vijay Anand's multi-starrer *Rajput* (1982). When his father introduced Ajit to Dharmesh, the veteran actor, suave in a white safari suit, was his usual cultured and charming self. 'His son Shehzad and I had attended the same school, Bombay Scottish, and Ajit-sahab would sometimes visit during annual-day functions. There would be much excitement because he was a big villain in the mid-'70s, his "Mona Darling" making him a household name,' informs Dharmesh. When Otters Club opened on Bandra's Carter Road, the Darshans, along with Rajesh Khanna and Ajit, were among its first members. 'Like Pran-sahab and Jeevan-sahab, Ajit-sahab was classy even when playing to the gallery,' the filmmaker asserts.

Rajput was in the making for eight years, with Ranjeeta Kaur stepping in for Neetu Singh as Kamli, and Vinod Khanna replacing Amitabh Bachchan as Bhanu Pratap. Before the film was released, Vinod Khanna announced his retirement and followed his guru Osho Rajneesh to the US. He finished shooting his portions and even completed his dubbing before he left. When his director got in touch with him for some extra scenes, he shot them in an American studio and sent the reels back to India. Owing to the long delay, Ajit could not juggle his dates and passed the baton to Rehman, who went on to play Hema Malini's father. It was the last major film of the *Sahib Bibi Aur Ghulam* (1962) actor, who succumbed to throat cancer two years later.

By the '80s, Ajit's health had also begun to fail following heart problems and a bypass surgery. Midway through the decade, he moved back to Hyderabad. He cultivated grapes, mangoes, pomegranates and other fruits, grew vegetables on his farm, and kept poultry and cattle. He was happy and could not be persuaded by producer-director Harmesh Malhotra, with whom he had worked in *Sangram* (1976), *Choron Ki Baaraat* (1980) and *Phaansi Ke Baad* (1985), to come out of retirement for his 1986 film *Nagina*. Disappointed, but unwilling to make a film without him, Harmesh cast him as Rishi Kapoor's deceased father and hung his garlanded photograph on the wall of the bedroom.

Ajit was eventually lured into making a comeback by

Salim Akhtar in *Police Officer* (1992) and *Jigar* (1992). Over the next three years, he worked in around half a dozen films— he plays the underworld don Uncle in Sanjay Gupta's *Aatish: Feel the Fire* (1994), a rich village jeweller, Chandulal Seth, in Dev Anand's *Gangster* (1994), Khan Chacha in Iqbal Durrani's *Betaaj Badshah* (1994) and Jagdish Prasad in Mahesh Bhatt's *Criminal* (1994), even as he continued to battle health problems. On 22 October 1998, at the age of 76, he was felled by a sudden heart attack. The Lion never roared again.

During my visit to Florida Apartments, after a couple of hours of conversation, Ajit apologized for not being able to offer me even a cup of tea. 'My wife is in Hyderabad and I don't know how to cook,' he confessed. I assured him I wasn't hungry. He reacted by saying he was and wondered if I knew how to cook. 'There's chicken in the fridge and some vegetables too,' he said hopefully. Unfortunately, I was on a deadline and had to hurry back to the office, so I couldn't rustle up a meal for him. I was apologetic. I thought he would be upset I had left him hungry despite him giving me so many priceless nuggets of information. But whenever I called after that day, his familiar baritone would greet me fondly, and he would happily address all my queries. After meeting him, I realized that the Ajit jokes didn't do the man justice. They are indeed silly. Today, I associate him with one of his lines in *Zanjeer*: '*Jis tarah kuch aadmiyon ki kamzori beimaani hoti hai, issi tarah kuch aadmiyon ki kamzori imaandari hoti hai* [Just as some people's shortcoming is corruption, honesty is the failing of others].' Cheers!

✕

JEEVAN AND KIRAN KUMAR

LIKE FATHER, LIKE SON

'Narayan, Narayan…'

Over the decades, the familiar chant of 'Narayan, Narayan' has come to be associated with Jeevan, who was inevitably the first choice for the role of Devarshi Narad Muni, the king of the sages.

'Can you imagine, my father played Narad in 61 films! It is a feat unprecedented in the world, which no other actor can boast of, not even Sean Connery as James Bond. He should be in the *Guinness Book of World Records*!' exclaims Jeevan's son Kiran Kumar. A popular screen actor himself, he shares that a week before his father was to start shooting as Narad, he would give up meat and other non-vegetarian food, as well as alcohol, until the film was complete. 'It was his way of cleansing his body and soul for the character. In fact, such was his dedication, that he would even shave his head,' he adds.

Several other actors have played the character, including Asrani in the film *Narad Vivaah* (1989) and the TV mini-series *Ayodhya Ki Ramleela* (2020). But it is Jeevan whom people immediately identify with the sage after films like *Bhakta*

Dhruva (1947), *Har Har Mahadev* (1950), *Jai Mahalaxmi Maa* (1976), *Har Har Gange* (1979) and *Gopal Krishna* (1979). 'There was a time when even in calendars, Narad Muni wore my father's face, while on screen the sage's "Narayan, Narayan" greeting was always spoken with his signature twang. Such was the impact of his performances,' Kiran Kumar beams with understandable pride.

Omkar Nath Dhar was born on 24 October 1915 in Gilgit in a wealthy and aristocratic Kashmiri Pandit family. His grandfather had been the governor of Gilgit Agency during British rule. His father was also the wazir (minister) of the maharaja and the Dhars were considered nobility in the valley. Omkar lost his mother in childbirth and his father when he was three. But despite the twin tragedies, he grew up a happy, boisterous child in the company of 23 siblings.

At the age of 18, during his college vacation, he came to Bombay with just ₹26 in his pocket. The plan was to pick up some tricks of the trade so he could open a photography studio in Srinagar after he graduated the following year. On his request, an older brother introduced him to writer, lyricist and director Dina Nath Madhok, who pulled a few strings and got Omkar an apprenticeship with a film studio.

The initial excitement of entering the world of glamour quickly faded as boredom set in. With just 13 days left before college opened, Omkar was beginning to get seriously worried because he had not even touched the camera till then, forget clicking pictures. It was at this point, when his future was clouded with uncertainty, that he landed an opportunity that would change the direction of his life.

He had become the 'reflector boy' by then and had been entrusted with the job of pasting silver foil on two plywood reflectors and putting them in the shade to dry.

One afternoon, he put them out in the sun and soon enough, the gleam of the foil began to make his eyes water. Looking for shade, he strolled in the direction of a big mango tree in the studio compound. On reaching it, as he narrated in an interview to Vividh Bharati*, he found a group of young actors sitting under the tree, rehearsing their lines for an upcoming film, *Fashionable India* (1935). The boys had come to the city dreaming of becoming the next Prithviraj Kapoor or Master Vithal, the biggest stars of the time. There were three or four beautiful girls too in the group. Omkar stood, looking at them curiously as they read out their dialogue. Suddenly, there was a break in the reading as the upcoming film's director, Mohan Sinha, realized that one of the boys who was playing a leading role hadn't turned up. Looking around, he noticed Omkar, who was the same age as the boys, standing in front of him. Something about the teenager caught the eye of the filmmaker, the grandfather of *Rajnigandha* (1974) actress Vidya Sinha. Looking him straight in the eye, Mohan Sinha urged, 'You there, say something.'

Omkar was taken aback and shaking his head, mumbled, 'I'm not an actor, I'm from the technical side.' But the filmmaker would not take no for an answer. Finally, having read William Shakespeare when in school, and performed a few plays in college, he started reciting lines from popular playwright Pandit Narayan Prasad Betab's *Mahabharat*. Slipping into the character of Duryodhana with ease, Omkar vowed to make his cousins' lives difficult, making them sleep on stones instead of the soft beds they were used to. The words flowed from memory, including the eldest Kaurava's mocking laugh.

---

*Asheesh Pandey, 'Jeevan (Actor) Tells about His Journey (Recorded in the Year 1967)', *YouTube*, 5 July 2015, https://tinyurl.com/bdeydmut. Accessed on 7 May 2024.

As he basked in the spotlight, his friend and fellow apprentice Dwarka Divecha, who later became the cameraman of movies like *Rattan* (1944), *Dillagi* (1949), *Dil-E-Nadaan* (1953) and *Yasmin* (1955), and the director of photography of *Dil Diya Dard Liya* (1966), *Khilona* (1970) and *Sholay* (1975), among others, watched from a distance. Encouraged by his rapt audience, Omkar switched from prose to tragic verse with a *sher* from Agha Hashr Kashmiri's book *Nek Parveen Urf Silver King*. Divecha cleverly turned the reflectors so the silver foil caught the sun and shone directly on his friend's face. As he recited the tragic verse, his right eye started twitching. By the time he ended with a flourish, his eyes were streaming tears. For a moment there was a pin-drop silence, and then, thrilled that the boy could tear up without glycerine, Mohan Sinha embraced Omkar, booming, '*Wah wah, wah wah barkhurdar* [Wonderful, my child], you are a born artiste! Forget photography, act in films, I will make your life!' And just like that Omkar Nath Dhar, who had been dreaming of a career behind the camera, found himself facing one instead.

Fashionable India was a big-budget romantic drama, revolving around Kusum, played by Pushpa, and the three men in her life. One is a fellow student, Ramesh, enacted by R.D. Shukla, the man Kusum loves. Then there is Wadilal, who portrays the raja who plans to wed her by paying off her father's debts. Omkar was cast as the third suitor, the villainous Madhav. He is credited as O.K. Dhar in this film. He went on to do other films with the director, including *Swaraj Ke Sipahi* (1937), *Anuradha* (1940) and *Vanmala* (1941). After a while, he adopted the screen name Jeevan—given to him by producer-director Vijay Bhatt, in whose *Bhakta Dhruva* (1947) he played Narad for the first time.

The seeds of villainy were sown in his very first film, but for over half a century, Jeevan went on to do every role possible, from a sly *muni* (sage) to a scheming munim (accountant), from a thakur (landlord) to a *diwan* (minister), and from the warden of an orphanage to a kidnapper. Later, he even played Duryodhana's uncle Shakuni, who brings the Pandavas to ruin with a game of dice, in Babubhai Mistry's *Mahabharat* (1965). 'My father was passionate about his craft and would often say that he was being paid to do what he loved most in the world,' recalls Kiran Kumar.

For him, his father's best performance is in B.R. Chopra's *Kanoon* (1960), despite him having just one scene in the film. The courtroom drama opens with Jeevan's Kalidas pleading guilty for the murder of Ganpat. When Judge Badri Prasad (played by Ashok Kumar) reminds him that he can be hanged for the crime, Kalidas shocks everyone by saying he cannot be punished twice for killing the same man. In an impassioned performance, he then goes on to reveal that 10 years ago, he was sentenced to life imprisonment for snuffing out the life of this very man who had still been alive then, despite all his protestations of innocence. After a decade, filled with venom, he had gone after Ganpat once he was released from jail, this time actually killing him. He berates the law for ruining not just his life, but that of his wife's (played by Leela Chitnis) too, asking the judge if he can give her back her lost youth. Even as the tirade continues, punctuated with coughing bouts, Kalidas clutches his chest and gasping for breath, falls in the witness box. He dies before another sentence can be delivered.

Though Jeevan himself never believed his mentor Mohan Sinha's conviction that he was a natural-born actor, with this one-scene appearance he proved it true. For someone who had no training in the craft, to make such a lasting impact, without any props or costumes, and with just two scenes in a film that boasted of several big names like Ashok Kumar, Rajendra Kumar and Nanda, is nothing short of incredible.

Jeevan had earlier acted in Chopra's directorial debut, *Afsana* (1951). Six years later, he collaborated again with the filmmaker for *Naya Daur* (1957), in which he plays the son of a rich landlord, Kundan, who brings a bus to ferry people into the village, much to the dismay of the local tongawallas, triggering a dramatic race between man and machine. 'B.R. Chopra, Narendra Bedi and Manmohan Desai were my father's friends and wanted to repeat him in every film they made,' informs Kiran Kumar. He goes on to list Jeevan's roles as Motilal, the loving older brother of the heroine, in the Dilip-Kumar–Mumtaz-Shanti-starrer *Ghar Ki Izzat* (1948); Paul in *Hulchul* (1951), another Dilip Kumar film, based on the 1847 novel *Wuthering Heights*; and Robert, the don of *Amar Akbar Anthony* (1977), as his other favourites from his father's vast and rich repertoire.

Amar Akbar Anthony brings back an amusing memory. 'My father enjoyed playing Christian characters and had the anglicized accent down pat. Several church-going fisherfolk were his friends and he would spend a lot of time with them in Bandra, which is how we always got the best fish and crabs,' laughs Kiran Kumar. He would sometimes accompany his father to the Khar Danda fish market in Mumbai where the fisherwomen were crazy about him. 'As soon as they spotted us, they would shout excitedly, "*Hamara hero aa gaya* [Our hero is here]!" There was one particular fisherwoman who was really possessive about my father and would insist, "*Yeh mera hero hai* [He is my hero]!" It was all very heart-warming,' he recounts.

The '60s star Biswajit Chatterjee, who worked with Jeevan in *Pardesi* (1970), remembers him as a sincere actor and a seasoned artiste who was brilliant as the villainous munim Dharmpal. 'Anita Guha's husband, Manik Dutt, once visited me on the set. He was an actor too, and spotting Jeevan-sahab from far, warned me to scale up my performance or he would overshadow me completely,' reminisces Biswajit, who, having been wowed by Jeevan's performances and his unique dialogue delivery in films like *Mela* (1948), *Shabnam* (1949) and *Kohinoor* (1960), knew this was no idle threat.

He was delighted when soon after they started shooting, the senior actor told him graciously, 'You have come from the Bengal film industry, *aapke saath kaam karne mein bada mazaa aayega* [I will enjoy working with you].' They only did that one film together, but for Biswajit, working with his neighbour was an unforgettable experience. 'I lived in Bandra at the time and Jeevan-sahab's son Kiran Kumar would boast to his friends that a big hero lived opposite their bungalow. According to me, his father was a bigger hero,' he asserts.

After *Fashionable India*, Mohan Sinha cast Jeevan as the lead in *Romantic India* (1936), with Noor Jehan as the daredevil Princess Chandrakala. This was followed by *Badhe Chalo* (1937), in which he again played the hero. But in due course, Jeevan moved to negative roles, and later to character roles.

∞

Interestingly, Kiran Kumar's career followed the same trajectory. As he says, it made no difference to him whether he was playing the leading man or the villain, whether it was a Hindi or a regional film or even a television series. 'From a very young age, when I would accompany my father to the set to watch him shoot, I wanted to be a part of the film industry and just getting opportunities to act was enough for me,' he states.

Born Deepak Dhar, Jeevan's young son was destined for excellence from a young age. Head boy and captain of the cricket team at his boarding school, the Daly College, he was kept away from the glitter of the film industry during the formative years of his childhood. He joined the acting course at the Film and Television Institute of India (FTII) in Pune on the advice of Shatrughan Sinha. He was the gold-medal-winning graduate of the 1967 batch. After graduating from the institute, Deepak adopted his mother's name Kiran and made his debut as a leading man, playing the '*lambu* engineer' in K.A. Abbas's film *Do Boond Pani* (1971). Set in a small village in Rajasthan, this critically acclaimed film on water scarcity bagged the Nargis Dutt Award for Best Feature Film on National Integration.

This film was followed by *Bindiya Aur Bandook* (1972), *Jangal Mein Mangal* (1972), *Hum Junglee Hain* (1973) and *Aaj Ki Taaza Khabar* (1973). However, after *Jangal Mein Mangal* flopped, having watched his father and uncles Ajit and Pran effortlessly carry off villainous roles, the handsome young man accepted a character with shades of grey in Subhash Mukherjee's *Mr. Romeo* (1974). 'The film has Shashi Kapoor, whom I idolized, in the lead. I play his younger brother, Suresh, who befriends the son of a man who hates their father. Under the influence of these two men, my character becomes a wastrel and a drug addict,' Kiran Kumar narrates. 'I wasn't too enamoured with playing the hero and was happy playing an anti-hero. I have always found negative roles challenging,' he says simply.

A couple of years later, Kiran Kumar moved to Gujarati cinema and acquired a cult following there. Even in his first

Gujarati film *Kulvadhu* (1977), produced by Asha Parekh (who also acted in it), he plays the bad guy. Over the course of a decade, he worked in 82 Gujarati films, quickly moving to leading roles, and came to be known as the Amitabh Bachchan of Gujarati cinema.

He once remarked that even though Mumbai is his *janmabhoomi* (birthplace), Gujarat will always hold a special place in his heart as his *karmabhoomi* (workplace) because this is where he met his wife, state-award-winning actress Sushma Verma, his co-star in films like *Albeli Naar* (1981), *Pocketmaar* (1982), *Rasta No Raja* (1982) and *Tadka Chhayan* (1995).

However, after a series of superhits, he felt he was stagnating and returned to Mumbai. 'I had always been close to Salim-sahab [scriptwriter Salim Khan], who had pushed my dad to send me to the Daly College, a boarding school in his hometown Indore. After returning to Mumbai, I got in touch with him and asked if there were any good roles going. He had just written a revenge drama, *Falak* [1988], and told me that while Jackie Shroff and Mohan Bhandari had already been signed to play the brothers, there was the role of a baddie, Bagga, and suggested I take it up,' informs the actor. *Falak*, directed by Shashilal K. Nair, flopped. But fortunately for him, Rakesh Roshan's *Khudgarz* (1987)—in which his character Sudhir drives a wedge between two friends, Jeetendra's Amar and Shatrughan Sinha's Bihari—was released the previous year and was a huge hit. It marked a triumphant comeback to Bollywood for the actor.

The character Kiran Kumar is remembered for even today, though, is that of the dreaded gangster Lotiya Pathan, Madhuri Dixit's tormentor and Anil Kapoor's nemesis, in *Tezaab* (1988). 'My director [N. Chandra] understood the dark world Lotiya inhabited and helped me flesh out the character. Like Amjad Khan's Gabbar Singh in *Sholay* [1975], Ajit uncle's Lion in *Kalicharan* [1976], Anupam Kher's Dr Dang in *Karma* [1986] and Amrish Puri-ji's Mogambo in *Mr. India* [1987], *Tezaab*'s Lotiya Pathan has come to be instantly identified with me. For 30 years, he has been the monkey on my back and refuses to get off,' the actor guffaws. You can almost hear him roar, '*Babban ne jo kiya wo mujh par karz hai, aur pathan duniya chhod sakta hai lekin karz nahin chhod sakta* [After what Babban did to me, I owe him something too, and a pathan cannot leave this world without paying his debt],' and shiver in anticipation of his retribution.

Six feet tall, with a great physique and a rich baritone, it was easy for Kiran Kumar to pass himself off as a pathan. He plays one to perfection in another film, Mukul S. Anand's *Khuda Gawah* (1992). 'Like Lotiya, Pasha is a man blinded by revenge. He carries out his threats mercilessly and shows streaks of insanity. What makes him even more exciting is that this pathan is an Afghan,' the actor points out.

Khuda Gawah was shot in Kabul and Mazar-i-Sharif. Kiran Kumar did not cross the border into Afghanistan, but he did shoot in another neighbouring country, Nepal. There was a long, tough schedule in Jomsom, a small village nestled in the lap of Mount Dhaulagiri and the Nilgiri Himal range, the terminus for treks that are a part of the arduous Annapurna Circuit. 'It's one of the remotest regions, completely cut off from the world. There's a tenuous connection to Beni now, but back then there were no roads or public transport and we had to travel to the location on mules, along dirt roads cut into the mountains. The constant threat of a loose, sharp-edged boulder hurtling down at us like a missile made these daily treks hazardous,' Kiran Kumar reminisces. Food and water were also scarce and the unit survived only on potatoes and rationed drinking water. 'By the time I returned home, I was 10 kilograms lighter, and my mother was shocked by my gaunt appearance,' he chuckles at the memory.

The film remains special because it gave him a chance to share the screen with Sridevi. 'Even though she did not interact much on the set, going into a shell as soon as the shot was okayed, Madam Sridevi was a gorgeous woman and an absolute dynamite on camera,' the actor raves.

He was equally wowed by Amitabh Bachchan's sincerity, passion and commitment. The actor had worked with his father. Kiran Kumar reminisces how whenever there was a shoot in the city during the filming of *Amar Akbar Anthony* (1977), Manmohan Desai would insist that along with his father's lunch, his mother, who was a terrific cook excelling in Kashmiri cuisine, send *kofta*s (meatballs) and *paaya* (mutton soup) for him, Pran, Amitabh Bachchan and the rest of actors. 'Big tiffin carriers would arrive on the set before the unit broke for lunch and the meals were much appreciated,' he says.

Manmohan Desai was the only one from the film industry whom Jeevan, a conservative man, allowed the women of his family to interact with. When she was eight, Kiran's sister Nikki cajoled their father to let her accompany him to Pune for a three-week schedule for *Amar Akbar Anthony*. She was pampered by everyone and had a blast. When she returned, Nikki boasted that she had met 'the' Amitabh Bachchan and that they shared the same birthday, 11 October, and became the 'star' in her school—until the film opened in theatres, that is.

When the students saw the film, in particular the scene where Jeevan, as Robert, deliberately pours whiskey on his shoes and orders his chauffeur, Kishanlal, to wipe them, they were appalled. Desperate for money to treat his ailing wife and feed his starving children, Kishanlal, played by Pran, polishes the loafers with the sleeve of his jacket, only for a coin to be tossed to him, humiliating him further. That scene made Jeevan a villain for real, and one day, his daughter came home crying, wondering why he would play such a horrible character. Jeevan simply told Nikki, '*Bachcha* [child], ask your friends if anyone knows their daddies like they know yours?' Touché!

Kiran Kumar remembers his father as an excellent teacher who would impart life lessons without preaching. He was also more of a friend than a parent, who played cricket with him and his friends on Sunday, then took them out for ice cream and chocolates. 'He was absolutely fearless, not afraid of anything, not even death. I inherited his strength of will and it stood me in good stead during the pandemic in 2020, when I contracted the dreaded Covid-19,' the actor shares.

His father was very close to his wife and children. Kiran Kumar recalls that when they sat down for a meal, if there was something he particularly liked, such as a favourite chicken dish, his father would spoon it up from his plate into his son's. 'There were times when he would return from shooting late at night with a box of gulab jamuns from Jhama, a famous sweet shop in Mumbai. If we had fallen asleep by then, he would tiptoe into our bedrooms, lift our heads from the pillow, coax us to open our mouths and feed us the *mithai* before sitting down to savour the dessert. He never ate anything special without first sharing it with us,' he recounts.

Jeevan was equally close to his friends. Every evening, he would either host a dinner at his home or drive over to Dilip Kumar, Mukri, Johnny Walker, Pran or Naushad's place. 'He was particularly close to Chandrashekhar [actor-writer-filmmaker Chandrashekhar Vaidya] uncle. That was a different era, when personal equations ruled,' points out his actor son.

After returning to Hindi cinema with *Khudgarz* and *Tezaab*, Kiran Kumar himself played an array of characters in shades of black, grey or black and white. He is quick to add that he has always been careful not to imbibe any of the negativity he portrays on screen. 'My father never carried home any of his characters. He would say, "*Sab villains ko set pe chhod deta hoon* [I leave all the villains behind on the set] and I return home with a clean heart." His words still resonate with me,' he admits.

One remembers him as Narendra Chauhan, the urbane dad of Shilpa Shetty's Anjali in Dharmesh Darshan's *Dhadkan* (2000), who gets his daughter married to Akshay Kumar's Ram knowing that she is in love with Suniel Shetty's Dev. 'And despite being an educated girl with a mind of her own, Anjali gives in to his wishes not only because she idolizes her father, but also because he justifies his choice to her,' says Dharmesh Darshan, reminding me that Kiran Kumar is in the film for just 20 minutes at the beginning, and for 20 minutes towards the end, and yet he is still remembered for that performance.

The filmmaker lived close to Jeevan's bungalow, 'Jeevan Kiran', and recalls watching a 10-year-old Kiran Kumar play cricket. 'We moved to our own bungalow in Pali Hill when I was five, but my mother continued to speak affectionately about the Dhar family,' he says, adding that Kiran Kumar's debut film, *Do Boond Pani*, was distributed by his father, Darshan Sabharwal.

They had lost touch when the actor moved to Gujarati cinema. Around 1986–87, though, they had bumped into each other at a pizza outlet and Dharmesh Darshan's mother, Sheila, introduced her teenage son to the good-looking Kiran Kumar who had just made a successful comeback to Bollywood. Almost 15 years later, when the filmmaker, riding high on the super success of *Raja Hindustani* (1996), was looking for an actor to play Shilpa Shetty's father in *Dhadkan*, his mother, who didn't usually interfere with his career decisions, surprised him by recommending Jeevan's son for the role.

'He met me very warmly. Even his wife Sushma, who had been an actress and knew my parents well, swung by for a few minutes. Kiran Kumar told me he would be happy to do my film, but added that he had just signed a big film with a top star and could give me only 15 days,' informs Dharmesh Darshan, admitting with a laugh that at that time, neither of them knew the fortnight would be spread over two to three years as the film kept getting delayed. 'We wrapped up his portions exactly on the fifteenth day, but by then, he would have given me extra dates if required,' says the director, who was delighted that though he could not work with Jeevan, who had passed away before he entered the industry, he got to work with his son.

Dharmesh Darshan admits that many well-wishers tried to dissuade him from casting Kiran Kumar in that strong supporting role in *Dhadkan* because by then, with Lotiya and Pasha, he had established himself as a villain. However, since every actor in the film had been cast against type, including Akshay Kumar and Suniel Shetty, there was no one better than him to play Narendra Chauhan according to the director. 'He was a disciplined professional and an approachable actor, excited to play the role and respectful towards a director many years his junior,' reminisces

Dharmesh Darshan. He reasons that exposure to the film industry at a young age and a decade-long tenure in regional cinema had made the actor grounded and he was also not prone to star tantrums. 'Losing his brother Bhushan [he was an actor and producer who passed away following a heart attack in 1997] had brought an emotional depth to his performances. Like his father, he could fit into any role with admirable ease,' he lauds.

Kiran Kumar himself admits that he found the *Dhadkan* character interesting because Narendra Chauhan is so different from him. 'As a father, I left it to my kids [daughter Srishti and son Shaurya] to choose their own paths. As far as I was concerned, my father called me "Baaghi Shehzada" because I was a rebel and would question everything I was told. At the same time, he respected my judgement and did not stop me from moving to Gujarati cinema. In fact, he encouraged me, saying it is better to be a big fish in a small pond than get lost in the ocean,' he remembers fondly.

For him, the transition has continued—from Hindi cinema to Gujarati films, then back to Bollywood and on to television. In 1986, he seamlessly moved to television with Cinevista's *Katha Sagar*. Directed by Shyam Benegal, the series included 37 stories on different subjects by famous authors, including 'The Overcoat' by Nikolai Gogol, Leo Tolstoy's 'Where Love Is, God Is', O. Henry's 'The Clarion Call' and 'The Last Leaf', and so on. He featured in other shows on the national broadcaster, among them *Ghutan* (it aired on Doordarshan in 1997 and as *Manzil* on StarPlus in 1998), *Detective Karan* and *Agneepath* (2006). Kiran Kumar was also seen in the Aruna Irani-produced *Vaidehi: Ek Aur Agni Pareeksha* as the protagonist's rich father-in-law harbouring a dark secret. He appeared in shows on Sony

Entertainment Television as well, including the fun-filled *Chhajje Chhajje Ka Pyaar*, about owners and tenants, and the historical series *Prithvi Vallabh: Itihaas Bhi, Rahasya Bhi*, in which he plays Sultan Sabuktigin of Ghazni. On StarPlus, he was memorable as Air Commodore AOC Suraj Singh in *Saara Akaash*, and as the protagonist's biological father, Vishal Rastogi, in *Miilee*.

On Zee TV, he was a part of *Aandhi*, a story of mistaken identity similar to *Kati Patang* (1970), and the crime drama series *Waaris*, about a don's search for his heir. 'On television, my audience wants to see me play strong, central characters, while in films, I can experiment with negative roles too. This way, I have the best of both worlds,' beams the actor who, over two decades, has featured in more than 5,000 episodes in different TV shows, worked in over 450 films with more to come, and has now moved to OTT content with web series like *The Trial* with Kajol and the upcoming *The Showstopper* with Zeenat Aman. He completed a golden run, 50 years in show business, in 2021.

He is quick to point out that he has never copied his father, not even when he moved to negative roles. 'My father acted in over 600 films. He was a legend. As an actor, he will always be miles ahead, distinctive for his unique mannerisms and voice that have been imitated by many other actors over the years. But I have the satisfaction of having made my own place in the industry,' Kiran Kumar asserts. Today, his only regret is that his father didn't live to see him return to Bollywood in a big way, *Khudgarz* having released on 31 July 1987, and Jeevan having passed away a month earlier, on 10 June 1987.

Among Jeevan's last films was Sanjay Khan's action thriller *Kala Dhanda Goray Log* (1986) in which he plays a kidnapper.

'My father breathed life into the characters he played, leaving an indelible mark on our hearts. His contribution to cinema, his artistry, dedication and passion for the craft will inspire generations of actors and movie enthusiasts,' Kiran Kumar signs off proudly.

RANJEET
LUCK BY CHANCE

'Dine, wine, maaro line… I am free after nine…
Place is yours or mine?'

—*Housefull 2* (2012)

As I enter his bungalow in a sylvan bylane of Mumbai, a Shivalinga on a canvas catches my eye. It comes as a surprise to know that the painter is none other than the bad man I have come to meet, Ranjeet. On another wall is an artwork of an elderly tailor neck-deep in a monsoon deluge, holding afloat a sewing machine that is his only means of livelihood. Every wrinkle on his face, every strand of hair, the light and shade on the muddy flood waters—it is all meticulously detailed. 'I saw this photograph by American photojournalist Steve McCurry in a magazine and replicated it,' the actor informs with quiet pride as I stand transfixed before it.

Upstairs, in his cozy study that resembles a tree house more than a villain's den, whose walls, floor and even ceiling Ranjeet has painted himself, there's a smaller canvas of a young couple. Serene in shades of white, it grew out of a friend's New Year's card from London. 'There are more canvases here,' he says, opening a cabinet cut into the wall.

He surprises me again with the admission that he learnt art through online tutorials. 'I've experimented all my life,' Ranjeet smiles.

Acting also happened quite by chance, from the desire to experience something new. Back in 1966–67, Ranjeet, or Gopal Bedi as he was called then, was sitting in the canteen of New Delhi's Hindu College. Some friends were discussing the full-page ads released by the Indian Air Force (IAF) for the selection and training of pilots, talking about how the Union Public Service Commission (UPSC), which recruits candidates for the armed forces, was very stringent and only 10–12 per cent from across the country made it. 'Wanting to know what made the selection so difficult, four of us filled out the application form. I paid the registration fees from my pocket money without informing my parents,' he recounts.

To their surprise, all four passed the Air Force Common Admission Test (AFCAT) written examination. They were called to Jabalpur for the Air Force Selection Board (AFSB) test, and cleared that too. During medicals, one was rejected, but Gopal and three others were accepted. 'That's when I informed my father [Dwarkaprasad Bedi] that I had been accepted by the IAF, since I needed his signature on a bond. My family was really proud and I left for training at the National Defence Academy,' he informs.

Unfortunately, in Coimbatore, he had a run-in with a senior officer who lived in the cantonment with his family and suspected the new recruit of hitting on his daughter. 'His suspicions were baseless, but he abused me roundly and threatened to ruin my career. Upset, I showered some choicest Punjabi *gaalis* [abuses] on him and was thrown out of the academy,' Gopal admits sheepishly. So it was back to Delhi and the Hindu College canteen, waiting for the term to end so he could enroll and complete his graduation. 'Since I was a well-known goalkeeper—that's how I got my nickname Goli—and played football for a local club as well as the college team, I was allowed inside the college premises despite no longer being a student,' he adds.

One day, on his way to Connaught Place for coffee, Gopal dropped by a friend's place. His father was having a small get-together and called out to him, enquiring how his air force training was going. Gopal confessed that he had been sacked and after a few minutes of polite conversation, as he turned to leave, someone tapped him from behind and asked, 'Hey, would you like to act in a film?' The stranger was a good-looking man, fashionably togged out in a blazer and cravat, waving a cigarette holder. His proposal was unexpected, to say the least.

'Coming from a conservative family, I had not seen a single film till then, naively believing they would rob me of my stamina and affect my football. I had also never acted in plays when in school and college, not even the local Ramleela,' Gopal shares. As he stood there pondering over the offer, the stranger invited him to lunch the following day at The Claridges, a five-star hotel in central Delhi. He nodded his acceptance and left.

Afraid of being ridiculed, he did not tell his friends about the film offer, and definitely not his family, knowing that he would get hell. But he did go for lunch to The Claridges, where the gentleman introduced himself as Ranjeet Singh, fondly called Ronnie, and sketched out the story of his film, which revolved around a truck driver who encountered dacoits in the jungles and goondas on the highways while driving at night. 'Jayant-sahab, Amjad Khan's father, had been signed to play the truck driver. I was offered the parallel lead of his cleaner, Raj, aka Raju, who shines the windows, gets the chai at the dhaba and occasionally accompanies the boss to *kotha*s to watch the *naach-gaana* [song and dance]. I wasn't a looker, but being a footballer, I had the physique of a panther, and I guess that's how I caught Ronnie's eye,' he surmises.

The film was titled *Zindagi Ki Raahein*. After getting his nod, Ronnie left for Mumbai to sign the rest of his cast, promising to call Gopal over soon. In the interim, following his producer's advice to watch a few films, he watched reruns of old movies like *Gunga Jumna* (1961), *Hum Dono* (1961) and *Mujhe Jeene Do* (1963) at reduced rates. He would sneak into morning shows, praying that no one would spot him and rat him out to his parents. 'Three months passed and there was no news from Ronnie. I had heard of filmmakers exploiting youngsters, and believing that Ronnie was a fraud too, I returned to my old, familiar routine,' he shares.

Then, one day, Gopal was surprised by a postcard from Ronnie. He apologized for not being able to cast him as the second lead, but offered him another role with shades of grey. 'If you are interested, I can send you the money for a plane ticket,' the filmmaker wrote. Gopal accepted the offer and told his parents he wanted to go to Bombay with his football team to play some matches. They agreed immediately. As he was leaving, his mother put a gold chain around his neck, and gave him an expensive watch and some rings to wear. When he protested, pointing out that he might lose them, his mother told him that she had heard there were plenty of pickpockets in Bombay. If he got robbed, he could sell some of the jewellery and buy a return ticket home.

So, travelling by plane for the first time, Gopal Bedi reached Bombay, where he was picked up by Ronnie in

Chetan Anand's black Fiat and driven to the actor-filmmaker's shack on Juhu Beach, where he had been staying.

Over the next few days, Ronnie made Gopal meet the legends of the Hindi film industry. The young man accompanied Sunil Dutt to his Pali Hill bungalow, where 'Mother India' Nargis herself served him a late dinner, and was whisked off to R.K. Studios, where he watched footage from Raj Kapoor's film *Mera Naam Joker* (1970), which was then under production, even seeing the legend edit a song reel with scissors and nail polish right in the preview theatre.

Meanwhile, Ronnie rented a four-bedroom bungalow near Hema Malini's house in Juhu and opened a production office in Bombay. 'Occasionally I would visit Dilip [Kumar] sahab's bungalow and was welcomed enthusiastically by his younger brother, Ehsan, who had become a good friend. In the evening I would dress up in a suit and accompany Ronnie or Sanjay Khan to some of Bollywood's biggest parties. It was a good life and I was fortunate to be accepted so easily into the elite circle despite having no filmi connections,' Gopal recounts.

Life was rolling along smoothly, until the financiers pulled out. Ronnie left for London, promising to be back soon and make the film with his own money. 'Sanjay Khan dropped out and was replaced by Sanjeev Kumar, but after five to six reels, the film was shelved,' informs Gopal, who, by the end of the month, was beginning to worry about the rent and turned to Sunil Dutt for advice.

It was the senior actor who suggested he store all the furniture they had rented for the office in the garage and lock up the bungalow till Ronnie returned. 'You can move into my guest house meanwhile,' Sunil Dutt offered. Embarrassed to accept his hospitality, Gopal asked one of the boys at the office to fix him a paying-guest rental. 'Since Ronnie had never introduced me as an actor, his friends had simply assumed that I was one of his relatives and had come to help him with the production. They had no idea I was living on the ₹750 he was paying me as a monthly remuneration, and without him around, I had begun to wonder if I would be able to make a place for myself in the film industry among all these good-looking actors,' he admits.

Suddenly depressed, he cut himself off from his newfound friends and retreated to a hotel in Mahabaleshwar that belonged to a friend of his father. Impressed with him, the friend offered to send Gopal to Germany for training in hotel management. After staying at the hotel for a fortnight, though, he returned to Bombay, ready to go back home and decide what to do next. But destiny had other plans.

He was having lunch at Neelam Restaurant on Linking Road when the boy from Ronnie's office who had got him his paying-guest accommodation dropped by with a request. Could Gopal put in a word with Sunil Dutt for a job in any department during the two-month outdoor schedule in Rajasthan for his upcoming home production, *Reshma Aur Shera* (1971)? 'Knowing Ronnie's continued absence had hit him hard, too, and this would help him earn enough money to live out the year comfortably, I took him with me to Dutt-sahab's office, which was close by,' says Gopal.

He got a hero's welcome from the manager, who admitted they had been hunting high and low for him after he had gone off the radar. Gopal was told that Sunil Dutt wanted to cast him in the role of Waheeda Rehman's brother, coincidentally also called Gopal, in *Reshma Aur Shera*. 'Dutt-sahab thought I looked like a Rajput, and, moved that he had considered me for a film he was producing and directing, I agreed immediately. The boy with me got a job, too, and his train ticket was booked that very day,' he beams.

The next morning, when he dropped by the office to thank Sunil Dutt, who was returning from Madras that day, he was told by the manager that Mohan Segal had called the previous day after he had left, enquiring about Gopal's whereabouts. Segal was a big producer and director whose last film, *Sajan* (1969), had starred Manoj Kumar. Gopal called him from the office and was told he was making a film titled *Sawan Bhadon* (1970) with newcomers Navin Nischol and Rekha.

'I want you to play Rekha's brother. It's a small role, but a good one. Will you do it?' the filmmaker asked. Gopal wasn't sure he wanted to do another small role, but since Mohan Segal was a big name, he told him he would drop by that evening. 'It was in the elevator, on my way up to his fifth floor apartment, that I decided that since I had come to Bombay to act in films, I should accept the role,' he says.

Soon after, he took a couple of hopping flights to Rajasthan, driving down the last stretch to join the unit shooting *Reshma Aur Shera* in the desert. He shared a tent with actress Nimmi's husband, the screenwriter S. Ali Raza, associate director B.S. Thapa, and Amitabh Bachchan, who had already worked in *Saat Hindustani* (1969), his debut film. A close bond developed between the two young actors, both affectionately calling each other 'lale'. They went on to feature in several blockbusters, including *Muqaddar Ka Sikandar* (1978), *Suhaag* (1979), *Laawaris* (1981) and *Namak Halaal* (1982).

Meanwhile, one day, while driving to Jaisalmer, Sunil Dutt suddenly told Gopal he needed a more filmi name and asked him to pick an alphabet. He chose 'R', and his mentor suggested Ranjeet. 'It reminded me of Maharaja Ranjeet Singh, a great warrior king. "Done," I told Dutt-sahab, pointing out that eventually my work rather than my name would speak for me,' he narrates. In Jaisalmer, Sunil Dutt called his Bombay office and informed his publicist that Gopal would now be known as Ranjeet and should be promoted by that name. 'Dutt-sahab was like a father figure who loved me like his son. If ever he felt I was on the wrong track, he would quietly put me straight,' he adds fondly.

Sawan Bhadon was Ranjeet's first release and it was a superhit. *Reshma Aur Shera*, which released the following year, won three National Awards, was India's entry for the Oscars in the Best Foreign Language Film (now Best International Feature Film) category, and was nominated for the Golden Bear at the Berlin International Film Festival. It got him a lot of appreciation and also landed him *Sharmeelee* (1971), which kickstarted his journey as a villain. 'Raakhee, who is my bride in *Reshma Aur Shera*, told me on the flight that they were looking for someone to play her college boyfriend in *Sharmeelee*. One look, and the producer, Subodh Mukherji, decided I was his Kundan. The film made me a star,' Ranjeet says proudly.

As fans crowded around him for autographs and his photographs started appearing in magazines, Ranjeet decided it was time to reconcile with his parents, who had disowned him after learning that he had become an actor. Hoping to mollify them, he invited them to *Sharmeelee*'s premiere in Delhi. 'But after seeing me pulling Raakhee by her hair and tearing off her clothes, they left the film midway. I returned to the auditorium to find their chairs empty and at home was confronted by stony faces and dirty looks, my mother wailing that I had shamed the family with my black deeds and that my father would never be able to face relatives back home in Amritsar now,' he recounts. Ranjeet had to bring Raakhee, whom he had dropped off a few minutes ago, to his home to convince everyone that she held no grudges against him and what they had seen was just play-acting, even as his mother continued to apologize profusely to the *soni kudi* (beautiful girl) and berate him.

'In time, my parents accepted their prodigal son back into the fold, understanding that I was simply doing my job. *Chaiji* [mother] even started going to watch my films with her friends in the neighbourhood theatre, the owner refusing to let them pay for their tickets because I was the "*colony ka bachcha*" [the boy from the colony] who had made good. Once, though, when a bullet found its mark on screen, my mother started lamenting loudly that they had killed her beta [son], till it was explained to her that all this was make-believe and her son was fighting fit,' Ranjeet chuckles.

He was a popular villain by then, with distributors insisting on at least one rape scene with him in the film to bring in the crowds. 'I was shooting round the clock with around 80 films on the floors. Since many of the leading men back then arrived late on the sets, I started doing multiple shifts, reporting on an hourly basis, and was being paid handsomely for the dates my secretary squeezed out. I was clueless about how much I was making as he set the terms. I bought him a place of his own and a Fiat, then bought this bungalow and a few cars,' he informs.

So busy was Ranjeet that he would take the 6.00 a.m. flight out to outdoor locations. He would shoot from 9.00 a.m. till two in the afternoon, then catch the 4.00 p.m. flight back to Bombay. 'I would report for the 7.00 p.m. shift. It was usually a fight sequence at Murud-Janjira Fort, 165 kilometers south of the city, and I would often drive down myself, shoot till 2.00 a.m., catch a few winks or get pulled off to a party, then take the early morning flight out of town again. If I was needed in Bombay during the day, the schedule would reverse,' he laughs, recalling how he shot his death scene in *Haath Ki Safai* (1974) at Panvel railway station during a five-hour stopover in Bombay, while returning from Mauritius and en route to Beirut. In the car, on the way to Panvel, Ranjeet also reeled off a few shots for a Satyen Bose film.

Since he was a bachelor and his parents lived in Delhi, his bungalow, with a staff of seven to eight, became the go-to place for his colleagues. They would head there after pack-up. 'Moushumi [Chatterjee] would fry fish, Reena [Roy] would roll out parathas and Parveen [Babi] would mix drinks. Whenever I dropped by, the cook was asked to whip up a cold coffee and make a sandwich for "pandit-ji", since I am a vegetarian. I miss those carefree days when we were like one big happy family,' he recalls fondly.

Ranjeet's on-the-run lifestyle changed after a wake-up call from his father complaining that he didn't even have the time to drop his mother personally to the airport when she was visiting him. 'You want us to relocate to Bombay when you are never home,' he groused. The actor immediately instructed his secretary to stop signing any new films. While he wrapped up his earlier commitments, Ranjeet decided he wouldn't work on weekends and would start making his own films.

In 1990, Ranjeet turned writer, producer and director with *Kaarnaama*. He had signed Aloka as the leading lady opposite Vinod Khanna. She started attending story sessions, music sittings and taking a lot of interest in the production. 'People knew her as my girlfriend and as word got around, I found it difficult to get a second heroine despite it being a good role as many of the actresses were afraid of being overshadowed by Aloka,' he reveals.

Meanwhile, since their younger children were already

married, Ranjeet's parents wanted their eldest son to settle down too. 'They liked Aloka, who despite being a glamorous actress was a *sanskari* [cultured], homely girl and tentatively suggested that she would make me a good wife. When I pointed out that she was doing my film, they told me they would wait,' he recalls.

Ranjeet took Aloka into confidence then. She agreed to drop out of his film. He signed Kimi Katkar in her place and Farah Naaz as the other heroine. He married Aloka on his farm in Pen and also shot his film there. As a junior reporter, I had accompanied my features editor, Madhulika Verma, to the *Kaarnaama* shoot, much to the consternation of my mother, who didn't like the idea of me being in close proximity to the bad man. While Madhulika interviewed Vinod Khanna, I chatted with Ranjeet. He pointed out the different trees on his farm and even showed me the chalet-like cottages that he had had specially built for the film shoot. Aloka joined us for a while and I learnt that Ranjeet had remained a strict vegetarian, did not smoke, and only drank the occasional glass of rum at social gatherings. On our way back, I enlightened my senior, and later my mother, about this good bad man.

When I told him this recently, Ranjeet guffawed and recalled how after he had married Aloka quietly in his farm with only their parents, siblings and her uncle present, and with no big reception afterwards, his new mother-in-law broke the news to her sister who lived in Chandigarh. After the usual sulks because she had not been invited to the wedding, Aloka's maasi (aunt) had enquired who the *dulha* (groom) was. When told it was the actor Ranjeet, she screamed at her sister, 'If you wanted to kill Naazi [Aloka's nickname], you could have poisoned her, strangled her, even drowned her in the sea, you didn't have to marry her off to that blackguard.

Call her home, take off her clothes and see how many bruises he has left on her with his hunter [whip].' His mother-in-law laughingly retorted that it was more likely her daredevil daughter was whipping him. They have been happily married for 37 years and are blessed with two beautiful children.

Kaarnaama turned out to be a good film, with none of the sex and sleaze one had expected, given Ranjeet's image as a molester, Kimi Katkar's as a sex siren, and Vinod Khanna's as a desirable *sanyasi*. 'Hrishi-*da* [filmmaker Hrishikesh Mukherjee] hugged me after watching it and even the censor board members congratulated me. The film was passed with a 'U' certificate. I got an invitation for a special screening for Members of Parliament and might have got tax exemption had I sent the print, but I didn't know the art of self-promotion,' he rues.

Two years later, he made *Gajab Tamaasa* (1992), about employers and employees, featuring Anu Aggarwal and Rahul Roy. 'I didn't lose money, but I learnt I was not a good businessman,' Ranjeet acknowledges.

He continued to act and caught the eye in *Housefull 2* (2012) as Akshay Kumar's father, John Abraham's mentor and Asin's father-in-law. He shares that when producer Sajid Nadiadwala and director Sajid Khan approached him, he had turned them down, pointing out that his fans didn't want to see him in small roles. That's when they sheepishly admitted that they had already shot a few scenes with his photograph. "*Hum mar jayenge* [we will die], just give us five days," they entreated, and not wanting anyone to suffer on my account, I agreed,' he says. They eventually wrapped up his scenes in just a day.

At the studio, when he was introduced to Asin, he greeted her with his usual hug. Noticing that she looked somewhat uncomfortable in his presence, Akshay reassured her with a laugh, 'Don't be afraid, you are like his *beti* [daughter].' That exchange inspired the hilarious 'Beauty, beauty, beauty... Beti, beti, beti,' scene, written then and there. In the film, Ranjeet berates Akshay's Sunny for not being able to woo even one girl despite being the son of an unapologetic womanizer.

This scene, which portrayed Ranjeet as 'the rapist' with the aid of a crooked 'e' on the signboard of his therapist practice, was a reference to his image in the '70s and '80s as a villain with over 300 rape scenes to his (dis)credit. He strutted around with his shirt unbuttoned to the waist, a locket dangling from a gold chain on his hairy chest. Decades later, he shares that when his daughter Divyanka was working in Delhi, as a protective father, he would fly over frequently to check on her and take her out to dinner. As soon as they stepped into the restaurant, his beautiful daughter on his arm, towering over him in her fashionable heels, the whispers would start, 'Dirty old man, won't even leave alone a girl young enough to be his daughter.'

Occasionally, someone sitting at the next table would reprimand his wife and daughter for gawking at them disapprovingly. Ranjeet came up with a way of ensuring that Divyanka was not embarrassed. When the waiter would come to take their order, he would say loudly, 'I will eat whatever my daughter decides to order.' Immediately, there would be a shift in public perception, and by the time they had finished their dinner, fans would be waiting to take his autograph.

Today, after making a name for herself as a fashion and jewellery designer, Divyanka has opened her own fitness studio. 'She helps people become healthy,' informs the proud father. His son Jeeva was among the top 10 racing drivers in Asia who tried breaking into the F1 circuit, but it was near impossible to raise the ₹180 crore needed. So, Jeeva followed in his father's footsteps, making his debut in the Karan Johar production *Govinda Naam Mera* (2022).

'I had offered to launch Jeeva, but pointing out that I had made it despite having no father and godfather backing me, my son insisted he, too, would do it on his own. He got this film on his own merit and was noticed in a challenging role. I saw it for the first time at a preview show and Jeeva made me so proud,' he exults.

On his part, Ranjeet has continued to experiment, moving from film to television and theatre. 'I did three plays and even toured the US with *Hanky Panky*. I agreed only because my wife had scoffed that I was a chance *ka* actor and would never be able to pull off a live performance,' he confesses. He recalls rehearsals in his own swimming pool and how his younger co-actors, Parvin Dabas and Babloo (actor Keshto Mukherjee's son), had promised to give him cues if he forgot his lines. But on the day of the premiere, an intimidated Babloo turned his face in the wrong direction and actually got slapped by Ranjeet, following which he blanked out. 'I ended up ad-libbing on stage and desperately trying not to laugh, much to the amusement of my friends. I went on to do a Hinglish play, *Papa Don't Preach*, and *Taak Jhaank* with Rekha Sahay. It was fun,' he smiles.

Ranjeet still gets offers for films and web series, and while he is open to good projects, most, according to him, have no story, no role, no music and no soul. 'There is a lot of nudity and vulgarity on screen today and I won't be a party to that just to increase the zeroes in my bank balance. I may have been a crude villain, but I was never a vulgar villain,' he states. One is reminded of his famous dialogue in *Raampur Ka Lakshman* (1972), '*Main paidaishi imaandaar hoon, beimaan ki maut marna mere liye beizzati hai* [I was born honest, to die dishonest would be an insult to my reputation].'

Ranjeet proves how strong his work ethic is by talking about how, after his father suddenly succumbed to a heart attack, he took the first flight out to Hyderabad and shot on the day of the *chautha* (fourth day of pooja and prayers), leaving behind a houseful of relatives from Punjab. He reasons that his father had never inconvenienced anyone in his life, and after his demise, he wouldn't want anyone to say that his death had ruined them.

It was a big film, with an expensive set standing, and with busy stars like Sunil Dutt, Shatrughan Sinha and Sridevi. Ranjeet was playing the usual villain and between shots, he would lock himself in the make-up room and howl his heart out. 'But as soon as I was told the next shot was ready, I would splash chilled soda on my face, red and swollen from the crying, and step in front of the camera to laugh, leer and wield the hunter,' he reminisces, acknowledging that it was the toughest shoot of his life. But despite being drained of all his energy, and shaking like a leaf, he managed to complete all his close-ups and mid-shots before leaving his duplicate to finish the schedule, and flew back home. As they say in filmi parlance, 'The show must go on.'

Today, Ranjeet is happy pottering around his terrace garden, growing flowers and vegetables, painting and remembering the good old days. As he comes to the gate to courteously see me off, I rewind to our first meeting in Pen on the sets of *Kaarnaama* and realize anew why even in my early twenties, I was never scared of one of Bollywood's most notorious villains. He doesn't claim to be a saint, but he is no sinner either.

⋊

DANNY DENZONGPA

A CLASS APART

'Apna usool kehta hai har galti ki sazaa maut hai,
sirf maut...'

—*Agneepath* (1990)

The youngest of seven brothers and four sisters, Tshering Phintso Denzongpa was born in Yuksom, Sikkim. His father, Rinzing Yongda, was one of the heads of the royal monastery of Tashiding, one of the biggest and most sacred monasteries in Sikkim. Two of his brothers were lamas who gave up their robes to start a small hotel business and today are owners of five-star hotels. He himself wanted to join the army, like his first hero, a six-foot-tall soldier in the hills, and had even been accepted by the Armed Forces Medical College in Pune. But when he shared the news with his mother, she promptly burst into tears. Many from their own village, as well as nearby villages, were in the Indian Army, and during the India–China War, some soldiers returned home in closed coffins. Daily curfews added to the fear. Not wanting to upset his mother any more, Danny, as he is popularly known today, started looking at alternative careers.

An advertisement in the film weekly *Screen* for a diploma course in acting at the FTII in Pune caught his eye. One of the subjects being taught was music, and since he sang well, played the flute and had performed on stage, he thought he could train at the institute to become a professional singer. He applied and was among the 10 students to be accepted. 'On my first day at the institute, during the orientation session, the new students gathered in the assembly hall were asked to introduce ourselves. I came in for a fair share of ribbing from my seniors because of my unusual name. Even my classmates found it hard to pronounce Tshering Phintso, and Jaya [Bachchan, née Bhaduri] suggested I shorten it to a simple Danny. I agreed, and the name stuck,' he recounts with a laugh.

While at the FTII, Danny Denzongpa impressed several of his instructors, including well-known producer-director B.R. Chopra who came as an examiner during the final exams. However, after graduation, it was a struggle to get work as he did not fit into the *saas–bahu* (mother-in-law and daughter-in-law) kind of films being made at the time because of his unconventional looks. Some of his well-wishers suggested pragmatically that he return to Sikkim, but that wasn't an option for him. Instead, he took up a job as an acting instructor, confident that he would soon get a break as an actor.

Meanwhile, one of his FTII classmates, Anil Dhawan, landed the lead role in writer-director B.R. Ishara's *Chetna* (1970) opposite Rehana Sultan. It was a bold film on the rehabilitation of prostitutes and they were shooting in Pune. One day, Danny landed up on the set to meet Anil. He was introduced to the director, who liked him and immediately signed him for his next film, *Nai Duniya Naye*

Log (1973), a love triangle featuring two other newcomers, Reena Roy and Satyen.

Meanwhile, an announcement of a film, *Mere Apne* (1971), in *Screen* sparked Danny's interest. He had seen the original Bengali film, *Apanjan* (1968), which had won the National Film Award for Best Feature Film in Bengali. Directed by Tapan Sinha, it revolves around two rival street gangs. 'I wanted to play Chhenu, one of the gang leaders, a lout who flourishes because of political patronage, and wrote to Gulzar-sahab expressing my interest. He replied back saying Shatru-ji [Shatrughan Sinha] had already been signed for the role,' the actor sighs, remembering how disappointed he was.

Once again, Jaya came to his rescue. The actress had started shooting for Hrishikesh Mukherjee's coming-of-age drama *Guddi* (1971). It was written by Gulzar and she strongly recommended Danny to him. He was asked to come and meet the writer-director after he returned to Bombay from a shoot in Bangalore (now Bengaluru). He ended up playing the ventriloquist Sanju in *Mere Apne*, with Vinod Khanna as the rival gang leader and Meena Kumari as an elderly widow.

Mere Apne, which opened on 10 September 1971, was Danny Denzongpa's first release. It got him good reviews and he was signed by B.R. Ishara for a second film, *Zaroorat* (1972), which starred Reena Roy and another FTII colleague, Vijay Arora, as a young, financially strapped couple in love. Danny plays their friend in a positive parallel role.

Around this time, B.R. Chopra, who while visiting the institute had told Danny to meet him after he graduated, assuring him of a role in one of his forthcoming films, called him for the narration of a murder mystery, *Dhund* (1973). 'There were several top writers present at the narration. Chopra-sahab told me to listen carefully and if there was something I didn't think was working in the story, I was free to point it out and suggest how it could be rectified. I was just a newcomer while Chopra-sahab was a successful filmmaker. For him to solicit my opinion was amazing and I was really touched!' he recalls.

At the end of the narration, Danny was offered the role of the inspector investigating the case. Since the story is set in a hill station, Chopra thought he looked the part. To his surprise, the young actor told him that he wanted to play Thakur Ranjit Singh, the frustrated, wheelchair-bound husband of Zeenat Aman's Rani whose murder is the trigger for the courtroom drama that follows. 'Chopra-sahab told me that Amitabh Bachchan had already been signed for the role, but after *Anand*'s (1971) success, Amit-ji decided he would only accept lead roles,' he shares.

Elated upon hearing the news, the actor went back to the producer-director and asked to play Thakur Ranjit Singh. Once again, he was disappointed as another actor, Shatrughan Sinha, had already been finalized. B.R. Chopra urged him to accept the inspector's role, pointing out that he is there throughout the film, while Thakur appears only post interval and is shot dead after a few scenes. But to his exasperation, Danny was set on the negative role.

'I had a friend from FTII who worked as an assistant to Chopra-sahab. He would update me on any new developments on the *Dhund* front. One day, I learnt from him that Shatru-ji had turned up late for a sitting and was no longer in the film. I immediately went back to Chopra-sahab with the same request. This time, he agreed to audition me,' he reminisces.

The filmmaker wasn't entirely convinced that the fresh-faced newcomer, barely out of his teens, could pull off this character of a much older, embittered man. The screen test was held at the director's Juhu bungalow and Pandhari Dada was called to do Danny's make-up. Dada gave him a beard and a streak of white in his hair which instantly made him look 10 years older. 'The camera was set up in the hall and a gun was put in my hands. When the scene ended, everyone present, from the DoP [director of photography], Chopra-sahab's brother Dharam Chopra, to the light man, broke into spontaneous applause. And that's how I landed my first role as a villain,' he exults.

Danny, however, continued to exasperate the filmmaker, insisting that Thakur Ranjit Singh be introduced just before the interval rather than immediately after as in the script. He had even planned an impactful entry for his character, throwing a plate at the camera in a way that it seemed to fly straight at the audience, making them instinctively recoil. 'I pleaded with Chopra-sahab for days to shoot it, but he always laughed me off. Then one day, I caught him just as he was leaving, and he instructed his brother Dharam to take the shot the way I wanted, warning me that it might well be left out on the editing table,' Danny recounts.

To his satisfaction, it was eventually retained, and when his 'introduction' was widely appreciated by audiences, B.R. Chopra publicly acknowledged that it had been the 21-year-old actor's brainwave. He also put to rest growing rumours that Danny's voice had been dubbed in the film because no one could believe his Hindi diction was so impeccable.

Dhund made Danny Denzongpa an overnight star, but not a villain. He continued to play positive supporting roles. He was the hero's friend in *Chor Machaye Shor* (1974) and *Kaala Sona* (1975), and Shashi Kapoor's lost brother in *Fakira* (1976). While dramatic, emotional scenes were never a problem for him, he disliked naach–gaana. 'Having watched films of Akira Kurosawa and Ingmar Bergman at the institute and evolved as an actor, I found the dance moves demonstrated by the choreographers ridiculous and uncomfortable. As a trained actor, I told myself that I was not going to run around the trees,' he reasons, explaining why he preferred villainous turns in films like *Aashiq Hoon Baharon Ka* (1977), *Paapi* (1977), *Lahu Ke Do Rang* (1979), *Bandish* (1980) and *The Burning Train* (1980). He also hated exaggerated theatrics and tried to hold on to his natural style of acting. But there were times when he had to up the pitch of his performance or risk sticking out like a sore thumb in the crowd.

Mera Gaon Mera Desh (1971) and *Sholay* (1975), which had iconic villains in Vinod Khanna's Jabbar Singh and Amjad Khan's Gabbar Singh, had flagged off a new trend of dacoit dramas. 'I went from one film set to the next with my gang of dakus on horseback, looting innocents. The roles were similar; I was even mouthing the same lines and often was even surrounded by the same actors playing my henchmen. It got really monotonous and boring after a while,' Danny grouses.

Eventually, he instructed his secretary to give the producers he had committed to bulk dates so they could wrap up the films as soon as possible and not accept any new projects. So, while his colleagues were shooting round the clock, Danny was only doing one shift a day and did not work on Sundays. After he had cleared the backlog, he took off to Sikkim. For months, he trekked in the mountains and returned to Bombay rejuvenated, determined to do something different.

Soon after his return, N.N. Sippy, with whom he had collaborated in jubilee hits like *Chor Machaye Shor* (1974), *Kalicharan* (1976), *Fakira* (1976) and *Devata* (1978), dropped by to welcome him back to the city. When the producer asked him what he had done when away, Danny shared that he had written a script in Sikkim. N.N. Sippy was so impressed, he immediately decided to produce the film. Famous for introducing new directors like C.P. Dixit (*Paras*, 1971), Ashok Roy (*Chor Machaye Shor*, 1974) and Subhash Ghai (*Kalicharan*, 1976), he even suggested that the actor direct the film himself, and *Phir Wohi Raat* (1980) went on the floors.

The suspense-horror thriller featured Kim as Asha who is tormented by a nightmare, and Rajesh Khanna as her psychologist-lover, who tries to help her decode her terrifying past. 'I wanted Shashi-ji [Shashi Kapoor] to play Dr Vijay, but he was already over-committed, doing three shifts a day and flitting from one set to the next, some put up at the same studio on his insistence to save time. So, I took the role to Kaka-ji [Rajesh Khanna] instead. The film wasn't a huge hit, but I enjoyed the experience of directing it. *Phir Wohi Raat* was a welcome break from the usual masala movies of the time and gave me a lot of creative satisfaction,' says Danny, who plays Asha's cousin, Ashok, whose wife is killed by her.

On the same trip, he had written another script. Around this time, Mohinder Batra, a colleague from the FTII, dropped by his place. Batra was distraught because the film he had produced was banned. 'I have lost all my life's savings. What will I do now?' he wailed. To take his mind off his troubles, Danny narrated his script to Batra who loved it. The actor had wanted to direct this film himself, but before he could take it to any producer, Batra returned, looking much happier. 'He had found a producer, Ashish Roy, who was ready to invest in a Hindi–Bengali bilingual. "Please give me your script," he begged,' Danny reminisces.

Lal Kothi or *Lalkuthi* (1978) features Danny in the lead alongside Tanuja, Ranjit Mallick and Master Partho Mukherjee. Utpal Dutt is the scheming villain. Danny didn't even take credit as the writer. Mohinder Batra is credited with both the story and the screenplay. The film ended up celebrating a diamond jubilee. 'I also wrote a script titled *Shyahi*, meaning "darkness". Later, Mohinder Batra directed me in a fabulous Hindi action film, *Pehredaar* (1979), which was dubbed in Bengali as *Prohari* (1982). It was much appreciated by the press and well received by the audience,' he says proudly.

His nephew Ugyen Chhopel then directed him in a Nepalese film, *Saino* (1988), whose story the actor had penned. He also sang for the film under the baton of Ranjit Gazmer, with 'Suna Katha Eauta Geet' becoming very popular. He had earlier crooned a duet with Lata Mangeshkar, 'Mera Naam Aao Mere Paas Aao', under the baton of S.D. Burman for the Dev Anand–Sharmila Tagore-starrer *Ye Gulistan Hamara* (1972), and 'Sun Sun Qasam Se' for R.D. Burman in *Kaala Sona* (1975) with Asha Bhosle. There were other songs, including a duet with Kishore Kumar ('Paani Ke Badley Me Peekar Sharab') and one song with Mohammed Rafi and Asha Bhosle ('Mujhey Doston Tum Galey Se Laga Loh') for Mahesh Bhatt's *Naya Daur* (1978). So, in a way, Danny Denzongpa lived his dream of becoming a professional singer too.

He also penned *Bandhu* (1992) for his best friend, producer Romesh Sharma. It is reported to be the Hindi remake of *Saino*, and Danny, who plays the title role, lent his voice to the song 'Kaun Ho Mere Tum', a version of Ranjit Gazmer's 'Suna Katha Eauta Geet'. The Hindi film was directed by Ugyen Chhopel, who also directed *Ajnabi* with Batra. Produced by Romesh Sharma, the story for the

75-episode television drama series was written by the actor. 'Those days, no star wanted to be on television, which was derogatorily referred to as the "idiot box". I was the first star to appear on TV. In fact, the TV awards too started after *Ajnabi*'s TRPs touched 70, and I was the recipient of the first award,' he says with satisfaction.

Acting roles continued to pour in, but they were mostly run-of-the-mill, in mainstream Hindi movies, and Danny had always wanted to do something out of the box. He had written other scripts, but whenever he narrated them to producers, they would shake their heads doubtfully and say, '*Yeh to Hollywood film jaise lagta hai, yeh nahin chalengi* [This sounds like a Hollywood film, it won't work]. Now, listen to this script we have.' Usually, it would be something he had done many times before. 'So, then, I just started picking the best from the rest,' he sighs.

Some films had roles that challenged him as an actor, like Esmayeel Shroff's *Bulundi* (1981), which stars him in a double role as both father and son, Ranjeet and Manjeet Singh Lobo; the Pranlal Mehta production *Dharm Aur Qanoon* (1984), in which he holds his own against Dharmendra and Rajesh Khanna, the latter playing a double role; and J. Om Prakash's *Bhagwaan Dada* (1986), which pits him against Rajinikanth in the lead. Romu and Raj N. Sippy's *Andar Baahar* (1984), inspired by the Hollywood hit *48 Hrs.* (1982), was another interesting role with him as the notorious criminal Shamsher Singh, aka Shera, while *Oonche Log* (1985), inspired by Emily Brontë's 1847 novel *Wuthering Heights*, is memorable for his Thakur Maan Singh.

However, the film that has attained cult status over the years is Mukul S. Anand's crime drama *Agneepath* (1990), with Danny as the underworld don Kancha Cheena and

Amitabh Bachchan as the gang lord Vijay Deenanath Chauhan. 'Agneepath was my first film with Amit-ji. What a phenomenal actor! I turned down countless offers, including Man-ji's [Manmohan Desai's] Coolie [1983] and Mard [1985], before I accepted Agneepath because I knew that to match up to him, I needed a role of equal importance or I would be overshadowed. I waited 18 years till Mukul came to me with the role of Kancha,' he shares.

Danny was the one who suggested they add a Cheena to Kancha. 'When I joined the FTII, I couldn't go into town alone because the locals, mistaking me as Chinese, would call me Cheena and throw stones at me. The India–China War had led to a deep-rooted dislike for the Chinese. "Cheena" stuck in my mind and when Mukul agreed to incorporate it in my character's name, I could finally convert a bad memory into something positive,' he informs.

Six years before Agneepath, Anand had signed Danny for his debut directorial Kanoon Kya Karega (1984), inspired by J. Lee Thompson's American noir psychological thriller, Cape Fear (1962). He plays the terrifying Raghuvir Singh, who toys with the law without crossing the line. He reveals that no actor wanted to play the lawyer, Gautam Mehra, because the antagonist was such a powerful character. 'Suresh Oberoi was from the FTII and had played the inspector's role in Phir Wohi Raat. I pointed out to Mukul that he has a good personality and voice and suggested he take him,' Danny informs.

A year later, the trio of Danny Denzongpa, Mukul Anand and Suresh Oberoi reunited for Aitbaar (1985), inspired by the Alfred Hitchcock film Dial M for Murder (1954), with Danny playing the role of Inspector Barua. 'After that, Mukul came to me with Agneepath, a film in which the villain is the hero. It was a radical concept and again, none of the leading actors would accept the role of Vijay Deenanath Chauhan, fearing it would tarnish their image. I told Amit-ji about this bright, young director, and having seen and liked Mukul's work in *Sultanat* [1986], he agreed to do the role,' Danny says.

Agneepath failed commercially, primarily because Amitabh Bachchan experimented with his voice, his familiar baritone replaced with a raspy whisper. It did not go down well with the audience. The actor later re-dubbed his lines, but by then, it was too late to salvage the film. He, however, won the National Film Award for Best Actor for that performance; and today, *Agneepath* is regarded as a cult classic.

The following year, Romesh Sharma produced *Hum* (1991), also directed by Mukul Anand, with Amitabh Bachchan as Tiger, and Rajinikanth and Govinda as his brothers. Danny plays Bakhtawar, his sworn enemy. *Hum* was a blockbuster and the song 'Jumma Chumma De De' a chart-topper.

Buoyed by its phenomenal success, Mukul Anand, Amitabh Bachchan and Danny Denzongpa then joined hands for an ambitious epic drama, *Khuda Gawah* (1992). Produced by Manoj Desai, it was shot in and around the shrine of Mazar-i-Sharif in Afghanistan. Danny remembers that the Russians had just left the country after decades of occupation and the Taliban was at large, so the actors were reluctant to cross the border. Having travelled to Afghanistan for Feroz Khan's *Dharmatma* (1975), Danny assured his director that he would be happy to return there.

Sridevi, who plays a double role of mother and daughter in *Khuda Gawah*, could not be persuaded to make the trip even though the mother, Benazir, belongs to an Afghan tribe. They had to shoot her scenes in Afghanistan with a duplicate. But Danny, who plays Khuda Baksh, a friend of Amitabh

Bachchan's Baadshah Khan, was able to coax the actor to accompany them, assuring him that they would be safe because the Afghan government had promised to provide them with tight security.

From the Kabul airport, where they received a red-carpet welcome, they flew to Mazar-i-Sharif where, given the Taliban threat, they were not put up at a hotel, but at the governor's residence inside a fort. 'Would you believe the governor vacated his home for us? Wherever we went, we were surrounded by Afghan soldiers carrying machine guns. There was a tank in front of my car and one bringing up the rear, with two more on either side,' Danny reminisces.

Helicopters kept vigil from the top and the entire region was carefully inspected before they arrived for the shooting. 'We could see guns poking out from the peaks of the hillocks, and had to wave a white flag when we neared to signal that we were the film unit, to avoid being shot,' he shares.

The Afghanistan shooting schedule ended with a taste of royalty, as they were invited by the king of the Kayan valley in northeastern Afghanistan for a short visit. They were welcomed with open arms and gun barrels tipped with flowers that showered petals as they walked, served local cuisine and bid farewell to with expensive gifts, including a coal black horse of a rare breed that was presented to Amitabh Bachchan.

Khuda Gawah opened in the theatres on 8 May 1992. It became the third highest-grossing film of the year, entering the *Limca Book of Records* as the first Indian film to use surround sound. It was dubbed in Telugu and even adapted into a Pakistani television series of the same name. In Afghanistan, it became one of the most popular Indian films, with both Sridevi and Amitabh Bachchan being honoured by the Afghan government. Back home, Mukul Anand bagged the Filmfare Award for Best Director for it, while Danny Denzongpa received the Filmfare Award for Best Supporting Actor.

He also took home the Filmfare statuette for Best Supporting Actor for Saawan Kumar Tak's *Sanam Bewafa* (1991), in which Pran and he play two feuding pathans. 'I was nominated five times for Best Performance in a Negative Role, but surprisingly, the two Filmfare awards I won were for supporting characters,' points out the actor, who in 2003 was honoured for his contribution to cinema with the Padma Shri, the fourth-highest civilian award presented by the government of India.

Twenty-five years after *Khuda Gawah*, Danny Denzongpa was cast as an Afghan again in *Bioscopewala* (2017). The film was inspired by Rabindranath Tagore's 'Kabuliwala', but took a few creative liberties with the original. Danny, who had loved the Bimal Roy-produced *Kabuliwala* (1961), was excited about playing Rehmat Khan. 'But unfortunately the film didn't do well—perhaps because it did not have a popular hero and heroine dancing around the trees,' he sighs.

The actor has always tried to make every character he plays different, delving into their backstories and finding a reason to explain why the character behaves the way he does. 'Even serial killers believe that what they are doing is right and the one pursuing them is the villain. You must have that conviction when you are playing negative characters. Only when you believe that the villain is the hero can you carry him off convincingly. For me, no character is completely black or white. Even a hero has grey shades because he is human. And a villain, however inhuman, is human too,' he argues with irrefutable logic.

Interestingly, Danny Denzongpa is one of the few actors who has worked with three generations of actors from the same family. He collaborated with Dharmendra in *The Burning Train* (1980), *Dharm Aur Qanoon* (1984), *Aag Hi Aag* (1987), *Zalzala* (1988) and *Jagira* (2001). He took on Sunny Deol's *dhai kilo ka haath* in *Yateem* (1988), *Paap Ki Duniya* (1988), *Yodha* (1991), *Ghatak* (1996) and *Indian* (2001). And when Bobby Deol was about to be launched, Dharmendra called him to confide that they were looking for a strong, powerful guy his younger son could have a face-off with in the climax of *Barsaat* (1995). After that, Danny and Bobby went on to do *Ab Tumhare Hawale Watan Sathiyo* (2004) and *Chamku* (2008). 'I have been fighting the Deol family for years, yet we have remained friends,' he chuckles.

The actor recalls how miffed Dharmendra had been upon being nominated for the Filmfare Award for Best Supporting Actor for *Ayee Milan Ki Bela* (1964). 'Dharam-ji pointed out that despite the grey shades, he was the film's hero and not a supporting actor so he refused to accept the award. After that, he stuck to playing the romantic lead, not experimenting with negative characters till he moved to character roles,' Danny reveals.

Actors today have no such qualms, because with the boom in foreign films and the advent of television, the Internet and now OTT, the audience has evolved. 'In the '70s and '80s, for the hero to appear heroic, the villain had to pack a punch. The distinction between the two was very marked. Today, that demarcation has been erased to the extent that if a story has a good villainous role, the hero wants to play it. Amit-ji and Shah Rukh Khan have made bad good. The filmmaker too likes the idea because having two heroes in the film makes it a bigger draw with the audience, irrespective of whether the actor is a perfect fit or not,' he reasons.

As a result, many villains have faded away into oblivion. For Danny Denzongpa, the offers continue to pour in, but it is a Catch-22 situation. 'Many of today's directors are kids from the '70s and '80s. The films they saw left a lasting impression on them, with the result that 90 per cent of the roles I get are what I have already played before. And since I don't want to repeat myself, I say "no" to many of the offers,' he points out.

The few that have got his nod include the Rajinikanth-starrer *Robot* or *Enthiran* (2010), in which he plays a rogue scientist working with a terrorist organization, and Hrithik Roshan's *Bang Bang!* (2014), in which he portrays the wanted terrorist Omar Zafar. 'I also enjoyed playing Feroze Ali Khan in Neeraj Pandey's espionage thriller *Baby* [2015]. Following the 9/11 attacks, he is made head of a temporary task force whose job is to find and eliminate those planning attacks on India. It was a well scripted and believable film,' says Danny, who was equally impressive in *Manikarnika: The Queen of Jhansi* (2019) as Ghulam Ghaus Khan, who goes to battle with Kangana Ranaut's Manikarnika. And in Sooraj Barjatya's *Uunchai* (2022), his demise motivates his three senior citizen friends to trek to the Everest base camp to fulfil his last wish.

While the actor decided not to accept a role unless there's something really exciting for him, his son, Rinzing Denzongpa, who grew up playing on his sets, breaking a few props and later getting a degree in theatre, made his debut as a leading man with the action-packed *Squad* (2021), shot during the pandemic. His father admits that Rinzing, who towers over him at six feet four inches, has a better physique.

Yet, unlike many of his colleagues, Danny did not want to launch his son, leaving Rinzing to find his mentor in actress Zaheeda's son, Nilesh Sahay, who was not just the director, but also the co-writer and co-producer of *Squad* (2021).

Sahay remembers seeing *Hum* when he was eight years old. He instantly fell in love with Kimi Katkar's Juma and was bowled over by Danny's Bakhtawar. 'A hero can only be as powerful as the villain, and in *Hum*, Danny sir was a towering bad man. Unlike the typical '90s' dakus and thakurs who looted and raped, Bakhtawar had class; and Danny sir, in his three-piece suits, puffing a pipe, has always been a class apart,' he asserts.

What, according to him, is the reason for Danny Denzongpa's longevity? 'Danny sir is still around because he has evolved as an actor. Over the years, the style of filmmaking has changed and to survive, you have to adapt to the changing times. That's the reason 90 per cent actors of his generation have disappeared or look dated on screen. But Danny sir has upped his game, reinvented himself, and resonates not just with his legion of loyal fans, but also cuts a dashing figure with the new-age audiences,' opines Sahay.

Today, at 75, Danny Denzongpa is still a much-respected actor. He may not always want to do a film, but once he gives his nod, he brings his panache to the character and professionalism to the set. Off the set, there is a certain nobility about him that transcends the evil he brings to the screen. For me, the real Danny is the regent of the Brad Pitt-starrer, *Seven Years in Tibet* (1997). Inspired by the true story of the Austrian mountaineer Heinrich Harrer and his friendship with the young Dalai Lama during World War II and China's takeover of Tibet, the Hollywood film took him back to his roots and completed the cycle of life for Danny, even as his son Rinzing, named after his grandfather, takes the Denzongpa name forward on screen.

AMJAD KHAN

THE BANDIT KING

'Gabbar ke taap se tumhe ek hi aadmi bacha sakta hai,
ek hi aadmi, khud Gabbar.'

—*Sholay* (1975)

In the '90s, after running around for weeks, I finally managed to pin down Salim Khan for an interview. As I sat opposite Prince Salim, the man who had started his career as an actor, wanting to be another Dilip Kumar, and had subsequently gone on to team up with Javed Akhtar to become part of the most successful screenwriter duo in Bollywood, I couldn't help but recall Salim–Javed's many blockbusters. From *Andaz* (1971), *Haathi Mere Saathi* (1971), *Seeta Aur Geeta* (1972), *Yaadon Ki Baaraat* (1973), *Sholay* (1975), *Deewaar* (1975), *Trishul* (1978), *Don* (1978) and *Shakti* (1982) to *Mr. India* (1987), image after image, like the famous montage in Sergei Eisenstein's silent film *Battleship Potemkin* (1925), flashed through my mind—but one recurred with disconcerting familiarity.

A man walks in khaki fatigues, the camera zooming in on his boots. Army boots. A bullet belt trails after him. His face is not in the frame, but his voice, laced with quiet menace, asks a shamefaced Kaalia who has just returned from the village after a trouncing, '*Hmmm... Kitne aadmi the* [How many men were there]?' You sense a tempest coming even before Ramgarh's dreaded dacoit, in response to his henchman's mumbled '*Sardar, do aadmi the* [Chief, two men]', explodes, '*Do aadmi! Soowar ke bachcho, woh do the aur tum teen, phir bhi wapas aa gaye... Khali haath... Kya samajh kar aaye the? Sardar bahut khus hoga, sabasi dega, kyun? Dhikkar hai!* [Two men! You pigs, they were two and you three, yet you returned empty-handed... What were you thinking? That the chief would be happy, he would congratulate you? Damn you!]' You cower in your seat as Gabbar Singh triggers a game of Russian roulette with his now-famous line, '*Iss pistol mein teen zindagi, teen maut bandh hai, dekhein kise kya milta hai* [There are three lives and three deaths locked in this pistol, let's see who gets what].' Three shots are fired. Three blanks. Gabbar bursts into maniacal laughter and the three condemned goons follow, believing they have survived the near-death encounter. Soon the rest of the gang joins in. Then, Gabbar fires. Three gunshots. Three corpses. A deafening silence engulfs the ravines till his voice booms out, '*Jo darr gaya, samjho mar gaya* [If you are scared, you are dead]!'

Today, Gabbar Singh, one of Hindi cinema's most awe-inspiring villains, has become synonymous with the much-loved Amjad Khan. It was Salim Khan who ran into the young actor one day and accompanied him to Ramesh Sippy's office. The director of *Sholay* (1975) had seen him on stage in an English play that had also featured his sister. When he walked into his office, Sippy was once again intrigued by his unusual face and voice. He told him to start growing a beard and return in a few days. The next time Amjad dropped by, a stubble darkened his chin, his teeth blackened so his smile appeared tobacco-stained, and the director knew he had found his daku from the hinterlands.

Before Amjad Khan, there was talk of other established actors like Prem Nath, Shatrughan Sinha, Danny Denzongpa and even Ranjeet being approached for the role of the now-famous dacoit. Danny himself has confirmed that he was the original choice for Gabbar Singh and had given his nod to *Sholay*. But by the time the film was ready to roll, the dates he had allotted to Ramesh Sippy clashed with those for *Dharmatma* (1975). Since Feroz Khan had already taken permission to shoot in Afghanistan, and he had allotted dates and taken money from the film's producer, director and actor, Danny, a principled actor, did not want to back out of *Dharmatma* at the last minute.

Both Amitabh Bachchan and Sanjeev Kumar, who had already been signed to play the brooding Jai and the vengeful Thakur Baldev Singh, were ready to switch roles and gamble with Gabbar Singh, but that would have meant finding other stars to replace them and delaying the film further. Salim Khan reasoned that since Amjad was a newcomer, dates would not be a problem. Also, not having an image of a stereotyped villain, he would take the audience by surprise and could perhaps make a bigger impact. That's how Amjad Khan entered the picture.

Sholay released on 15 August 1975 to scathing reviews. Writing for *India Today*, critic K.L. Amladi dismissed it as a 'dead ember'.* The initial collections weren't great, either. Almost 50 years later, I ask Amjad Khan's wife Shehla whether he was upset by the film's lukewarm opening. She shakes her

---

*Amladi, K.L., 'Sholay in Totality Is a Depressing Film', *India Today*, 15 December 1975, https://tinyurl.com/24kh6yev. Accessed on 10 June 2024.

head, negating the notion immediately: 'No, he came from a theatre background and had a different mindset. He wasn't scared by failure. If you fell, you just had to pick yourself up and start all over again.'

Shehla had gone to see the film with her mother-in-law and her friends. She had had to leave before the end and rush back home because her eldest son, Shadaab, who was around two years old then, suddenly got angry by the hammering his father was taking on screen and started screaming at the top of his voice, '*Haramzaade, daddy ko mat maaro* [Bastard, don't beat my father]!' To Shehla's embarrassment, the child had picked up the word 'haramzaade' from his father's on-screen vocabulary without knowing what it even meant.

Meanwhile, disappointed exhibitors who had been expecting a winning run from the much-hyped, big-budget action drama had started to think of ways to salvage it and cut their losses. This included considerations to trim its unwieldy three-hour-20-minute length, because of which they had to start early with a near-empty 9.00 a.m. show so that the last show would end by the government-regulated midnight deadline. Some theatre owners opined that the end should be changed and Amitabh Bachchan, a superstar after *Zanjeer* (1973) and *Deewaar* (1975), should be allowed to live. A few who didn't like Amjad's unusual voice suggested his lines be dubbed. Fortunately, collections picked up miraculously and *Sholay* went on to make box-office history.

Two days after its release, Amjad and Shehla took Shadaab to Juhu Beach. In the midst of a leisurely stroll, she recalls that he suddenly picked up their son, grabbed her hand and pulled her along, urging her to run, as he raced towards their car as fast as he could. They had just managed to get in and lock the doors when all hell broke loose, hundreds of fans banging on the car, demanding, 'Gabbar Singh *bahar niklo* [come out]!' The clamour left Shehla shell-shocked!

Veteran actor and National Award-winning filmmaker Ananth Narayan Mahadevan, who worked with Amjad Khan in Khalid Mohammad Sami's shelved film *Nargis*, reminds us that despite his seeming omnipresence, Gabbar Singh appeared in just nine scenes. 'But with his maniacal, almost-caricature of a laugh, Amjad-bhai took his villain from the edge of black comedy—"*Bahut yaarana lagta hai* [There seems to be love here]"—to cold-blooded menace—"*Yeh haath humko de de Thakur* [Give me these hands, Thakur]!" He made simple, throwaway lines iconic in the way he delivered them,' he raves.

Shehla remembers her father-in-law, actor Jayant, telling his son, '*Tum khaas ke nakal karoge to pehchane jaago, agar nakal hi karni hai to aam ke karo* [If you try to imitate a known person, you will be caught, if you have to imitate someone, let it be a common man].' The words resonated with him, and Amjad Khan found his muses in the people around him, including their domestic worker and the *dhobi* (laundry man). 'We had a dhobi who would call out to his wife, "*Arrey O Shanti*", and from that was born "*Arrey O Sambha*",' reveals Shehla. After *Sholay*'s release, not just music director R.D. Burman's chartbusters, 'Yeh Dosti' and 'Mehbooba Mehbooba', but even Gabbar Singh's one-liners, like '*Arrey O Sambha, kitna inaam rakhe hai sarkar hum par* [Hey Sambha, how much reward has the government put on me]?' and '*Tera kya hoga, Kaalia* [Now, what will happen to you, Kaalia]?', set records in audio sales and have been imitated by several generations of moviegoers.

Ironically, despite opening on India's twenty-sixth Independence Day, *Sholay* came in a year when Emergency had been imposed by then Prime Minister Indira Gandhi. Ramesh Sippy's creative liberty also came under fire, because the censors found the original ending that had Thakur pushing Gabbar Singh against a pillar embedded with spikes, literally crucifying him, too gory. They insisted on a more conventional path, letting the law take its own course. Eager to keep his 15 August date with the audience, Sippy got his writers to tweak the script, and the film ended somewhat tamely with the cops leading Gabbar away in handcuffs. 'It was a difficult time and a small change to make for the bigger picture,' Salim Khan admitted to me years later in an interview for *Filmfare*, pointing out that Javed Akhtar and he had anyway never propagated violence and vulgarity in their films.

However, despite the tame ending, such was the impact of *Sholay* that many to this day believe that it is Amjad Khan's debut film. But he had appeared as a child actor in *Nazneen* (1951), a performance that went uncredited, followed by *Char Paise* (1955), *Ab Dilli Dur Nahin* (1957), *Maya* (1961) and *Hindustan Ki Kasam* (1973).

He had even signed the action thriller *Charas* (1976) before *Sholay*, his father being a good friend of the writer, producer and director Ramanand Sagar, having worked in his film *Zindagi* (1964). Ramanand Sagar's son, Shanti Sagar, who was entrusted with the job of raising funds for needy workers, came up with the idea of a talent hunt contest. The incentive was that the winner would land a role in a top-ranking producer's film. Amjad and his brother Imtiaz, who were still studying, were brilliant actors and regulars at inter-collegiate competitions. They even had their own theatre group, United Stage Artistes. In fact, it was in a play staged in Delhi in 1963, *Ai Mere Watan Ke Logon*, that Javed

Akhtar had spotted Amjad, and had been raving about him to Salim Khan since watching the performance. He was picked as the winner at the Wadala Junior Chamber's talent hunt contest and Shanti Sagar requested his father to give the talented actor a role.

He was sent to the darkroom above the Sagar office at Natraj Studio for a screen test. 'We gave Amjad a black suit and a wig to wear. I put a gun in his hand and a huge burn mark on his cheek, which I had created from potato peels and make-up. After seeing those photographs, papa-ji [Ramanand Sagar] signed him for *Charas* [1976] as one of Ajit-sahab's henchmen, Robert,' Prem Sagar, who had photographed Amjad, shared while discussing the iconic villain.

Charas was released on 24 May 1976, almost a year after *Sholay*. By then, Amjad Khan was a sensation and his distributors wanted Ramanand Sagar to give him as much footage as the hero, Dharmendra. So, the screenplay was hurriedly reworked and the last five reels re-shot. 'From being one of the goons, Robert turns into a mafia boss lording it in Europe while Ajit-sahab's Kalicharan commands the underworld in India. The climax was filmed in Malta with Amjad taking centre stage,' informs Prem Sagar, who cast the actor three years later in his directorial *Hum Tere Aashiq Hain* (1979), and remembers him as a perfect gentleman who, despite his phenomenal success, never negotiated his price or even discussed his role.

Even Pankaj Parashar recalls that when he approached him for *Peechha Karro* (1986), the actor didn't know him at all despite having worked in *Achha Bura* (1983), a film produced by his brother, Deepak Parashar. 'Kahani sunao [Tell me the story],' the director was asked. Amjad looked somewhat baffled at the end of the narration and admitted that he had not understood head or tail of his crazy story. 'But I like you and I will do your film,' he assured a delighted Parashar.

During the shoot in Hyderabad, they bonded over food. Amjad would call the young director to his five-star hotel, where his co-star Farooq Shaikh, another foodie, and he only spoke about the different types of mutton he had discovered in the city or which dhaba served the best boti kebabs, much to the bemusement of the film's villain Anupam Kher. 'Anupam worshipped Amjad and tried to initiate a conversation with him on *Sholay* and his other great performances, but Amjad was only interested in discussing food. He and I did talk about cinema occasionally. He had very fixed notions about what he liked and what he didn't,' shares Parashar.

∞

The real start of Amjad Khan's story though, even before *Nazneen*, can be traced all the way back to the start of his father's story. Rewind to the early 1930s. Amjad's father, then going by his birth name Zakaria Khan, had come to Bombay from Peshawar to become an actor. After a period of struggle, the burly Pashtun pathan landed a Gujarati film, *Sansaar Leela* (1933), whose director, Vijay Bhatt, gave him the screen name Jayant. The film was remade in Hindi as *Nai Duniya* (1934). Jayant went on to feature in other films, including *Bombay Mail* (1935), *His Highness* (1937), *Mala* (1941), *Shirin Farhad* (1945) and *Doli* (1947). After Partition, his family and friends tried to persuade him to move to the newly formed Pakistan, but Jayant only shifted as far as Bandra with his wife and two sons, Amjad and Imtiaz.

After appearing for his matriculation exams, Amjad dropped by Filmalaya Studio one day. His father was shooting with Dilip Kumar for the Sashadhar Mukherjee-produced political drama *Leader* (1964), and when told that the teenager was waiting for his results to come out to join college, the thespian suggested Amjad join the unit as an assistant director and learn something of his father's profession. Over the next few months, the boy toiled on the sets, hoping to make some quick pocket money. He later admitted good-naturedly that he wasn't paid even a rupee.

In 1963, Amjad Khan started going to college and distinguished himself in debating and elocution; excelled in cricket, badminton and NCC; and ruled the stage. He also started assisting on another project, the *Mughal-E-Azam* director K. Asif's ambitious colour film *Love and God* (1986). It starred Jayant as Emir-e-Basra, the father of Laila, who was played by Nimmi. Guru Dutt was cast as the lovelorn Qais who, after being separated from Laila by a family feud, wanders in the desert chanting her name. He soon starts being referred to as 'Majnu', a crazy, obsessed lover. One day, the director asked Amjad if he would play an Abyssinian slave sent by his mother to bring Qais home. He accepted the offer.

Guru Dutt's untimely demise the following year brought shooting to an abrupt halt. It resumed only six years later, in 1970, with Sanjeev Kumar replacing Guru Dutt. But the next year, on 9 March 1971, the director himself passed away; the film was only released 15 years later, on 27 May 1986, after K. Asif's widow, Akhtar Asif, and producer-director K.C. Bokadia, salvaged some usable portions of film from three different studios and pieced them together to complete his celluloid dream. By then, even Sanjeev Kumar was no more and his scenes and a song had to be shot with a duplicate, with Sudesh Bhonsle dubbing his voice. Jayant, too, was gone.

While Amjad had been shooting in Jaisalmer for *Love and God*, his father had fallen ill. He was later diagnosed with cancer of the larynx. That's when Amjad's parents went with a formal proposal to Shehla's parents asking for her hand, which her father, Akhtar ul Iman, accepted. The wedding, which took place on 17 August 1972, was rushed through because of Jayant's failing health, even though Shehla still had a year to go to complete her master's in Aligarh.

Their first child, Shadaab, was born on 20 September 1973. The same day, Amjad signed *Sholay*. When his son was two months old, he boarded a flight to Bangalore for the first schedule of the film in Ramanagara. It was a difficult shoot, his father's illness preying on his mind. Jayant passed away on 2 June 1975, just two-and-a-half months before his son's first blockbuster was unveiled to the world. However, Shehla informs that producer G.P. Sippy had screened a rush print of *Sholay* for him to see ahead of the release, and Jayant had loved Amjad's performance as Gabbar.

After *Sholay*, Amjad Khan became a busy star who featured in around 50 films in the '70s. Some, like *Hum Kisise Kum Naheen* (1977, Saudagar Singh), *Parvarish* (1977, Mangal Singh), *Ganga Ki Saugand* (1978, Thakur Jashwant Singh), *Des Pardes* (1978, Bhoot Singh and Avtar Singh), *Muqaddar Ka Sikandar* (1978, Dilawar), *Mr. Natwarlal* (1979, Vikram Singh) and *Suhaag* (1979, Vikram Kapoor), were big hits. Some disappeared without a trace. Almost all of them had him playing a typical Bollywood villain.

In the crowd of releases, one performance stands out— Wajid Ali Shah, the profligate, hedonistic Nawab of Oudh, an artist, a poet, a chess player and a gentle soul. Reportedly, Satyajit Ray cast Amjad Khan in *Shatranj Ke Khilari* (1977) after seeing him in *Sholay*, but this Nawab had no traces of Gabbar Singh. 'Amjad himself liked the film so much that he even bought the Nizam territory and distributed it. The timing was wrong as it was released during the month of Ramadan, when morning and night shows don't pull in crowds in Hyderabad because people are busy with prayers. He lost money, but *Shatranj Ke Khilari* remains one of my favourite performances. He was such a wonderful actor!' Shehla applauds.

It is said Satyajit Ray was so keen on Amjad that he even delayed the shoot to give the actor time to recover from a near-fatal road accident. Shehla confirms this, sharing that the Oscar-winning filmmaker even visited her husband when he was in hospital at a time when his condition was critical and not many were sure he would even pull through. 'He urged Amjad emotionally to get well soon, saying that if he didn't do the film, he would shelve *Shatranj Ke Khilari*. Shabana [Azmi] later pointed out that Satyajit Ray saying he would not make a film without him was the biggest compliment any actor could receive. She was right,' she acknowledges.

The accident happened when they were on the way to Goa for the shoot of Shakti Samanta's *The Great Gambler* (1979). The actor was supposed to take an evening flight to Goa, but the shooting of the (now-shelved) film *Watan* in Mumbai had got extended because his co-star, Sunil Dutt, also had to leave the next day. By the time they packed up, he had missed his flight. To ensure that he reported for the 9.00 a.m. shift on time, he decided to drive through the night. Shehla was six months pregnant then and he called her gynaecologist to check if he could take his wife along for the trip. When she gave the go-ahead, along with advice to avoid bumpy routes, Amjad, Shehla and Shadaab took off for Goa in their car.

The actor dozed off soon, but Shehla stayed up most of the night, giving their chauffeur directions on the route from the back seat. At around 6.00 a.m., they stopped at a wayside eatery for tea and a snack. When they resumed their journey, Amjad sent the driver to the back seat to grab some sleep and, with his wife beside him, took the wheel. He urged Shehla to take off her glasses and get some rest too. He himself looked fresh and rested, driving fast, wanting to reach the set on time. She remembers seeing him flip a cassette in the deck, his eyes on it—then bang! The world shattered around her.

When she returned to consciousness, she was lying in a pool of blood, the car having rammed into a big tree. Dazed and disoriented, Shehla kept repeating, 'Who are we? Where are we going?' Her husband had broken his left leg and 13 ribs, but he was conscious and alert. The driver, maid and their son were instructed to jump out. Then, breaking the steering wheel that had ruptured a lung, Amjad pushed Shehla out of the car too, and holding his broken leg, he threw himself out. They were all huddled by the side of the road, when the driver of a state transport bus passing by recognized the star. Clearing out the other passengers, telling them to take the next bus, he drove them to Sawantwadi Hospital. 'There Amjad, unconcerned about his own injuries, urged the doctors to check on me, telling them I was six months pregnant,' Shehla remembers.

From there an ambulance took them to Panjim, where the unit was stationed, and they were admitted to Panjim Medical Hospital. Amjad was wheeled in for an emergency surgery. 'Since my right hand was broken, Amit-ji [Amitabh Bachchan], who had rushed over on getting the news, signed the consent forms for the tracheostomy. He must have been so nervous because Amjad's condition was not good, but both Jaya and Amit-ji were by my side all day, consulting the doctors and making all the arrangements,' Shehla relives the horror.

Throughout his stay at the Panjim Medical Hospital, Amjad Khan's *The Great Gambler* co-star and good friend, Amitabh Bachchan, would visit the hospital every day, urging him to get well soon. Later, when the actor himself was in hospital for months after being injured on the sets of *Coolie* (1983), Amjad sat by his bedside and boosted his spirits. Their *yaarana* (friendship) was real!

While Shehla healed and delivered a healthy daughter, Ahlam, in February the next year, followed by another son Seemab, the road to recovery for Amjad was a long one and he was never the same again. 'The accident happened on 15 October 1976. After spending his birthday in a hospital in Goa, he was flown back to Bombay and admitted to Nanavati Hospital. Amjad stayed there for almost three months, till mid-January, then was home for another 15–20 days, before he got permission to resuming shooting,' relates Shehla, adding that during the first schedule of *The Great Gambler*, he had to jump from a height, and despite all the precautions, he hurt his foot and had to return home. He was eventually replaced by Utpal Dutt.

'Then he wanted to buy a new car, and during the test drive, met with an accident. Since there was a long schedule in Hyderabad, he asked the doctor to pump him with steroids so he could get back on his feet fast. Amjad was so busy running from one set to the next that there was no time to rest, recuperate or even follow his usual fitness regime,' rues his wife.

The frequent falls and the steroids, the lack of exercise and his mother's failing health after she was diagnosed with cancer, followed by her subsequent demise, took their toll. Amjad put on a lot of weight and slowly, the bad man roles he had been flooded with stopped coming because they required plenty of action. 'He didn't eat much, but he loved sweets. *Gulab jamuns, rasgullas*, even chocolates. When he came home late from a shoot, he would not want dinner, but he hunted for the bars of chocolate I had hidden away. Then there was the chai, 30–40 cups of over-sweetened tea that he would drink all day, every day,' Shehla remembers.

Ananth Narayan Mahadevan recalls going to watch the actor at Prithvi Theatre once. As usual his performance was matchless, but what the actor-filmmaker remembers is an amusing story he heard from when the actors had been rehearsing for the play. 'Amjad-bhai had called for tea from Prithvi Café, and after a long wait, he was informed that there was no milk. The next day, he apparently brought a buffalo along and tied it to a post outside the café, telling the manager that now they would never be short of milk,' he laughs.

It was this deliciously wicked humour that helped Amjad make a smooth transition from villainy to comedy. Some of his performances, be it the police inspector in *Qurbani* (1980) or the irreverent sex guru in *Utsav* (1984), got him rave reviews. 'I loved him in *Hum Se Badhkar Kaun* [1981]. He is hilarious! Then there was Havaldar Sher Singh in *Love Story* [1981], who is assigned the job of finding the runaway couple, Bunty and Pinky, but ends up sympathizing with them and becomes their ally,' Shehla smiles. She recalls that after watching *Love Story*, which launched Kumar Gaurav and Vijayata Pandit, B.R. Chopra called up Amjad and congratulated him on his performance and his distinctive dialect.

Pankaj Parashar remembers a drunken scene in *Peechha Karro* (1986). When he took the dialogue sheets across, Amjad waved them away, saying, '*Tu abhi chhod hum ko, hum theatre ke bande hain* [You leave us now, we are from the stage].' Farooq Shaikh and he did the scene in one take, improvising as they went along. 'It was fantastic!' the director recounts with awe.

They remained friends, with Amjad sometimes calling the director, who lived five minutes away from him, over to his place. Parashar showed him his television detective series *Karamchand* and got the thumbs up. The actor also saw *Chaalbaaz* (1989) on video and called to tell the director that he had liked the film. 'What are you doing next?' he asked curiously. When told he was directing a children's film, *Aasman Se Gira* (1992), Amjad asked him what role he was playing in it. When told that they had a budget of just ₹40 lakh and could not afford him, he retorted, 'When did I ask for money? You can give me a carton of Benson & Hedges cigarettes as payment.'

And that's how he came to play God in the fantasy comic adventure film, starring Raghubir Yadav as an alien who comes to earth by mistake and befriends a young prince dissatisfied with his royal life. When he returns to his parallel universe, God runs down mankind, saying they are ruining earth and should be eradicated even as his subject defends the human race, insisting they will learn from their mistakes. 'Amjad had just three days of work. He was brilliant!' Parashar raves.

After acting in over 200 films, Amjad Khan turned to directing with *Adhura Aadmi* (1982), followed by a crime drama, *Chor Police* (1983). Then came *Ameer Aadmi Ghareeb Aadmi* (1985) and *Abhi To Main Jawan Hoon* (1989). 'I remember in one scene in *Hum Tere Aashiq Hain* where I told him [Amjad] to give some money to Shriram Lagoo's character, he insisted on arrogantly throwing the notes instead of handing them over in keeping with his character. He even suggested I put in some sound effects to enhance the moment. Like Kamal Haasan, Amjad understood the language of cinema because of his experience on stage. I knew that he would direct films one day,' says Prem Sagar.

Amjad was going to act and direct his fifth film and had set up a meeting with a senior cop at Carter Road police station on 27 July 1992 as part of his prep. The previous day, he had been busy from nine in the morning to midnight, trying to mediate a dispute between producers/directors and actors as president of the Actors' Guild Association. 'Since he had been on his feet for long hours, I sent him to his doctor at Nanavati Hospital late at night for a quick check-up. He returned to say all was well,' remembers Shehla.

The next morning, the calls started early, and continued all day, regarding the previous day's issue. Amjad was drifting in and out of sleep as he answered them. At around 4.30 p.m., Shehla went up to wake him and urged him to take a shower. He asked for tea and she pointed to the cup by the bedside. He picked it up, promising to get ready soon.

When Shadaab returned from college, Shehla sent him up to hurry his father along or he would be late for his 7.30 p.m. appointment with the police inspector. Her son returned in a few minutes looking shaken, saying Amjad was sweating profusely and had turned cold. Protesting that he had been fine just 15 minutes ago when she had checked on him, Shehla raced up, her sister, who was visiting, at her heels. He did not look good.

'He wasn't responding to our efforts, so I called his father and brother who arrived soon after. I also called his doctor, but before he could arrive, Shadaab, who was in junior college then, showing great presence of mind, got a local doctor who immediately prescribed an injection. It was past 8.00 p.m. by then, but after trying several hospitals, Shadaab finally got it at Asha Parekh hospital, and rushed back home. When the doctor told him it was too late, my son insisted he still give it, hoping for another miracle. But this time there was none,' mourns Shehla, who kept urging Amjad's doctor who had arrived to do something till he told her gently, '*Bhabhi*, let him go.'

Amjad Khan was born prematurely at seven months. He passed away prematurely too, on 27 July 1992, from a cardiac arrest. Thirty-two years have passed. Shadaab has turned into an actor and a writer. Ahlam is passionate about theatre like her father and writes, acts and produces plays. Her husband, Zafar Karachiwala, is a popular theatre actor. Seemab wants to be an actor and a director like Amjad someday. 'I have two lovely daughters-in-law and two grandchildren, Suraayah and Mihaail. It's a full house. He would have loved it. He was crazy about the children and would cry if any of his babies were ill or hurt. When I would tell him matter-of-factly that they would be fine soon, Amjad would say, "You won't understand, you are not a father." And I would tell myself, "No, I'm not, but I am their mother!" He was such a baby sometimes,' Shehla smiles fondly.

She remembers her husband saying, 'Take one day at a time.' That's what she has been doing all these years, still unable to believe that Amjad is not around. 'He was a lovely, funny man with the softest heart and simple tastes. Every birthday or anniversary, I invariably gifted him a lighter or a watch because those were the only two things he loved. He had over a hundred watches, but he ran out of time too soon,' Shehla sighs.

Amjad Khan is gone. But he hasn't been forgotten. Almost half a century after he exploded on screen as Gabbar Singh, one can still hear him saying, '*Yahaan se pachas pachas kos door gaon mein, jab bachcha raat ko rota hai, to maa kehti hai, bete so ja, so ja nahin to Gabbar Singh aa jayega* [Fifty miles from here, when a child cries at night in a village, the mother hushes him up saying, son, go to sleep, or else Gabbar

Singh will come].' Shehla herself admits that even today, at any function or show, she hears these cult lines. 'Some characters are there to stay, and actors too,' she signs off.

AMRISH PURI
THE DON OF A NEW ERA

'Mogambo khush hua.'

—*Mr. India* (1987)

To my best villain, you are unique in all the world as a bad guy and in the real world we live in. You are a terrific human being. I loved every minute of our work together, can't wait to work with you again.*

This handwritten letter from Steven Spielberg was Amrish Puri's most treasured possession, the experience of working with the Oscar-winning director on *Indiana Jones and the Temple of Doom* (1984) one he cherished all his life. So, it came as a surprise to me to learn that he was sorely disappointed after reading the script when he landed in London for the costume and make-up trials. In fact, he admitted that he might well have turned down the film, which was part of a blockbuster, multi-million-dollar franchise, and returned home—had it not been for Sir Richard Attenborough.

---

*"Steven Spielberg Was "Amazed" Amrish Puri Was Doing 22 Films at the Same Time, Came to India to Audition Him: "You Are Terrific Human Being"', *The Indian Express*, 9 June 2023, https://tinyurl.com/w9w4esr4. Accessed on 8 May 2024.

While working on the Oscar-winning epic biographical film *Gandhi* (1982), the British actor-filmmaker had developed a close bond with the Indian actor, who plays Khan, a friend to Ben Kingsley's Gandhi during his stay in South Africa. After reading the script of *Indiana Jones and the Temple of Doom*, Amrish Puri called up Sir Richard Attenborough and groused, 'This is like any masala [commercial] Hindi movie, I don't think I want to do it.' The latter convinced him to stay back in London, and even lent him his own agent to negotiate a favourable deal for him. It was thanks to Sir Attenborough's timely intervention that he made his Hollywood debut as Mola Ram in the 1984 action-adventure, which became the year's highest-grossing film and the tenth top grosser of all time when it was released.

In an interview with *Scroll.in*, Amrish Puri revealed that he had landed the film after casting directors Dolly Thakore and Shama Habibullah sent across some stills to the producers from Aruna Raje and Vikas Desai's horror thriller, *Gehrayee* (1980), an Indianized *Exorcist*, in which he had played an evil *tantrik* (magician). Surprisingly, the actor himself was not keen on doing a Hollywood film and had refused to come for an audition when the casting directors arrived in Bombay, instead calling them to one of his film shoots.[*]

When he was handed a full page of dialogue in English and asked to memorize the lines in 10 minutes, he told the casting director that was impossible and he would improvise on camera. 'What I suggested was unheard of, but they had no option but to agree. Most of what I said during that audition

---

[*]Ramnath, Nandini, '"Temple of Doom" Is the Indiana Jones Movie that Indians Won't Forget in a Hurry', *Scroll.in*, 31 March 2016, https://tinyurl.com/wsf4uxfa. Accessed on 9 May 2024.

was meaningless gibberish,' he admitted with a guffaw. But the innovative twist he gave his lines and the hypnotic power of his histrionics caught Spielberg's eye, and Amrish Puri landed the coveted role. He was one short of 50 when *Indiana Jones and the Temple of Doom* released. It made him a global star and brought along a flood of offers from the West, but he turned them all down and continued working in Indian cinema.

He entered films pretty late, despite an early interest in acting. The fourth of five children, Amrish Lal Puri was born in Nawanshahr in Punjab. He went to school in Delhi, where his father, Lala Nihal Chand Puri, had been posted, but finished his matriculation in Simla, where the senior Puri settled after retirement. He then proceeded to Hoshiarpur to do his intermediate at D.A.V. College, but returned to Simla to enroll in BM College. That's when the acting bug bit him, and he featured in a few plays staged by the Amateur Artists' Association.

Meanwhile, despite their father's aversion to cinema, his two elder brothers—Chaman Puri and Madan Puri—inspired by their first cousin, legendary actor-singer Kundan Lal Saigal, had made a career in acting. Madan Puri went on to become a top-ranking Bollywood villain, and the two brothers featured in Shakti Samanta's crime thriller, *Howrah Bridge* (1958).

In 1953, after completing his graduation in Simla, Amrish Puri, following in the footsteps of his brothers, also relocated to Bombay. He was only 21 then and started doing the rounds of producers' offices for a hero's role, which proved elusive. So, a year later, he took up a government job and worked with the Employees' State Insurance Corporation (ESIC) in the Ministry of Labour & Employment for 21 years, till 1975.

It was here that he met Urmila Divekar and fell in love. The couple later tied the knot.

After marriage, the acting bug resurfaced, and in 1961, he enrolled for a one-year course at Ebrahim Alkazi's Natya Academy. After he passed out of the academy, adjudged best student, Satyadev Dubey, who had directed him in a class play titled *Bichhoo*, offered him the role of the blind king Dhritarashtra in his stage production, *Andha Yug*. He would sell insurance during the day, but the evenings were for theatre. Amrish Puri quickly became a well-known name in Hindi theatre, following his histrionics in plays like *Andha Yug*, *Hayavadana*, *Aadhe Adhure* and *Yayati*. He was honoured with the prestigious Sangeet Natak Akademi Award in 1979.

His screen debut, at the age of 38, wasn't as impressive. He played Jerry, a henchman in a church in Spain, in Dev Anand's spy thriller *Prem Pujari* (1970). The first film he signed, however, was Sunil Dutt's crime drama *Reshma Aur Shera* (1971), which released a year after *Prem Pujari*, and revolved around violent family feuds and star-crossed lovers. Amrish Puri played Rehmat Khan and was disappointed because several of his scenes were edited out.

It was in Shyam Benegal's *Nishant* (1975) that he first caught the eye as the eldest *jagirdar*, whose younger brother Vishwam's obsession with Shabana Azmi's Sushila, the abducted wife of the schoolmaster, sparks off a rebellion in the village. *Nishant* bagged the National Film Award for Best Feature Film in Hindi. The filmmaker had seen the actor in a play and confided that his first thought was 'this man is all evil.' Impressed with his rich baritone, which had landed him some plays, and even a radio show, *Hawa Mahal* on All India Radio, Shyam Benegal used Amrish Puri's voice in the documentaries he was making then, before offering him the role of Anna in *Nishant*.

Anna had reportedly been written with Utpal Dutt in mind. Based on a true story, *Nishant* had grown out of the Telangana movement, an armed peasant uprising against oppressive landlords, between 1946 and 1951. The screenplay was penned by noted playwright Vijay Tendulkar, and Satyadev Dubey had written the hard-hitting dialogue. The film was banned by the Central Board of Film Certification (CBFC) for being 'anti-establishment'. In an interview to *Huffington Post*, Shyam Benegal shared how following the ban, he met the then Prime Minister Indira Gandhi and screened the film for her at the Film Division in New Delhi. She liked it and agreed with him that *Nishant* should be released in India, having won accolades at several prestigious film festivals around the world, including Cannes. Following her intervention, it was passed without a single cut, which was surprising because Emergency had been declared and the constitutional right to freedom of speech and expression severely curtailed. However, he had to add a disclaimer at the beginning of the film that the events depicted on screen took place in pre-Independence India, which he found quite funny as it was obvious the film was set in the '50s.

Interestingly, the man who stands up to Amrish Puri in *Nishant*, Girish Karnad, had earlier written a Kannada play, *Yayati*, which had been translated into Hindi by Satyadev Dubey. Impressed by this giant of a performer who ruled the stage in the Hindi play, Karnad offered him a role in the Kannada film he was directing. *Kaadu* (1973), based on

---

*Pathak, Ankur, 'As a Filmmaker, I'm a Critic of the Present: Shyam Benegal Reflects on His Best films', *Huffpost*, 30 May 2020, https://tinyurl.com/mrymsees. Accessed on 23 April 2024.

Srikrishna Alanahalli's novel of the same name, features him as the village headman, Chandre Gowda, whose affair with a woman in a neighbouring village leads to family discord and a feud between the two villages with far-reaching consequences. It took the director three months to convince the film's producers, G.N. Lakshmipathy and K.N. Narayan, that a Punjabi actor who couldn't speak a word of Kannada should play this all-important role.

Kaadu bagged three National Film Awards and introduced Amrish Puri to the film's cinematographer, Govind Nihalani. He went on to feature in Nihalani's directorial debut, *Aakrosh* (1980), a scathing satire on corruption in the judicial system. He plays Public Prosecutor Dushane, who is the system himself, till he starts getting threatening calls reminding him of his indigeneous origins. This film was also written by Vijay Tendulkar and Satyadev Dubey, and bagged the National Film Award for Best Feature Film in Hindi.

Two years later, Govind Nihalani and Amrish Puri reunited for the coming-of-age film, *Vijeta* (1982), after the former prevailed upon his producer, Shashi Kapoor, to sign the bad man for the more sympathetic and supportive role of Chief Instructor Verghese.

The duo collaborated for a third time for the iconic *Ardh Satya* (1983). Vijay Tendulkar had recommended S.D. Panvalkar's book of Marathi short stories to Nihalani and the film has its genesis in a story titled 'Surya'. It revolves around a retired village constable, Velankar, who beats up his wife at the slightest pretext while their son Anant watches helplessly. When the latter expresses a desire to go abroad for higher studies, his father forces him to become a cop against his will. Tendulkar fleshed out Panvalkar's story, which initially ended with Smita Patil's Jyotsna Gokhale finding

Om Puri's Anant dead. However, wanting his protagonist to win at least one war, the director had Anant kill Sadashiv Amrapurkar's mafia-don-turned-politician Rama Shetty. He shot both endings, then went with his own, after getting the writer's approval. Both Tendulkar and Nihalani agreed that Amrish Puri should play Om Puri's father. The actor gave his nod immediately. 'I loved the scenes between the father and son, particularly the ones where they are drinking together and end up quarrelling,' he reminisced years later. The following year, he went on to also feature in Nihalani's *Party* (1984).

In the '90s, Amrish Puri came into his own, playing the face of evil in films like *Tridev* (1989), *Saudagar* (1991), *Tahalka* (1992), *Damini* (1993), *Karan Arjun* (1995), *Kaalapani* (1996) and *Koyla* (1997). 'There's grace and grandeur in black, but none of my characters have ever been totally black,' the man, who personally preferred spotless white, would say, pointing out that even Mogambo had streaks of grey.

Mogambo, the bad man of the Boney Kapoor-produced fantasy action-adventure *Mr. India* (1987), is the character that has come to be most closely associated with the actor.

In Boney Kapoor's first production, *Hum Paanch* (1980), a contemporary re-telling of the Mahabharata, he was cast as the lecherous landlord Thakur Vir Pratap Singh, a modern-day Duryodhana, who gets the men of his fiefdom hooked on gambling, molests the women, and kills anyone who opposes his tyranny. Amjad Khan had reportedly been the unanimous choice for the role after becoming a household name as *Sholay*'s (1975) dreaded dacoit Gabbar Singh, but the film's director, Bapu, who had seen Amrish Puri in *Kaadu*, insisted on him. His remuneration for *Hum Paanch* was ₹40,000, but Boney Kapoor admitted while speaking to me for *Mumbai Mirror* in August 2015 that he paid the actor an extra ₹10,000 as a promised bonus when the film became a hit.

The producer returned to his *Hum Paanch* Thakur with Mogambo and *Mr. India*. But Amrish Puri was a super busy star by then and had no dates to spare. The late Satish Kaushik, memorable as the cook and the children's caretaker Calendar in the fantasy adventure, revealed in our 2014 interview for *Mumbai Mirror* that after Puri reluctantly turned Boney Kapoor away, several actors were considered for the role. Eventually, Anupam Kher was finalized and his costumes were also stitched; but just before they were to start shooting, everyone came to the agreement that Mogambo needed someone more menacing, despite being a comic-book villain.

Like Girish Karnad and Govind Nihalani before him, director Shekhar Kapur fought tooth and nail to get Amrish Puri on board. When Boney Kapoor pointed out that he was not just a busy actor but also an expensive star and they could not afford him, his director simply turned around and told him that it was better to go a little over budget and get the right actor. He refused to make *Mr. India* without him. They called the actor in Ooty where he was shooting and the producer offered Amrish Puri the role again. This time, he agreed; later, he even got his niece Kanchan to design a chair for his home that looked like Mogambo's throne.

Amrish Puri's grandson, Vardhan Puri, an actor himself, asserts that there were no hard feelings between his grandfather and Anupam Kher over *Mr. India*. 'They were good friends and when they spoke about it, Anupam assured *Dadu* [grandfather] that if anyone else had to do the role, he was glad it was Amrish Puri,' he shares.

After Amrish Puri signed *Mr. India*, he would frequently call Satish Kaushik home early in the morning, along with the costume designer and make-up man. He would wear his costume and full make-up and read out his scenes. The same process continued during *Badhaai Ho Badhaai* (2002), which Kaushik directed. The actor-filmmaker had idolized the senior actor since his NSD days in Delhi, not just for his passion for the stage, but also because he had managed to break into the dazzling world of Hindi cinema.

Unlike other theatre actors, Amrish Puri not only featured in off-beat films, but was also a part of big-budget, mainstream cinema. His success inspired stage actors like Satish Kaushik, who had met Amrish Puri for the first time during the shooting of Shyam Benegal's *Mandi* (1983), in which he plays the councillor and Amrish Puri has a cameo as Darvish.

I met Amrish Puri for an interview for *Zee Premiere* magazine on 22 June 1998, which, coincidentally, was his sixty-sixth birthday, a fact that explained the bouquets strewn around his Juhu bungalow. When I arrived, he scrutinized me for a long time, and then called every member of the family present in the house to confirm that I looked like one of his nieces. For a while I was disconcerted, even embarrassed by all the attention given that he was the star, but his childlike glee soon melted my natural reserve and I understood why Shekhar Kapur had been so convinced only Amrish Puri could play the comic-strip villain of *Mr. India*. It came as no surprise to learn from Vardhan that his grandfather had loved watching *Tom and Jerry* and played the cartoons on a loop on Sundays. 'Even on other days, Dadu would study a scene carefully as he stepped out of the shower and dressed for work, then watch it again, telling us that he was learning from watching the cat and mouse at play,' informs the younger Puri, who is a scriptwriter himself.

Vardhan's first acting guru was his grandfather, who till his last day would tell him, 'Your roots are in theatre, never forget that. Don't get lured by parties, nightlife and all the *moh maaya* [temptations] of this glamorous world, live for your craft.' The stage was Amrish Puri's passion and even when he was struggling to support his family, he would invest whatever money he could in Satyadev Dubey's path-breaking plays. The financial assistance continued even after he became a successful star. Occasionally, he would watch a play, sitting in the audience, going backstage after the curtain came down to congratulate the actors.

By then he was doing two, three, even four shifts a day, and if a producer wanted to sign him, he had to approach Amrish Puri for dates eight to 10 months in advance. From being paid a paltry ₹100 per show during his theatre days, he became Bollywood's highest-paid villain in the '90s, reportedly charging as much as ₹1 crore per film, and in some cases even double that—a remuneration only the heroes commanded back then.

He never confirmed the figure or his status as leader of the pricey khalnayak pack, but acknowledged that he never compromised on his price. His reasoning was simple: since the producer was earning 10, sometimes even 20 times in return, there was no reason for him to charge less. He, however, made concessions for a deserving few. Among the directors Amrish Puri respected and enjoyed working with were Shyam Benegal, Govind Nihalani, Yash Chopra and Subhash Ghai.

Subhash Ghai first met him on the sets of his revenge drama *Vishwanath* (1978), which features Shatrughan Sinha and Reena Roy in the lead, and a gallery of villains, from Prem Nath as the underworld don GNK and Pran as Golu Gawah, to Madan Puri as Pukhraj, Ranjeet as Khokha and Sudhir as Jimmy. 'One day, Amrish-ji dropped by to meet his brother. His eyes and voice impressed me and I asked Madan-ji why his brother didn't act in films. He replied that Amrish-ji was committed to theatre and wasn't too enamoured of commercial Hindi cinema,' the filmmaker recounts.

Undeterred, Subhash Ghai asked Madan Puri on the fourth day of the shoot to tell his brother to meet him. He explains that having graduated from the FTII, he has an eye for talent and his gut instinct told him Amrish Puri *lambi race ka ghoda hai* (he was a horse who would go far in the race). When the actor came over, Ghai offered him a small role in his next film, *Krodhi* (1981), telling him frankly that the main villain was Dharmendra, a mafia-don-turned-saint. Amrish Puri's character, Madhavan, is killed after just two scenes. The actor surprised him by saying he needed time to think, even though back then newcomers like him grabbed any role in a big project. Meanwhile, Ghai went to watch one of the actor's plays and was bowled over by his performance. 'The next time we met, I admitted that the role I had offered him did not do justice to his phenomenal talent. But I urged Amrish-ji to accept it, promising to give him something more substantial soon. That's how we started our journey together, and even in those two scenes he shone bright,' lauds the writer-director. They went on to do nine more films together, including *Hero* (1983), *Meri Jung* (1985), *Ram Lakhan* (1989), *Saudagar* (1991), *Pardes* (1997), *Taal* (1999) and *Yaadein...* (2001).

While Amrish Puri is best known as a Bollywood bad man, he had excellent comic timing. He was a riot as Durgaprasad Bhardwaj, Tabu's businessman father, in *Chachi 420* (1997), an Indianized *Mrs. Doubtfire* (1993). 'My grandfather would return from the studio in splits when he was shooting for the film,' recalls Vardhan with a smile.

He also enjoyed doing Priyadarshan's *Muskurahat* (1992), *Gardish* (1993), *Kaalapani* (1996) and *Virasat* (1997), which helped him break away from his villain image. Many had tried to dissuade Priyadarshan from casting Amrish Puri as Anil Kapoor's father, Raja Thakur, in *Virasat*, whose sudden heart attack changes the course of his foreign-returned son's life. They argued that as a certified villain, he would never be accepted in a role played by Sivaji Ganesan in the Tamil original, *Thevar Magan* (1992).

Buzz is, Dilip Kumar, Raaj Kumar and Sunil Dutt were considered for this all-important role. Vardhan confirms that Dilip Kumar was the first choice and producer duo Mushir–Riaz, director Priyadarshan and Boney Kapoor had even approached the thespian. 'But after listening to the narration, Dilip-sahab told them that he could see only Amrish Puri as Raja Thakur. After hearing this, a phone call was made to Kamal Haasan, on whose story the film is based. After consulting him, my grandfather was approached,' Vardhan shares, adding that his dadu later had a word with Dilip Kumar, who reiterated what he had said. 'His endorsement meant a lot to my grandfather because he had grown up idolizing Dilip-sahab, mesmerized by his performances on screen.'

Amrish Puri later acknowledged that Raja Thakur was unlike his usual roles. But in real life too, he was a dutiful father and a lovable grandfather.

He also experimented with Tamil films. He plays a gangster, Kalivardhan, in Mani Ratnam's *Thalapathi* (1991), which was dubbed in Hindi as *Dalapathi*. *Thalapati* is a cult classic today. He is also an evil tantrik in the Rajinikanth-starrer *Baba* (2002).

There were Telugu films as well, like *Jagadeka Veerudu Athiloka Sundari* (1990), *Kondaveeti Donga* (1990), *Aditya 369* (1991) and *Major Chandrakanth* (1993). And he will always be remembered as the zamindar Zalam Singh in the Punjabi film *Sat Sri Akal* (1977), the Sufi saint in *Shaheed Uddham Singh: Alias Ram Mohammed Singh Azad* (2000), and the villainous Jagirdaar Joginder Singh in *Chann Pardesi* (1981). Amrish Puri himself handpicked *Chann Pardesi* as one of his best performances. The scheming Dulla Singh from *Waaris* (1988) was another favourite.

I remember him as the ageing don, Nageshwar, in *Phool Aur Kaante* (1991), who has a change of heart after his grandson is abducted. Vardhan recalls hearing from his father Rajeev Puri that action choreographer Veeru Devgan had come to their home with a request for Amrish Puri. 'He told Dadu that he wanted a promise from him given that both of them were Punjabis who shared a close bond. When my grandfather insisted on first being told what he wanted, Veeru-ji refused to say anything more, simply stating that he would not take a "no" for an answer. When Dadu gave him his word, he was told about this role,' informs the younger Puri.

The film launched Veeru Devgan's son Ajay Devgn, as well as the heroine Madhoo and director Kuku Kohli. Amrish Puri was the biggest name in the cast and the only established star. His 'yes' was just the boost they needed. *Phool Aur Kaante* released on 22 November 1991, clashing with the release of Yash Chopra's *Lamhe* (1991). The film fraternity was expecting Anil Kapoor and Sridevi's unconventional love story to be a blockbuster, while Ajay Devgn's debut film, they predicted, would at best be an average grosser.

'In fact, at a big function some industry bigwigs even reprimanded Dadu, telling him he should not be working with newcomers at this stage in his career. My grandfather insisted that *Phool Aur Kaante* would be a sleeper hit. And that's what happened!' exults Vardhan.

As Shambu Nath, a former freedom fighter and Sunny Deol's father in Rajkumar Santoshi's *Ghatak* (1996), who is dying of throat cancer, he was impressive. Vardhan informs that his grandfather's fans were very upset with the scene where the antagonist Katya, played by Danny Denzongpa, puts a dog's collar and a leash around his neck. That performance bagged Amrish Puri Filmfare's Black Lady and Screen's Golden Lady for Best Supporting Actor.

Then there was the wealthy NRI Kishorilal in *Pardes* (1997) who, even after living in the USA for 40 years and embracing American culture, still croons, '*Yeh mera India, I love my India.*' The song plays every year during Independence Day and Republic Day celebrations. I remember Amrish asserting in that booming voice, 'I love my India too.'

Subhash Ghai admits that he had a special fondness for the actor who, with his distinctive features, bodybuilder's physique and larger-than-life persona, always stood out in a crowd. 'Amrish-ji looked like one of the heroes from Greek mythology, the mighty Hercules or the monster-slaying Theseus. He was gifted with a deep baritone, which he used to good effect to whip up both fear and empathy. Then, there were those eyes—fiery one moment and gentle the next, depending on who he was playing in the film,' the showman rhapsodizes.

These attributes were further amplified by the actor's tricks of the trade. He would find an animal parallel and study its traits carefully so he could embody them in the character he was playing. Vardhan informs that Mogambo's maniacal laugh in *Mr. India* came from imitating a hyena, while Balwant Rai, the crooked businessman in *Ghayal* (1990), emerged from a tiger. 'Chaudhry Baldev Singh, Kajol's father in *Dilwale Dulhania Le Jayenge* [1995], was modelled on an old lion, no longer physically agile, but still commanding fear and respect,' confides the younger Puri as he reflects on when *DDLJ*'s writer-director, Aditya Chopra, had come to their house for a narration. 'Adi Sir wasn't carrying a script, but he knew every character by heart and enacted all of them with different voice modulations.'

His grandfather was enchanted. He did not utter a single word all through the narration. 'When it ended, Adi Sir told him that he had written the role of Simran's *bauji* [father] with him in mind and would not make the film if he turned it down. With tears in his eyes, Dadu told him that he would love to be a part of his directorial debut,' reveals Vardhan, instantly bringing to mind that iconic last scene where he suddenly lets go of Kajol's hand, urging her to get on the train that is taking away Shah Rukh Khan's Raj and his father, played by Anupam Kher. His words are oft-quoted by doting dads today, '*Jaa Simran jaa, jee le apni zindagi* [Go Simran go, live your life].'

Despite his formidable persona on screen, Amrish Puri was an amiable giant off it who, while he avoided film parties, was not averse to calling friends home for dinner. His grandson recalls that once, Amitabh Bachchan called before dinner with a request that *kaali* dal (lentils) and his favourite *gobi sabzi* (cauliflower curry) be served. Vardhan adds that while Amrish Puri's friends were all big names, they were also simple people who enjoyed good food and the Punjabi songs that played during the meal. 'My grandfather himself was very particular about his diet and mostly stuck to vegetarian food, but enjoyed fish,' he informs.

Amrish Puri was also a style icon who even picked out suits, shirts, ties and hats for his film wardrobe. He loved hats in particular and had many in different shapes, sizes and colours. Parading some of them for my photographer Jagdish Mali's camera, he had revealed that his love for hats dated back to 1981, when he had shaved his head and started wearing a cap to save himself from the agony of an over-bright sun beating down on his bald pate. 'After that, whenever I spotted a hat I liked, I would buy it if it was a good fit,' he stated. Vardhan confirms this, and informs that he had over 500 hats, from America, Australia, Switzerland and France, which are preserved in a special room in an apartment in Madh Island with a monthly maintenance drill carried out diligently.

The actor also collected expensive watches and shoes. Since it was difficult to get shoes in his size, when he was in Agra for *Pardes*, Amrish Puri picked up 65 pairs and gave them to his costume designer. When that stock was exhausted, he bought another 30 pairs. As his love for shoes grew, he kept adding to his personal collection, sometimes bringing home a favourite pair he had worn in a film after shooting wrapped up.

The man who seemed invincible met with an accident while on a location shoot for Guddu Dhanoa's *Jaal: The Trap* (2003) in Himachal Pradesh. He suffered serious injuries on his face and eyes. He lost a lot of blood; moreover, during the transfusion, something went wrong and he developed a rare blood disorder. He lost his appetite, began to suffer severe headaches and grew weaker by the day—but Amrish Puri, ever the diligent actor, refused to hang up his boots and leave his producers in the lurch. He continued shooting and by 30 December 2004, had wrapped up all his pending films, including *Mujhse Shaadi Karogi* (2004), *Hulchul* (2004), *Aitraaz* (2004), *Kisna: The Warrior Poet* (2005) and *Kachchi Sadak* (2006).

Soon after, he tripped and fell at home and suffered a massive brain haemorrhage. The doctors pointed out that his only hope for a complete recovery was to undergo a brain surgery, warning that his chances of survival were only 50 per cent since he was 72 years old. 'Dadu spoke to my parents and aunt, pointing out that having lived his life like a lion, it was getting increasingly difficult to live with the excruciating pain. "I have to take a chance," he begged.' They lost him on the operation table.

Amrish Puri passed away on 12 January 2005. He worked in around 500 films, though not all of them were released. But 22 years after it opened on 15 June 2001, *Gadar: Ek Prem Katha*, one of Hindi cinema's biggest grossers, returned to the theatres on 9 June 2023 for a repeat run. A sequel, *Gadar 2*, followed on 11 August 2023, and was also a blockbuster. Amrish Puri had impressed as Major Ashraf Ali, the father of Ameesha Patel's Sakeena. Vardhan, who attended a special screening of the film with his family, was amazed by the kind of excitement *Gadar: Ek Prem Katha* still evoked. 'People reacted to the scene where Dadu urges Sunny Deol's Tara Singh to say "*Hindustan murdabad*" to prove that he is willing to adopt Pakistan for the love of his wife, repeating after Sunny, "*Hamara Hindustan zindabad tha, zindabad hai, aur zindabad rahega* [India was, is and will live on, forever glorious]!" It was unbelievable!' he marvels.

Anil Sharma, the director of the blockbuster, remembered the actor fondly at the show, asserting that Amrish Puri had been an integral part of the film's success. The younger Puri assured him that his grandfather was showering his blessings on them from above.

Reminiscing about the film's premiere in 2001, at Mumbai's Metro Cinema, Vardhan informs that the 8.00 p.m. show was delayed because of a huge traffic jam. Crowds of excited fans would not let Sunny Deol or Amrish Puri step out of their cars. A larger-than-life cutout of his grandfather loomed large in the foyer. After the show, all the big names present, from filmmakers Yash Chopra, Subhash Ghai and Rakesh Roshan to stars like Amitabh Bachchan and Shah Rukh Khan, praised Amrish Puri for a bravura performance. 'It was a joyous moment for Dadu,' his grandson smiles at the memory.

A couple of days after *Gadar*'s release, Amrish Puri took his grandchildren to the nearby JW Marriott Hotel to meet a guest from the UAE. 'As soon as Dadu entered the lobby, we were surrounded by around 4,000 fans. He must have signed around 500 autographs that day before the police were called to escort us to our car. It took 30 minutes to exit with fans screaming my grandfather's name. That was the first time I saw his stardom from up close and it was insane! Both Major Ashraf Ali and Amrish Puri live on,' Vardhan concludes.

)X(

PREM CHOPRA
IT'S ALL IN THE NAME

'Prem naam hai mera, Prem Chopra.'

—*Bobby* (1973)

Which other villain can boast of having a film that has made his name a brand name? Fifty years after Raj Kapoor's *Bobby* (1973) was released, Prem Chopra admits that by popular demand he is still mouthing the line, *'Prem naam hai mera, Prem Chopra,'* every time he is called on stage.

There's a family connection here. Raj Kapoor's wife, the late Krishna Kapoor, and Prem Chopra's wife, Uma, were sisters. So, it was difficult for him to refuse his brother-in-law, particularly one as charmingly persistent as Raj Kapoor, when he requested him to do a cameo in a teenage love story. *Bobby* (1973), which he was producing and directing, was an important film for Raj Kapoor as he was not only introducing his son Rishi Kapoor in the lead opposite the fresh-faced Dimple Kapadia, but also because he desperately needed a hit to pay off the debts that had piled up after the debacle of *Mera Naam Joker* (1970).

'I was the No.1 baddie at the time, and while Raj-sahab was a great filmmaker whose film I would love to do, as I pointed out to him, I wasn't doing just negative roles. There were also parallel roles, strong supporting characters, in the films of Yash Chopra, Shakti Samanta and several other big filmmakers. If I were to make a guest appearance in Raj-sahab's film, I would be expected to oblige others as well,' Prem Chopra shares, adding with a laugh that Raj Kapoor brushed off all his misgivings and arguments, simply telling him that he had to make this special appearance that played an integral part in the narrative, period.

By the time Prem Chopra jumped on board, almost 80 per cent of *Bobby* had been shot. On the appointed day, the actor turned up for the shoot, clueless about what he was expected to do because despite repeated requests, Raj Kapoor had refused to divulge any details about his role. He had not even shared the script. It was only when he braked to a stop on the Pune–Solapur Highway, near Raj Kapoor's farmhouse in Loni where they were to shoot, that the filmmaker quickly sketched out the scene to him.

The young couple, Raj and Bobby, have eloped because their parents won't agree to their match. On the run, they stop at a roadside dhaba. 'I am sitting at one of the tables with my cronies, reading the newspaper. Suddenly, spotting his face staring up from the back page, Bobby alerts her beau. Raj rudely snatches away the paper, revealing my face to the audience,' the actor recounts.

By then, films like *Woh Kaun Thi?* (1964), *Mera Saaya* (1966), *Teesri Manzil* (1966), *Upkar* (1967), *Do Raaste* (1969), *Purab Aur Pachhim* (1970), *Kati Patang* (1970), *Apradh* (1972), *Jugnu* (1973) and *Daag* (1973) had released and were huge hits, making Prem Chopra an infamous khalnayak. Raj Kapoor knew that the sight of him would make the audience shiver with anticipation and apprehension, instinctively realizing that his sudden appearance did not augur well for the runaway couple.

Meanwhile, on screen, Raj scans the advertisement his businessman-father Ram Nath, played by an imperious Pran, has placed, offering a reward of ₹25,000 to anyone who can offer information about his 18-year-old son. Realizing that any of those hanging out at the dhaba, including the man reading the paper, could happen to see the ad and identify him, Raj hurries away with his girl. As they are passing his table, Prem Chopra reaches out and grabs Bobby's hand. 'I want you to introduce yourself at this point, saying, "*Prem naam hai mera, Prem Chopra* [My name is Prem, Prem Chopra],"' Raj Kapoor told him. The bemused actor stuttered, 'Isn't that how James Bond introduces himself? "My name is Bond, James Bond."' His brother-in-law simply smiled in response, telling him he could go have some tea and snacks while they set up the shot.

The actor wandered off, bumping into Prem Nath, who was playing Dimple's fisherman father Jack Braganza. When the senior actor enquired about his scene, he nervously blurted out the line Raj Kapoor wanted him to say. Prem Nath, who was Uma's brother, laughed and assured his nervous co-star that the dialogue would become a 'superhit'. His morale boosted by one brother-in-law's words and another's conviction, Prem Chopra confidently faced the camera, pulling off his introduction scene with the panache of James Bond.

Raj Kapoor was delighted and made him repeat the line a second time, when he accosts Raj and Bobby on the cliff, after they jump out of his Tempo. This time he is brandishing a knife, and instead of a lecherous leer, he says the dialogue with chilling menace, '*Prem naam hai mera, Prem Chopra.*' He roughs up Raj, warning him that if he tries to run away again, he will break his leg. The second time around, the actor added his trademark devilish laugh to enhance his evil intent. 'Cut. Print!' the actor-director shouted, his delight obvious. And after the film's release, as Prem Nath had predicted, the single line, penned by Jainendra Jain, became a craze, immortalizing Prem Chopra. 'Yes, even the younger generation knows this cult dialogue now. At every show, in the UK and the US, I have to repeat it,' he reiterated to me during an interview for *Rediff.com* on 18 October 2023.

The third of six children, Prem Chopra was born to Ranbir Lal and Rooprani Chopra on 23 September 1935 in Lahore. The family moved to Simla following Partition. He did a number of plays in Hindi, Punjabi, Urdu and English when he was in college. A much-applauded performance was that of Shylock in an adaptation of William Shakespeare's popular play *The Merchant of Venice*. In retrospect, one can say that his career in villainy, which has spanned almost 400 films across five decades, started with the heartless moneylender.

When his father learnt that he wanted to become a Hindi film actor, the senior Chopra was horrified, having always imagined his bright son as an IAS officer or a doctor. He told Prem brusquely that as a government officer already providing for a large family, he wouldn't be able to support him while he chased after his starry dream. 'You are a graduate now; find a nice, steady job that will make you financially stable. Then, you can stay in Bombay independently and pursue your acting aspirations,' he advised.

His dutiful son found a job in *The Times of India*'s circulation department on a monthly salary of ₹2,500, along with a daily allowance and a first-class local train pass. He had to be on the road for 20 days a month, touring Bengal,

Bihar and Madhya Pradesh, but he found ways to get his work done quickly so that he could be back in Bombay quickly and do the rounds of producer's offices. To his disappointment, he didn't land any roles.

Then, one day, while he was travelling by the local train, he got talking to a stranger who turned out to be a talent scout. On learning that he was an aspiring actor, the gentleman escorted him to Ranjit Studios. There he was introduced to actor Jagdish Sethi, who took an instant liking to the young man and asked if he would be interested in doing a Punjabi film. He nodded his consent, believing that *Chaudhry Karnail Singh* (1960) could be his window to Hindi cinema.

Prem Chopra, however, continued with *The Times of India* job, even though he had to make every excuse possible to bunk work and report for shooting because his contract strictly specified that he could not take up any other job while working with the publishing house. It was a wise decision because his first film was in the making for three years. Without a steady job, he might well have been in dire straits.

The first schedule at Bombay's Chandivali Studio went off smoothly; but during the next one at Famous Studios, Prem Chopra, who was playing a snake-charmer, was told that the scene required him to take a live snake out of the basket and hold it in his hand, before whirling it away. The actor, who has a phobia of snakes, reached for the basket with shaking hands, knowing a live snake lay coiled inside. However, he could not bring himself to touch the reptile despite several retakes.

It was the same story the next day. This time, Krishan Kumar, the director, exasperatedly yelled at him, asking him if he wanted to be thrown out of the film. In response, the actor threw down his *pagdi* (turban) and took to his heels, shouting over his shoulder that he wanted out. It was only when the director and his two assistants caught up with him that they learnt that their hero was petrified of snakes. 'They tried telling me that its fangs had been removed and the reptile in the basket was harmless, but I was deaf to reason,' Prem Chopra reminisces with a laugh. He stated categorically that he was not going to hold the snake in his hand, even if it meant getting the boot. Since they had already shot one-fourth of the film and found him to be a good actor, they compromised and used a rubber snake to complete the scene.

Chaudhry Karnail Singh was a superhit. It even won a National Film Award. However, Prem Chopra's Hindi films from that time period did not work. He went uncredited in *Tonga-Wali* (1955), while *Hum Hindustani* (1960) and *Mud Mud Ke Na Dekh* (1960), which were released in the same year as his Punjabi film, disappeared without a trace. As a result, the actor soon found himself standing at the crossroads of life, wondering about his next move. There were plenty of offers for Punjabi films but he was not tempted, knowing that the appeal of regional cinema was restricted and he wanted to be a pan-India Hindi film hero. So, he accepted only one Punjabi film, *Sapni* (1963), opposite Nishi, a top-ranking heroine of the time, and decided to wait for his big break in Hindi cinema.

As luck would have it, Mehboob Khan, the director of *Mother India* (1957), spotted him one day sitting in the garden of his studio. They got to chatting. The filmmaker was impressed with the young actor and promised to launch Prem Chopra as the leading man in his next Hindi film. But unfortunately, since his *Son of India* (1962) had flopped and Mehboob Khan himself was unwell, the big break took its time coming.

Meanwhile, while shooting for *Main Shaadi Karne Chala* (1962), in which he plays one of six grooms, someone suggested that Prem Chopra switch to negative roles, pointing out that there was less competition for villainous roles because every star aspirant wanted to become a hero. So, impatient to make it big, when he was offered one in Raj Khosla's psychological thriller, *Woh Kaun Thi?* (1964), he grabbed it. The film featured Manoj Kumar, with whom he had done *Dr. Vidya* (1962) earlier, in the lead. He plays Manoj Kumar's scheming cousin, Ramesh, who spins a web of deceit to prove that his Dr Anand is mentally unstable so his inheritance passes on to him. Mehboob Khan was the chief guest at the film's premiere. The next day, the livid filmmaker walked up to the newly coronated villain whose performance was getting him rave reviews and ranted, '*Saala, maine kaha tha kuch gadbad mat kar, ab gadbad kiya to saari zindagi villain ban kar reh.* [I told you not to make any wrong moves, and now that you have, you can be a villain all your life].'

Woh Kaun Thi? was a superhit. Around this time, Manoj Kumar came to him with the role of the fearless revolutionary Sukhdev Thapar in *Shaheed* (1965), which he was unofficially directing. Prem Chopra grabbed the offer. Seventy-five per cent of the patriotic drama was shot in Ludhiana's Central Jail. In fact, among the 80–90 junior artistes featured in the film, some were actual death-row prisoners!

Among the condemned prisoners was an elderly sardar who, after watching the shoot for a few days, started walking up to Manoj Kumar every morning, respectfully touching his feet and striding away quietly, leaving him and the rest of the unit bemused. He opened up one night, in the darkness brought on by a power cut, informing them that he had been a warden in Lahore Central Jail when Bhagat Singh and the other freedom fighters were there. Impressed by how accurately Manoj Kumar was recreating the martyr's life, he expressed his appreciation through the daily salutations. By a strange twist of fate, the man had ended up in jail himself after committing a series of murders.

Prem Chopra confides that when he was walking to the gallows with Manoj Kumar and Anant Kumar, he felt a strange empathy with the nationalists Sukhdev, Bhagat Singh and Rajguru, and experienced the elation of patriots willingly laying down their lives for their country. 'There must have been some 25 films made on Bhagat Singh since, but people still cry when they see our *Shaheed* because it was such a pure and honest film,' he asserts.

Shaheed was followed by another Raj Khosla thriller, *Mera Saaya* (1966), and Vijay Anand's *Teesri Manzil* (1966). In *Mera Saaya*, Prem Chopra plays a dacoit who is the key to Sadhana's dual identity and redeems himself in court with a final confession. In the Shammi Kapoor murder mystery *Teesri Manzil*, he is the jealous fiancé of the victim and a strong suspect in Rupa's murder, till another twist in the tale unmasks the real villain. Both films were blockbusters. But the second turning point in his career came with Manoj Kumar's official directorial.

Upkar (1967) was made to take Lal Bahadur Shastri's slogan of '*Jai jawan, jai kisan* [Hail the soldier, hail the farmer]' to the masses. India's second prime minister was the chief guest at the premiere of *Shaheed* and after the film ended, his eyes suspiciously moist, he gave a 20-minute speech. Later that night, at around 2.00 a.m., Manoj Kumar was woken up by an unexpected call from the PMO extending an invitation to him and his team for breakfast with the Prime Minister the next morning. It was there that Babuji, as Lal Bahadur Shastri was fondly called, asked the actor to make a film about a farmer who becomes a soldier when the country is faced with a national crisis, outlining his message to every Indian. This was in the midst of the 1965 India–Pakistan War that was resolved with the signing of the Tashkent Declaration on 10 January 1966. A day later, Lal Bahadur Shastri passed away under mysterious circumstances.

Mr Bharat, however, kept his word to Babuji. *Upkar*, which was written in the train while Manoj Kumar was returning to Bombay after his momentous meeting with the Prime Minister, opened to theatres in 1967. It stars Prem Chopra as Puran, the polar opposite of his virtuous older brother Bharat, played by Manoj Kumar.

Chopra had not been the first choice for the role. During their days of struggle, sitting on a road roller outside Tardeo's Central Studio, Manoj Kumar and Shashi Kapoor had made a pact that whoever produced a film first would approach the other with a role. As promised, the actor-filmmaker took the role of Puran to his actor-friend first, who had such blind faith in him that he gave his nod without even listening to a narration. However, after a while, Manoj Kumar himself began to have second thoughts about casting Shashi Kapoor because Puran is most definitely a bad guy who goes against his selfless brother—who has toiled in the village to give him the best education in the city—by demanding his share of the property. Then, when the war breaks out, while Bharat goes off to the border to defend his motherland, Puran starts selling medicines in the black market to make a quick buck. Realizing that he would be betraying his friend and tarnishing his 'hero' image, he told Shashi Kapoor that *Upkar* wasn't for him. Again, there were no arguments.

The role was then taken to Rajesh Khanna, who

immediately gave his nod to the film, convinced it was a surefire winner. Six days later, though, he dropped by the actor-filmmaker's house. Manoj Kumar was out, and on his return, he was handed a letter the actor had left behind for him, regretfully turning down the offer. He had been warned by the panel of 10 big producers who had voted him the winner of the 1965 All India Talent Contest, organized by United Producers and Filmfare, that the role could work against him because it had shades of grey. Having already bitten the bullet, Prem Chopra had no such qualms.

Upkar wasn't an easy shoot. Manoj Kumar was a perfectionist and the last scene took them 72 hours to film because the director wanted shots of the rising sun and wouldn't let his actors stir from the location. 'We had to eat and sleep there till he got what he wanted,' Prem Chopra laughs, full of admiration for the actor who was also a producer, director and writer, could operate the camera when needed, had a cutting-edge knowledge of editing, and would attend music sittings to come up with one superhit score after another.

Upkar turned out to become the highest-grossing film of the year and with Malang Chacha changing his image, Pran moved to character roles. Prem Chopra took his place. What set them apart was that while Pran sported different get-ups, Chopra did so only in the occasional film like *Kaala Sona* (1975), in which he played a cocaine dealer, Poppy Singh, and looked every inch the maniacal villain with his bald pate, false eye and French beard. Mostly, though, he looked exactly as he did in real life, strutting around with his shirt unbuttoned, striking fear into the audience's heart with just his smile and his punchlines.

Till he quit *The Times of India*, the actor had been petrified of his pictures appearing in film magazines. He was afraid that they would alert his employers that he was moonlighting and he would then lose his job. But once *Upkar* became a superhit and Prem Chopra could finally quit the publishing house after six long years to become a full-fledged actor, he was delighted when a film magazine put him on the cover as a villain.

After that, not just filmmakers, but also prospective in-laws were queuing up outside his door with proposals for their daughters. The eligible bachelor, however, chose to tie the knot with Uma. It was an arranged match initiated by the bride's elder sister, Krishna Raj Kapoor. After just a couple of meetings, the actor lost his heart to Uma and they were married in 1969.

He made a career out of playing the devil incarnate who would find a way of getting a woman alone in a room. As he turned to lock the door, the damsel in distress, knowing what was to come, would plead with folded hands, '*Bhagwan ke liye mujhe chhod do* [For God's sake, spare me].' Prem Chopra's response, delivered with a sneer and a leer, is the classic one-liner, '*Itni khubsoorat cheez Bhagwan ke liye kaise chhod doon* [How can I leave such a beautiful object just for God]!', before pouncing on her. If it was the heroine, the hero often rushed to her rescue, wresting her away. But on occasion, he would get his way with her.

After *Upkar*, Manoj Kumar and Prem Chopra went on to do several films together, including *Purab Aur Pachhim* (1970), *Yaadgar* (1970), *Be-Imaan* (1972), *Sanyasi* (1975), *Kranti* (1981), *Kalyug Aur Ramayan* (1987), *Clerk* (1989), *Santosh* (1989) and *Jai Hind* (1999). Like Raj Kapoor, the actor-filmmaker gave the bad man a memorable line in his patriotic drama *Kranti*, which spans from 1825 to 1875, portraying a revolution against the ruling British. Chopra plays Shambhu

Singh, a man who helps the king's brother kill him and usurp his throne. His dialogue, '*Shambhu ka dimag do dhari talwar hai* [Shambhu's mind is like a double-edged sword]', quickly became a favourite with roadside urchins who would chant it whenever they spotted his car. He still brandishes this double-edged sword with the same flourish.

Two years after *Kranti*, Saawan Kumar Tak gave him some more cutting-edge lines in his love triangle *Souten* (1983), in which Prem Chopra plays Sampatlal, Tina Munim's step-uncle who creates a wedge between Rajesh Khanna and her. He delivers lines like '*Jinke ghar sheeshe ke hote hain, woh batti bujhaakar kapde badalte hain* [Those who live in glass houses should always douse the lights when changing their clothes]' and '*Main woh bala hoon jo sheeshe se patthar ko todta hoon* [I am that curse who breaks stones with glass]' with shattering impact.

In the Jackie Shroff-starrer, *Doodh Ka Karz* (1990), as Sampath, he deadpans with ironic humour, '*Baat jab apni maut par aati hai na, toh saari khidkiyaan khul jaati hain* [When the conversation moves to your death, all the windows fly open].' The words have a philosophical ring to them. In *Aag Ka Gola* (1989), as the don Raja Babu, he states pragmatically, '*Sharafat aur imaandari ka certificate yeh duniya sirf unhe deti hai jinke paas daulat hoti hai* [This world gives the certificate of dignity and honesty only to those with money].'

My personal favourites are the ones with a political ring. '*Agar opposition janta ko bhaashan deti hai, toh hum janta ko raashan dengey* [While the opposition lectures the masses, we give them ration],' states his *neta* (minister) Kailash Nath as the true *Khiladi* of the 1992 movie. '*Rajneeti ki bhains ke liye daulat ki lathi ki zaroorat hoti hai* [To tame this bull called politics, you need the stick of wealth]' is another gem from the same film.

Interestingly, Prem Chopra might have had a career in politics. After K.C. Bokadia's revenge drama, *Phool Bane Angaray* (1991), he was approached by a local delegation when shooting in Udaipur and offered a ticket to stand for the by-elections there. They were surprised when he turned down their offer despite having convincingly played the politician in so many films.

His rise as a super villain coincided with Rajesh Khanna's rise as a superstar. The two first came together in Raj Khosla's *Do Raaste* (1969). In Shakti Samanta's *Kati Patang* (1970), Prem Chopra plays the blackmailing Kailash, threatening to unmask Asha Parekh's real identity to Khanna. From *Doli* (1969) and *Do Raaste* (1969) to *Prem Nagar* (1974), *Mehbooba* (1976), *Souten* (1983), *Maqsad* (1984) and *Ghar Parivaar* (1991), they delivered 15 hits together, becoming the lucky *jodi* (pair) of the industry. However, Rajesh Khanna's lack of professionalism led to his downfall. After becoming the Phenomenon of the '70s, he went into oblivion—unlike his 'Babumoshai' from *Anand* (1971), Amitabh Bachchan, whom Prem Chopra remembers as a co-star who was never late for a shoot.

Beginning with *Pyar Ki Kahani* (1971), Amitabh Bachchan and Prem Chopra did innumerable films together. After having seen Hrishikesh Mukherjee's *Parwana* (1971) in a preview show, Chopra had told the film's leading man Navin Nischol frankly that the film wouldn't work. 'But who is this tall boy? He will spell trouble for other heroes,' he predicted. The 'tall boy' became Hindi cinema's 'angry young man'.

Their pairing proved lucky for Prem Chopra too. His performance as Ronjit Malik, who betrays his best friend Amit Roy in Dulal Guha's *Do Anjaane* (1976), bagged him the Filmfare Award for Best Supporting Actor. He had been nominated for the Black Lady before that, including for *Himmat* (1970), but had never won. This time, therefore, he hadn't been holding out much hope. 'We were in Amsterdam, shooting for *The Great Gambler* [1979]. My director, Shakti Samanta, came to my hotel room one morning. I was a little surprised to see him and told him apologetically that I was running a little late, but I would be on the set in a few minutes. He was quick to reassure me that he was not there to hurry me up, but to inform me that I had won the Filmfare Award for *Do Anjaane*,' Chopra reminisces, admitting that he found the news hard to believe till he made a call to his family in Bombay and they confirmed it. 'Unfortunately, since we were out of the country, I could not accept the trophy in person. But Amitabh and I had a small celebratory party that evening,' he shares with a smile.

He went on to win the Filmfare Lifetime Achievement Award in 2023, admitting on stage, '*Artist zinda rehta hai toh fans ki vajah se* [An artist survives because of his fans].' Earlier, at the 6th Punjab Film & Music Festival, he had been felicitated with the Lifetime Achievement honour for his contribution to Punjabi cinema. 'There have been other Lifetime Achievement awards too, from the UK, US, UAE, Germany and Norway. I was also honoured with the Bharat Ratna Dr Ambedkar Award in 2023. What was also very humbling was the Mother Teresa Award in 2011, for my five-decade-long career and humanitarian work that I don't like to speak about, whose previous recipients had been our former Prime Minister Rajiv Gandhi and the Dalai Lama,' Prem Chopra informs proudly.

The gentleman actor did not become a villain by choice. But once he did, there was no stopping him. By the '70s, Prem

Chopra had joined top-ranking khalnayaks like Amjad Khan, Amrish Puri, Ajit and Ranjeet. He continued to rule the '80s, and giving his bad man a comic touch, marched into the '90s, happy in a hell of his own making even if it occasionally brought along some awkward moments.

Once, when he was strolling in a public garden in Chandigarh with his father, a group of young men, spotting him, whisked their wives away, embarrassing his father. Unfazed, Prem Chopra boldly walked up to them and started chatting. By the end of the conversation, he had changed their impression of him and appeased his father. Like he says in *Kati Patang*, '*Main jo aag lagata hoon, usse bujhana bhi jaanta hoon* [I know how to extinguish the fire I set myself].'

Producer Ratan Jain who, as a seven-year-old, remembers seeing the actor in an advertisement for a hair gel and thinking what a good-looking man he was, went on to collaborate with him in *Khiladi* (1992). 'I found him to be a really sweet gentleman, who could get very nasty on screen,' he laughs.

Actor-filmmaker Ananth Narayan Mahadevan, who turns out to be the surprise killer in the same film, remembers Prem Chopra growling with mock anger, '*Arre miya, kyun hamare pet pe laat maar rahe ho* [Sir, why are you taking away my livelihood].' Mahadevan pointed out that he had no intention of becoming the villain in his life; he only wanted to experiment with a variety of roles. By then, the veteran actor had also started experimenting with more amiable roles and the two enjoyed a good laugh.

They got another opportunity to work together in Himesh Reshammiya's TV serial *Andaz*, which also featured Rajendra Kumar, Poonam Dhillon and Kanwaljit Singh. It was Prem Chopra's first brush with television, and Mahadevan recalls that they were shooting at Juhu's Hotel Horizon. By 8.00 p.m., the senior actor had realized that while they paid handsomely, TV producers also knew how to extract work from them. After he had shot 10 scenes, a rarity for a film actor in a day, he threw up his hands and told the assistant director that he was leaving at 9.00 p.m. 'I walked up to him and told him that having done a lot of television, I was his senior here and it would be better if we sat down and chatted companionably till our work was done. Being a professional, he finished his work for the day,' Mahadevan laughs.

Although the hustle-bustle of television was not his cup of tea, Prem Chopra went on to judge a talent hunt show, *No. 1 Dramebaaz*. Even in his 80s, the sprightly actor continues to be seen in the occasional film, like *Udanchhoo* (2018), *Main Hoon Khalnayak* (2020), *Bunty Aur Babli 2* (2021) and *Animal* (2023). He also acted in a short film, *Social Distancing* (2020), during the Covid-19 pandemic. There was the Punjabi film *Jindari* (2018), too, and an international project, *Line of Descent* (2019), with Brendan Fraser and Abhay Deol.

'I still get many offers, but now I like to pick and choose, find something that is interesting and significant. I had worked with Ranbir's grandfather Raj Kapoor [*Bobby*], his granduncle Shammi Kapoor [*Teesri Manzil*] and his father Rishi [*Raaja*, 1975, and *Sitamgar*, 1985], and then I did *Animal* with this fourth-generation Kapoor,' he points out with a laugh.

While he continues to intimidate on screen, away from the studio lights Prem Chopra is a genial gentleman who enjoys writing and reciting verses. He began with poems penned by others, then slowly started writing his own *shayari*. 'I was a *shayar* in my college days and was fondly called Prem Awargi,' he reveals with a laugh and recites a few lines of his own, '*Har raahein guzarne par shama jalana hai mujhko, tevar hai kya hawa ka, yeh main jaanta nahin* [I want to light a candle at each road I pass; what the mood of the wind is, I don't know].'

SHAKTI KAPOOR

CRIME MASTER

'Crime Master Gogo naam hai mera, aankhen nikaal ke gotiyaan khelta hoon main.'

—*Andaz Apna Apna* (1994)

Ask Shakti Kapoor 'what's in a name?', and he will tell you a story. Christened Sunil Kapoor by his parents, this Bollywood villain was signed for *Yari Dushmani* (1980), then *Rocky* (1981), with Sunil Dutt promising him a role in all the films made under his banner, Ajanta Arts, but insisting he needed a new name. Perhaps his mentor didn't want his protégé to be his namesake. Or like with Gopal Bedi, whom he had rechristened Ranjeet, Sunil Dutt wanted Sunil Kapoor to have a screen name that packed more power.

So, for around six days, he was called Karan Kapoor, but Nargis Dutt argued that even Karan seemed too mild. Then, one day, Sunil Dutt called him to the office for lunch, where he found a cake with 'Shakti' iced on top. From that day, Sunil Kapoor became Shakti Kapoor, and is a household name today.

Interestingly, while he was growing up, Shakti Kapoor had never imagined himself as an actor. Born in a Punjabi family in Delhi's Karol Bagh, his father, Sikander Lal Kapoor, had a cloth-cum-tailoring shop in Connaught Place. To his disappointment, his son showed little interest in academics or the family business. While studying at Kirori Mal College, he entered into a pact with his father that after he graduated, he would get half the shop to set up his own travel agency. 'With that in mind, I trained with Mercury Travels for six months, then with a BCom degree, approached my father,' says Shakti.

He was crushed when the senior Kapoor refused to keep his side of the bargain, reasoning that if he gave away half the shop, his business would diminish in size and his son's travel agency too would be a really small set-up and not attract much attention. Besides, he pointed out, people might assume that father and son have had a fight over property matters, leading to a division of the shop. It would be better if Shakti simply joined the family business.

Angry and upset, Shakti Kapoor stomped out of the house and headed straight for his usual haunt, the college cafeteria, where he narrated his tale of woe to his friends who, as part of the college theatre group, were rehearsing a play. One of them was a serious stage actor who aspired to join the FTII and was filling out the admission form. After Shakti Kapoor left, the friend consulted the others who agreed with him that the *gora chikna* (fair and good-looking) boy, who had started modelling by then, stood a good chance of getting selected. So, a form for the acting course at FTII, Pune, was filled on his behalf and posted.

'This was in 1973, when 40,000 aspiring actors from across the country were vying for the 10 seats that were up for grabs at the country's premier film school. And one of them had no idea he was even in the running till he got a letter from the institute informing him that he had been selected for the written test,' Shakti Kapoor reminisces with a laugh. Even as he was wondering how he had come to be selected, the friend called and admitted to having filled the form on his behalf, and persuaded him to take the test. He found it surprisingly easy and passed with flying colours.

He was then called for the audition, for which he was coached by his friends. He walked into the venue, a classroom of Delhi Public School, and did a double take. Seated before him were Ashok Kumar, Kamini Kaushal and Hrishikesh Mukherjee. 'I rushed forward and touched their feet, asking for their *ashirwad* [blessings] and admitting to being a huge fan. Smiling indulgently, they reminded me that I was there for an audition. Since time was short, I should start reading out my lines,' he shares.

Since he was pretty sure he wouldn't be selected because he had no background in acting, Shakti Kapoor was relaxed and unfazed even when he jumbled up his lines. He improvised as he went along, touched their feet once he had finished and left the veteran actors and director smiling. He hadn't expected to hear from the FTII again. So, it came as a shock when he got a telegram a month later informing him that of the three selected from Delhi, he was one. Naseeruddin Shah and Anil Varman were the other two. 'My friends were convinced my father had bribed the FTII board, which is how I had got through,' he chuckles.

There was one screen test still left to be cleared, but by then even he knew it was only a formality; for the first time, he began to think of himself as an actor. 'You may not have a godfather but God wants you to be an actor,' he would tell his reflection as he stood in front of the mirror. His doting mother agreed with him and urged him to reach for the stars.

In the second term of his second year at FTII, Arjun

Hingorani, who had launched Sadhana in his debut directorial, the Sindhi film *Abana* (1958), and two years later, Dharmendra in a Hindi film, *Dil Bhi Tera Hum Bhi Tere* (1960), came to the institute looking for three fresh faces to cast in his film *Khel Khilari Ka* (1977), which already boasted of big names like Dharmendra, Hema Malini and Shabana Azmi. He signed three students—Dhruv, Phunsok Ladhakhi and Shakti Kapoor. 'And that was how even before I passed out of the institute, I had started shooting for my first film,' shares the actor. Years later, Naseeruddin Shah acknowledged that Shakti was one of the best students in the class, while he himself was a backbencher.

Arjun Hingorani had an office in the now-defunct Roop Tara Studios in Dadar, Bombay. One day, while Shakti Kapoor was visiting, he learnt that Sunil Dutt was shooting in the studio. The next day, with some specially shot photographs, he went knocking on the door of the actor's make-up room during lunch break. A voice from inside shouted, 'Come in.' As he tentatively opened the door and peeped in, he saw Sunil Dutt sprawled out on the sofa inside, his head hanging over the edge. As he stood hovering nervously on the threshold, the senior actor looked up, straight at him. Even though he was disconcerted by the intense scrutiny, Shakti worked up the courage to walk up to Dutt and touch his feet respectfully. He was motioned to sit down, and taking a chair, he hesitatingly offered the photographs, telling Dutt that he wanted to be an actor like him. The senior actor, rifling through the photographs, told the boy he had expressive eyes and asked him to drop by his Ajanta Arts office. When Shakti Kapoor went across, he was offered a role in *Yari Dushmani* (1980). Produced by the senior actor's younger brother Som Dutt, it had Sunil Dutt in the lead, with Shakti playing a bandit. 'I became an Ajanta Arts boy and was put on a monthly retainer of ₹1,500,' he says.

Soon after, he was signed to play the villain, R.D., in *Rocky* (1981), produced and directed by Sunil Dutt. It marked the debut of his son, Sanjay Dutt. 'Dutt-sahab loved and treated me like his own son and I didn't have the guts to tell him that I had already signed Arjun Hingorani's film,' his protégé admits sheepishly.

Around this time, another actor-filmmaker, Feroz Khan, ran into Shakti Kapoor, quite literally. His swanky Mercedes hit the younger actor's 1961 Fiat from behind. Furious, Shakti got out to abuse the driver, but one look at Khan and his anger dissipated. 'I told him my name was Sunil Kapoor, I was a graduate of the FTII and wanted to be an actor, requesting him for a break,' he admits with a laugh, recalling that the star-filmmaker simply growled at him for damaging his car and drove off, even as the crowd of stargazers who had quickly gathered hooted at the younger actor.

That evening, after taking his car to the garage, a famished Shakti Kapoor dropped by K.K. Shukla's place. He was a favourite of the writer and his actress-wife Daisy Irani and was immediately invited to dinner by her. While he was sitting in the living room, Shukla, who had penned the screenplays of big films like *Khoon Pasina* (1977) and *Suhaag* (1979), walked in looking thoroughly disgruntled. Spotting Shakti, he grumbled, '*Tera kismet kharab hai* [Fortune doesn't favour you], I had been pushing for you for the villain's role in a very big film, but Feroz Khan now insists on casting some crazy actor who banged into his car this afternoon because of the menace he saw in his eyes.' Shakti couldn't believe his ears. Jumping up, he told the bemused writer that he was that crazy actor. Shukla immediately called the filmmaker to tell him he had found the boy, and Shakti went on to sign FK International's *Qurbani* (1980).

The film stars Aruna Irani and him as the scheming siblings, Jwala and Vikram. Feroz Khan is Rajesh, a motorcycle stuntman in a circus, who is a thief like his foe-turned-friend, Vinod Khanna's Amar, who eventually sacrifices his life for him, justifying the title of the film. '*Qurbani* was a film well ahead of its time, and the psychotic Vikram was one of my best performances,' asserts Shakti Kapoor, admitting that he had kept even Feroz Khan in the dark about having signed films with Arjun Hingorani and Sunil Dutt, afraid that he might lose out on *Qurbani*. When the actor-filmmaker learnt his secret, Shakti touched his feet and begged him for forgiveness.

'Feroz Khan-sahab confided later that he had known that I was doing *Rocky*, but had kept quiet. When Dutt-sahab learnt about my double game, he laughed and told Feroz Khan-sahab that he could introduce me in *Qurbani*, while the latter insisted that *Rocky* should be my launch pad. Both filmmakers were gentlemen and I ended up with two godfathers,' he says gratefully.

Qurbani opened on 20 June 1980. *Rocky* premiered 10 months later, on 8 May 1981. Both roles got him rave reviews, and Shakti gives full credit to his directors, pointing out that he was the first villain back then to sing and dance in a disco competition in *Rocky*, which was judged by none other than the *desi* Elvis Presley, Shammi Kapoor, who played himself. 'Tina [Munim] and I were up against Sanju [Sanjay Dutt] and Reena Roy dancing to Kishore Kumar and Asha Bhosle's "Aa Dekhen Zara, Kis Mein Kitna Hai Dum". I was in my element because dancing had been a passion since I was a child,' he reminisces.

Rocky brings back some unhappy memories too. While her son's debut film was being shot, Nargis Dutt was diagnosed with cancer and flown to the US for treatment. Knowing how much she doted on Sanjay, when the film was around 80 per cent complete, Sunil Dutt organized a special trial for his ailing wife at their home theatre. There were only a handful of people present at that screening, among them a few family members and Shakti. 'Nargis-ji saw 14 reels of the film and loved what we had shot. But after that she fell very ill and we couldn't even show her the first copy,' he rues. Nargis passed away on 3 May 1981. At the premiere, a grieving Sunil Dutt and a distraught Sanjay were seated together, a vacant chair between them in Nargis's memory.

Qurbani brings back memories of a different kind. On his way to Pune, with just ₹700 in his pocket, Shakti Kapoor had met Anil Varman, the second of the three boys to be selected for the FTII acting course from Delhi. The two aspiring actors had quickly become friends during the train journey. Once they reached Bombay, Shakti was all set to catch another train to Pune, but pointing out that there were still three days left for the institute to open, Varman invited him to stay with him at his sister's home in the city. As they stepped out of the station, Shakti found a Mercedes waiting to pick them up and asked Varman what his sister did. He was told that she was married to Vinod Khanna's brother, actor-producer Pramod Khanna, who later went on to play Salman Khan's father, Prajapati Pandey, in *Dabangg 3* (2019).

Within half an hour of them entering the house, Pramod Khanna's brother turned up. Over the next three days, Vinod Khanna took Anil Varman and Shakti Kapoor sightseeing. He even took the boys out for dinner. His mother took an instant liking to Shakti, and by the time he left, he was family for the

Khannas. 'Three months after passing out of FTII and moving to Bombay, I bumped into Vinod Khanna. On learning that I was staying as a paying guest, he offered me the use of his two-bedroom flat in Juhu, which was lying vacant. I was staying there for free when I landed *Qurbani*,' he shares.

In his first shot for the film, Shakti Kapoor had to kick Vinod Khanna on the shoulder. Excited to be acting in a Feroz Khan film, he kept kicking the star really hard, all over his body. Finally, an exasperated Khanna whispered in his ear, 'Shakti, you are hurting me, aim for my shoulder please.' But the younger actor couldn't seem to control his legs, which were moving of their own volition. Finally, Khanna threatened in an undertone, 'One more time and I will hit back, real hard.' With the warning ringing in his ears, he managed to rein in his flailing limbs and the shot was okayed after 17 takes. Didn't Vinod Khanna take offence, I ask Shakti Kapoor, and he shakes his head with a laugh, 'No, back then people just laughed off a youngster's excitement.' He is equally indebted to Mithun Chakraborty, his senior at the institute, who had chopped Shakti's hair as part of the initiation process by seniors, but ended up taking the youngster under his wing, sharing his meals with him and frequently offering him sound advice.

After *Rocky* and *Qurbani*, more roles started coming his way. The actor admits that back then he wasn't very selective, accepting whatever he was offered and interested only in making money. 'It soon became a joke in the industry that if you wanted to make a film, you needed raw stock and Shakti Kapoor,' laughs the actor who, in a career spanning close to five decades and almost 700 films, can boast of having worked in films in a myriad of Indian languages, including Hindi, Oriya, Punjabi, Bengali, Assamese, Telugu, Kannada and Malayalam. He also worked in a Bangladeshi film (*Eri Naam Dosti,* 2001) and a Bhojpuri film, *Hum Hain Hero Hindustani* (2009), dubbed in Nepali as *Pratikar* (2011).

'I have done the maximum number of films with Kader Khan [around 100], followed by Mithun Chakraborty [around 50]. I also featured in a number of films with Jeetendra, Govinda and Sridevi,' Shakti informs.

A turning point in his career was *Meri Awaaz Suno* (1981), an action-thriller with Jeetendra, Hema Malini and Parveen Babi. It is a remake of the Kannada film *Antha* (1981), which also spun Tamil (*Thyagi,* 1982) and Telugu (*Antham Kadidi Aarambam,* 1981) versions. The Padmalaya Studios production flagged off a South Indian sojourn for Shakti, with films like *Himmatwala* (1983), *Justice Chaudhury* (1983), *Mahaan* (1983), *Jaani Dost* (1983), *Mawaali* (1983), *Yeh Desh* (1984), *Tohfa* (1984), *Inquilaab* (1984), *Ghar Ek Mandir* (1984), *Maqsad* (1984), *Mera Saathi* (1985) and *Pataal Bhairavi* (1985). 'I quickly became a favourite with Padmalaya Studios and filmmakers like K. Bapayya, T. Rama Rao, D. Ramanaidu and K. Raghavendra Rao. For almost five years, I spent several months of the year in Chennai. My wife [Shivangi] with our two children [Shraddha and Siddhanth] would visit me sometimes during school vacations. The South producers were disciplined and paid very well, so everyone was happy,' he informs.

For a while, life was good and Shakti was putting in three to four shifts of filming a day. Then, boredom set in. 'The roles were the same, the scenes were the same, even the dialogue was the same, with me telling the hero to come and get his lady love to the count of ten...five...three...two...one. The only excitement was when I got to do a song with Amitabh Bachchan, Mithun or Govinda. I was the only baddie who did disco and ramba–samba. I was called "Disco Queen" by Amjad Khan,' he chuckles.

In 1982, Raj N. Sippy and Romu N. Sippy's action-comedy *Satte Pe Satta* came as a refreshing break. An adaptation of the English film *Seven Brides for Seven Brothers* (1954), it was a story about seven brothers, with Shakti Kapoor playing the second youngest, Mangal. He admits Mangal's speech defect was his idea. One of his favourite films, it brings back many fond memories; and for the industry, it underlined the fact that despite being a villain, Shakti had great comic timing.

Around this time, writer-actor Kader Khan was scripting a new trend in Hindi cinema, that of the comic villain. He was game to experiment with such roles with his guru. Soon their laugh riots became so popular, as did their father–son *jodi*, that producers even printed posters featuring Kader Khan and Shakti Kapoor to pull in the crowds. 'My *takiya kalam* [signature line] in *Tohfa* [1984] "*Aaaooo* [come] Lolita" became such a craze that after the film's release, four young boys were arrested in Hyderabad because they were standing outside a theatre and going "*Aaaooo*" every time they spotted a girl, imitating the way I eve-teased Sridevi in the film. Even after 30 years, *yeh aaaooo peechha nahin chhodta* [this *aaaooo* is still chasing after me],' he jokes.

Shakti Kapoor is the king of punchlines, from '*Tum meri zindagi mein full stop to kya, comma bhi nahin laga sake, lekin main tumhari zindagi mein full stop zaroor lagaunga* [Forget a full stop, you could not even put a comma in my life, but I will put a full stop to yours],' in *Khuddar* (1994), to '*Hum hain police ki naak ka baal, insaaf ki dhaal, Havildar Bankelal, chal do rupiya nikaal* [I am the hair in a policeman's nose, the armour of justice, Sergeant Bankelal, now give me two rupees],' in *Chauraha* (1994). Another quirky one-liner that is much quoted is from *Insaaf* (1987): '*Aala re aala Inspector Bhinde aala, haath mein le ke kanoon ka tala* [Here is Inspector Bhinde, come with the lock of the law in his hand].'

Equally memorable is a dialogue from *Chaalbaaz* (1989), '*Main ek nanha sa pyaara sa chhota sa bachcha hoon* [I am a small, cute child].' The actor reveals that one day, while shooting, Anupam Kher asked him between shots if his wife Shivangi and he ever had disagreements like other couples. When he replied that they did, Kher prodded, '*Phir kaun jhukta hai pehle* [So, who accepts defeat first]?' Shakti admitted that neither of them did, and he simply made his miffed wife laugh by saying, '*Main ek nanha sa pyaara sa chhota sa bachcha hoon.*' Kher found the line hilarious and suggested he use it in the film. 'I was wary, but on Anupam's urging, I spoke up. Pankaj [Parashar, the film's director] loved it, the whole unit laughed, and that was how "*Main ek nanha sa pyaar sa chhota sa bachcha hoon*" came to be incorporated,' he reveals.

In his first scene in the film, Shakti Kapoor, who plays Rohini Hattangadi's brother Batuknath Lalan Prasad Maalpani, fondly called Balma, tries to get Sridevi's scared, submissive avatar Anju to call him by his nickname. '*Pyar se bolo Balma, zor se bolo Balma, gaa ke bolo Balma* [Say Balma lovingly, say Balma loudly, say Balma musically],' he urges, even as she cowers in fright. The words are repeated later in the film, by his tormentor and Anju's daredevil twin Manju, who gives Balma a taste of his own medicine. 'Sridevi had impeccable comic timing and we had a wonderful tuning. It was her idea that I pronounce "Balma" in that distinctive way that she could imitate later. The gimmick caught on in a big way with the audience after the film's release,' he smiles with satisfaction.

Another favourite catchphrase is '*Main hoon Nandu, sabka bandhu* [I am Nandu, everyone's friend],' from David Dhawan's *Raja Babu* (1994), in which he plays Govinda's sidekick. What made the dialogue unique was the nasal tone in which Shakti spoke it. Dhawan had been the actor's junior at FTII, and starting from his directorial debut, *Taaqatwar* (1989), he cast Shakti Kapoor in almost all his films. One remembers *Aag Ka Gola*'s (1989) Inspector Popat Lal, *Bol Radha Bol*'s (1992) Gungu/Inspector Bhende and *Aankhen*'s (1993) Tejeshwar. These were followed by films like *Andaz* (1994), *Coolie No. 1* (1995), *Saajan Chale Sasural* (1996), *Judwaa* (1997) and *Hero No. 1.* (1997). *Raja Babu*'s Nandu bagged Shakti the Filmfare Award for Best Performance in a Comic Role. He gives credit for this performance to his producer Nandu Tolani and director David Dhawan, revealing that the duo had been told that he was miscast as the village buffoon, but had refused to replace him.

Dapper Delhi boy Shakti Kapoor himself hadn't been sure if he would be able to pull off the *ganji* (vest) and striped *chaddi* (underpants) look, but found an unexpected ally in the film's leading man, Govinda. On the first day of the shoot, Govinda suggested he speak his punchline, '*Samajhta nahin hai yaar* [You don't understand],' in a nasal tone. The dangling *naada* (pyjama drawstring) was also the actor's idea. 'I was reluctant, telling him I would look like a Pappu, but he pushed me to do it—and today, Nandu is unforgettable,' Shakti raves.

His wife, Shivangi, was confident the performance would bag him his first Filmfare Award, but the long-coveted Black Lady had passed him by many times in the past, and Shakti himself wasn't holding out much hope. 'My wife persuaded my mother to fly down from Delhi and attend the award show with us. Every five minutes, she wanted to know when I would be called on stage,' he reminisces. Halfway through the function, he was desperately praying that they would at least call him to present an award so that he could pretend to his mother that he had won it. Finally, when his name was announced and he was presented with an award of his own, there was reason to celebrate. The honour was particularly gratifying because after seeing him molesting Anita Raj's character as Shakti Singh in *Insaniyat Ke Dushman* (1987), his father, embarrassed by his 'black deeds', had railed at his mother. 'Finally, I made her proud of me,' he says emotionally.

Shakti Kapoor adopted the nasal tone again in David Dhawan's *Loafer* (1996), playing Bhiku, Anil Kapoor's uncle. This time, it was harder to speak in that style because he had to ensure he did not get into the *Raja Babu* zone. But by the time shooting wrapped up, the director was so happy with his performance that he added a song which was picturized on him and Upasana Singh, parodying the top heroes of the time and their superhit songs. 'It was a riot!' the actor crows.

Many of his films with David Dhawan, including *Aag Ka Gola* (1989), *Shola Aur Shabnam* (1992), *Aankhen* (1993) and *Andaz* (1994), were produced by Pahlaj Nihalani, who considers Shakti Kapoor one of the most versatile actors he has worked with. 'He can play both a villain and a comedian, a father and a son, and fill in any blanks in your cast. He has great screen presence and expressive eyes. He can fight, dance and emote. He is a complete actor whose comic turns with Kader Khan were one of a kind,' raves the producer, who ensured there was a scene for the actor in all his films.

He reveals that back then, Shakti Kapoor was so busy that he was only able to dole out two hours at a time. 'But whenever I told him, "Pappi, I want two hours of your time," he would make adjustments in his calendar without even enquiring about the role or character. That's the kind of person Shakti is, one of the finest I know,' says Nihalani.

Shakti's comic villain image, cemented by films like *Himmatwala*, *Tohfa*, *Raja Babu* and *Loafer*, was taken forward in the next decade by Priyadarshan's films, from *Hungama* (2003, Tejabhai or Kachara Seth) and *Hulchul* (2004, Kashinath Pathak), to *Chup Chup Ke* (2006, Natwar Jhunjhunwala) and *Malamaal Weekly* (2006, Joseph). He reveals that when the producer of *Hungama*, Ratan Jain, suggested his name to Priyadarshan, the director from the South agreed instantly. 'Priyan Sir told me later that once, when we were both shooting in Ooty for different films, he had watched me from a distance and marvelled that while just half a dozen fans hung around the hero, a big Bollywood star, more than 500 surrounded me for autographs, most of them women. He had decided that day itself that he would cast this good-looking villain in one of his films,' Shakti recounts.

Another director who made him unforgettable was Rajkumar Santoshi, with *Andaz Apna Apna*'s (1994) Crime Master Gogo. The cult classic turned the khalnayak into a comic superhero. Though short in footage and screen time, the character has had a long shelf life, going by his recall value. Interestingly, while Crime Master Gogo has become synonymous with Shakti Kapoor today, the role only came to him on the rebound because the original choice, actor Tinnu Anand, had to suddenly take off for a month-and-a-half to shoot for another film. Since he had left an expensive set standing at Bombay's Film City studio, the actor was approached to take his place. Back then, Shakti was doing three to four shifts a day, so the director let him decide for himself when he could shoot for the film. He usually reported late in the evening, and once, shot through the night.

Many of Shakti Kapoor's lines were improvised as they went along. Dialogues like '*Aaya hoon, kuch to loot ke jaoonga* [Now that I have come, I will steal something],' '*Mogambo ka bhateeja, Gogo* [Mogambo's nephew Gogo],' '*Gogo naam hai mera, aankhen nikaal ke gotiyan khelta hoon main* [My name is Gogo, I take out eyeballs and play marbles with them],' and '*Jab koi bachcha nahin sota to uski maa kehti hai, so ja, so ja, so ja, nahin to Gogo aa jayega* [Whenever a child refuses to sleep the mother warns him that if he doesn't, Gogo will come]'—the latter parodying Gabbar Singh's cult dialogue in *Sholay* (1975)—are instantly identifiable with the Crime Master.

Interestingly, while Shakti Kapoor went on to become a super successful bad man, and even an extremely popular comedian-villain, he failed as a hero—*Madine Ki Galian* (1981), *Begunaah Qaidi* (1982) and *Zakhmee Insaan* (1982) tumbled like ninepins. Pahlaj Nihalani was to launch him as a hero in a film called *Bhagya Vidhata*, and for a while, at the producer's behest, Shakti stopped signing films as a villain. *Bhagya Vidhata* was to feature Neelam, Sonam, and Bengal's matinee idol Prosenjit Chatterjee, who was making his Bollywood debut with *Aandhiyan* (1990). But *Aandhiyan*, which was Mumtaz's comeback film after marriage and a hiatus, ended up being a failure, and *Bhagya Vidhata* was shelved after five days of shooting. 'I was not happy with the way the film was shaping up. It was an off-beat subject, but those days we didn't work with a bound script. The scenes evolved on the day of the shoot and I wasn't satisfied with what I saw. So, rather than mess up Shakti's career as a villain, which was going great guns, I decided to put this film on hold and make it later, but that never happened,' rues the producer.

Shakti Kapoor has no regrets: 'Seeing my hero friends pack up while I continue to find work, I am glad I did not restrict myself to lead roles. Anyway, I got to do my share of singing and dancing.' His daughter, Shraddha Kapoor, is a top-ranking heroine today, while his son Siddhanth Kapoor, a trained actor, has made his mark in films like *Shootout at Wadala* (2013), *Haseena Parkar* (2017) and *Chehre* (2021). 'But that doesn't mean I have to retire,' points out the actor. 'There is always a role for a good actor, particularly one who had no godfather, but has God on his side.' Now that's a great punchline.

SADASHIV AMRAPURKAR

THE QUEEN OF THE MART

'Yahan ka raja, iss jism ke bazaar ka maharaja,
aur naam Maharani.'

—*Sadak* (1991)

In a career spanning three decades, Sadashiv Amrapurkar played innumerable characters, both on screen and on stage. Some were good, many were bad, and a few downright ugly. But not even the man himself could have imagined that he would be remembered forever as a eunuch by the name of Maharani, who lords over a red-light locality in Mahesh Bhatt's romantic-thriller *Sadak* (1991).

To understand how he came to walk this particular *sadak* (road), one has to go back to the early '90s, when Mahesh Bhatt was the messiah of middle-of-the-road mainstream Hindi cinema after hard-hitting, applause-worthy films like *Arth* (1982), *Saaransh* (1984), *Naam* (1986), and *Daddy* (1989). One afternoon, the filmmaker, impressed with Sadashiv's performance as the wily antagonist Rama Shetty in his first Hindi film *Ardh Satya* (1983), dropped by Bombay's Film City studio, where the actor was shooting, with a somewhat unusual offer for him.

Sadak, Mahesh Bhatt informed him, featured Sanjay Dutt and his own daughter Pooja Bhatt in the lead. He wanted Sadashiv Amrapurkar to play the villain in his film. The actor was on a high after the success of commercial blockbusters like *Aakhree Raasta* (1986), *Hukumat* (1987) and *Khatron Ke Khiladi* (1988). What made *Sadak* exciting for him was that this bad man is actually the 'madam' of a brothel from where Pooja flees one night, running into Sanjay's Ravi on the road. A tormented soul, the insomniac cab driver is determined to save the innocent young girl from the flesh trade so she doesn't end up committing suicide like his sister. Maharani, the transgender pimp of the brothel, is the roadblock. Having played a *gandharva* (celestial being) who enacts female roles in a Marathi play when in college, Sadashiv was immediately taken in by the character. But, as he pointed out to Mahesh Bhatt, the novelty of the character also upped the risk for both of them.

When I spoke to him for *Mumbai Mirror* on 29 April 2013 about *Sadak*, which in the 22 years since its release had grown to become a cult film, the actor revealed how, on a visit to Mumbai's red-light district Kamathipura with a friend who was researching an article for a newspaper, a photograph of a man draped in a sari and decked in heavy jewellery with a red *bindi* dotting his forehead had caught his eye. The actor subsequently heard from those who lived there that while Sethji was heterosexual, he liked cross-dressing and occasionally got himself photographed dressed as a woman.

The image of the drag queen stayed with Sadashiv Amrapurkar, and after sketching out the plot of *Sadak*, when Mahesh Bhatt showed him a picture of how he had envisioned his Maharani, the actor shook his head decisively and told him bluntly, 'No, this is not how your eunuch should look.' Recalling the meeting after Sadashiv Amrapurkar passed away on 3 November 2014, Bhatt shared that the actor then requested the director to get him a sari. The minute he stepped out, draped in a sari, Bhatt knew they had found their Maharani and *Sadak* would be a hit, acknowledging that his film would not have been as memorable without the actor's menacing presence as the ruthless brothel keeper.*

His hero shared his conviction. When Bhatt had narrated the script of *Sadak* to him, Sanjay Dutt had been as excited as Sadashiv, recalling a man in a Mumbai slum who would dress like a woman and boss over the residents. Even though he was the leading man, he staunchly believed the film's success rested solely on Maharani's shoulders. There is one particular scene in the car park towards the end, when Maharani, dressed as a man, turns up with her henchmen and tries to coax Pooja, Ravi and their friends, Gotya and Chanda, to come out of their hiding place. Like a cat, she purrs, '*Chuppa chuppi, o chuppi, aa tadpa tadpa ke re, chuhe baba, o baba, bhaag billi aayi re, billi boli meow, billi boli meow, kahe ghabrao...* [Run mouse run, the cat is here to torture you, but the cat says meow, why are you afraid...]' and a terrified Pooja cowers in Ravi's arms, finally letting loose an ear-splitting scream, hearing which Maharani blasts off a shower of bullets in their direction. After they had canned the scene, Sadashiv recalled Sanjay chortling, '*Tu hit hai to film hit hai* [If you are a hit, the film is a hit too]!'

The film opened on 20 December 1991, and despite nitpickers grousing that Maharani was 'gross' and not man

---

*Bhatt, Mahesh, '"He Requested Me to Let Him Wear a Sari"', *Mumbai Mirror*, 4 November 2014, https://tinyurl.com/jzmfx5yv. Accessed on 16 May 2024.

enough to take on the manly Sanjay Dutt, the film went on
to become one of the year's biggest grossers. Such was the
power of Sadashiv Amrapurkar's performance that Maharani's
appearance was not greeted with the usual hoots of laughter
and derisive sniggers that had been the bane of transgender
characters till then. This eunuch struck terror, not just in the
hearts of those who crossed her path on screen, but also sent
shivers down the spines of those watching the cat-and-mouse
drama play out in all its celluloid glory.

Sadak was one of the rare sets the actor's youngest
daughter, Rima, remembers visiting. 'I must have been
around nine or 10 at the time, and I have to admit that I
wasn't happy to see my *baba* [father] dancing with a group
of eunuchs. He was wearing a sari and acting so weird,'
she recounts with a laugh. Sadashiv Amrapurkar ended up
bagging the first ever Filmfare Award for Best Performance
in a Negative Role for the film.

Nine years later, *Sadak* was remade in Tamil as
Appu (2000), with Prakash Raj playing Maharani. Twenty-nine
years later, a sequel, *Sadak 2* (2020), was released on Disney+
Hotstar during the Covid-19 pandemic. Sanjay Dutt returned
as a much older Ravi who was depressed and suicidal after
losing his wife. Pooja Bhatt made a comeback as a garlanded
photograph who, even though she was dead, remained the
cab driver's conscience, urging him to help Aarya—played
by her sister Alia Bhatt—who, like her 30 years ago, was on
the run.

Sadak 2 was an eagerly awaited, much-hyped film
because of the nostalgia the original still evoked, but it could
not replicate the success of the 1991 film. Even its god-man
villain, Guru Gyan Prakash, played by a maniacal Makrand
Deshpande, was not in the league of Sadashiv Amrapurkar's

Maharani. Nor were the other actors who, down the decades, inspired by Maharani, attempted to play similar characters but only ended up looking like caricatures. Sadashiv Amrapurkar himself was never tempted to repeat his iconic act, even turning down the role of Nirmala Pandit, the mentor of the misogynist serial killer Dhiraj Pandey, in the Mukesh Bhatt production *Murder 2* (2011).

However, he did accept *Swayam* (1991), directed by Mahesh Bhatt, which brought Waheeda Rahman back from retirement as an elderly woman who in the course of her husband's illness learns the meaning of self-reliance. The subject of senior citizens was very close to the actor's heart. He plays an upright cop and reportedly did the film for free.

Soon after *Sadak* was released, Sadashiv Amrapurkar and his wife had gone out for a drive. When the car stopped at a red light, he was spotted by a group of hijras (eunuchs) begging at the traffic signal. 'With whoops of delight and cries of *"Apna Maharani aa gaya* [Our Maharani has come]," they started dancing around the car. My mother was momentarily aghast, wondering how her man had become the beloved of eunuchs. But having acted in plays when she was in school and college, she understood that such adulation grew out of the power of his histrionics,' Rima narrates.

She remembers a family trip to the Ellora caves that was far more terrifying. Word had quickly spread in the vicinity that Maharani was visiting and when they came out of the caves, they found a huge crowd had gathered. 'We had to literally fight our way through the excited mob to get to our car. That was the last vacation we took together,' she sighs, ruing the price they had to pay for their father's overnight fame.

Rima adds that she was asked all kinds of weird questions, like 'Does your father also clap his hands like Maharani?', while her mother was asked, 'Does your husband wear a sari in real life too?' 'It would have been ridiculous if it hadn't been so ludicrous. Some of my schoolmates even started calling me Maharani's child,' she grouses. If Rima and her sisters, Ketki and Sayali, were able to take all this in their stride, it was because at an early age their parents had sat them down and explained their father's job to them. 'If someone's father is a doctor, he goes to the hospital, right? Your father is an actor, so he goes out to shoot,' her mother would tell them matter-of-factly.

Rima herself was never interested in acting. She only wanted to write. After getting a postgraduate degree in Economics, she was working as a research assistant. Around that time, she happened to attend the Pune International Film Festival, her first film fest, where she was introduced to the genius of Japanese filmmaker Akira Kurosawa through his films *Rashomon* (1950) and *Ikiru* (1952). 'For the first time, I understood the power and reach of a film and my perception of cinema changed,' she shares.

She became a regular at all film screenings and fests. With every film she saw, Rima's interest in her father's profession grew. Eventually, she went to him and confessed that she too wanted to make a career in the movies. 'Are you sure you won't get bored 10 years from now?' he asked her worriedly. She assured him that she wouldn't. Reassured that this wasn't just a passing fancy but a carefully thought-out decision, her father suggested that since the FTII was on strike then, his daughter should go to New York and study filmmaking.

'Abhay Sir [producer-director B.R. Chopra's grandson, Abhay Chopra] was my senior at the New York Film Academy. After completing the course and getting my diploma, I called him, hoping he would know of some openings in Mumbai.

To my delight, he informed me that his dad [filmmaker Ravi Chopra] was starting a new film and invited me to join the unit,' informs Rima, who went on to assist on *Baabul* (2006), a film about widow remarriage, featuring Amitabh Bachchan, Hema Malini, John Abraham, Salman Khan and Rani Mukerji.

The following year, she worked as one of the chief assistants on Indra Kumar's laugh riot *Dhamaal* (2007), and the year after that, she went on to make her directorial debut with the socio-political Marathi satire, *Ara Ara Aaba Aata Tari Thamba* (2008). It had her father playing Aabha Patil, the sarpanch of a small village, who is so busy with politics that he has little time for the people and their problems. Then, suddenly, a young man returns to the village after completing his education in the city, and challenges him in the upcoming elections. The film also featured Nilu Phule, Milind Gawali and Tejaa Deokar.

'Directing Baba was tough because I was completely in awe of him as an actor. Sensing this, he called me one day and asked how I wanted him to play out a particular scene,' says Rima, revealing that when she told him he had read the script and could do the scene any way he wanted, Sadashiv was far from pleased. Pointing out that he was on the set not as her father but an actor whose job was to bring the director's vision to the screen, he suggested that if she was finding it difficult to cue him, she should send one of her assistants over with specific instructions. Rima immediately assured her father that she would instruct him henceforth, telling herself that if she could direct the legendary Nilu Phule, she could communicate with her baba, too, no matter how difficult it was. The film was a hit and got rave reviews. It bagged several awards, including the MaTa Sanman and the Maharashtra Shaasan Puraskar. Sadashiv was delighted.

Two years later, Rima's short fiction film, *Jananee* (2010), highlighting the evil of female foeticide, was released. The previous year, it had been adjudged the best short film at the 40th International Film Festival of India (IFFI) and was invited for a screening at the prestigious Cannes Film Festival. She remembers how excited her father was by the Cannes invitation and how he insisted on showing the film to all his friends, telling her proudly, 'This is *you* telling *your* story.' But when she suggested he come with her to the French Riviera so they could walk the red carpet together, Sadashiv Amrapurkar refused, telling her quietly, 'This is your moment, Rima, you must go alone.'

She points out that while her father did not have any formal training in acting—unlike his contemporaries Naseeruddin Shah and Om Puri, who had studied at the NSD—he was always very committed to his craft. It didn't matter how small a role was or how insignificant the character, he would put in a lot of time and effort to flesh it out. 'He did quite a few C-grade films and inconsequential roles in the early phase of his career to support his family. But even in them, Baba was always diligent,' Rima says appreciatively.

∞

Sadashiv Amrapurkar was born on 11 May 1950 into an affluent Maharashtrian Brahmin family in Ahmednagar. He developed an interest in the stage when still in school, and continued acting and directing plays all through college. What started as a hobby quickly became a passion—much to the displeasure of his father, who would frequently point out how Sadashiv's younger brother had made his mark in business and suggest he did the same. His son always refused, insisting that he would not be able to pursue any career other than acting. 'Livid, my grandfather locked Baba up at home to stop him from performing on stage. That's when my mother, who had known him since they were in kindergarten, jumped to his defence. She had done theatre in college and empathized with his passion,' says Rima.

Sadashiv and Sunanda had been married for five years by then and had two daughters. When his father asked him how he was planning to support his family, Sunanda assured her father-in-law that they would survive, pointing out that she had a job with the Life Insurance Corporation of India. She would earn while her husband tried his luck in films. And so, he left for Bombay, his wife's words ringing in his ears, 'You are free to do whatever your heart desires.' He never ceased to be grateful for Sunanda's unflinching support.

During those early years of struggle, he would come to Ahmednagar only once every two to three months. His wife never complained. The family finally moved to Bombay in 1982. A year later, *Ardh Satya* released.

He was spotted by director Govind Nihalani in a Marathi play, *Hands-Up!* Playwright Vijay Tendulkar, who had written the screenplay of *Ardh Satya*, had recommended the actor to the director for the role of Rama Shetty and suggested he watch him on stage. Halfway through the play, Nihalani decided to cast him as the head of the local mafia in his cop drama. The play was a comedy while the film was an intense drama, but Sadashiv Amrapurkar's eyes—sharp, alert, with a hint of mischief—convinced the filmmaker that he would be ideal to play the antagonist.

Ardh Satya was a surprise hit and the film's swarthy villain, Rama Shetty, with his distinctive Marathi-accented dialogue delivery, an instant hit. 'Baba has just two-and-a-half scenes in the film, yet his presence is felt in every scene even when he is not in the frame. He held his own despite so many brilliant actors like Om Puri, Amrish Puri, Smita Patil and Naseeruddin Shah,' his daughter observes proudly.

Sadashiv Amrapurkar won his first Filmfare Award in the category 'Best Supporting Actor' for this performance in his first Hindi film. It marked the beginning of a long and successful career in show business. He went on to do films like the Ramsay Brothers blockbuster *Purana Mandir* (1984), Ramesh Behl's teenage love story *Jawaani* (1984) and Vidhu Vinod Chopra's suspense thriller *Khamosh* (1986). But the film that catapulted him into the big league was K. Bhagyaraj's crime drama *Aakhree Raasta* (1986) in which he portrays the antagonist, Netaji Chaturvedi.

Aakhree Raasta was followed by Anil Sharma's *Hukumat* (1987), in which Sadashiv plays Mangal Singh, a corrupt cop who turns into a corrupt social-worker-cum-businessman, Deenbandhu Deenanath, aka D.B.D.N., and crosses swords with the hero, Dharmendra. He appeared in several movies over the next three years, including *Mohre* (1987), *Khatron Ke Khiladi* (1988), *Maar Dhaad* (1988), *Eeshwar* (1989), *Elaan-E-Jung* (1989) and *Gola Barood* (1989). By the '90s, he had transformed into a comic villain with films like *Aankhen* (1993), *Coolie No. 1* (1995), *Ishq* (1997) and *Aunty No. 1* (1998).

Usually kept away from film sets, Rima recalls visiting the bungalow of *Ishq*, which was erected on a playground close to their home, since Ashok Thakeria (the producer) and Indra Kumar (co-producer and director) were her father's friends. In the madcap comedy, Sadashiv Amrapurkar plays Ajay Devgn's father Ranjit Rai, who believes the poor are like mosquitoes and flies, sucking the blood of the rich and infecting them with the germs they carry. She would laugh as she watched the unit rib her baba over the sherwani he was wearing and crow over his exaggerated buffoonery.

Inspector Godbode in *Hum Hain Kamaal Ke* (1993) is another hilarious character, as is Anthony D'Costa in *Taarzan: The Wonder Car* (2004). 'Baba had great comic timing and enjoyed playing these roles, having done many on stage earlier,' says Rima.

Having majored in History from the University of Pune (now the Savitribai Phule Pune University), the actor was also delighted to play the social activist and nationalist Bal Gangadhar Tilak in the television series *Raj Se Swaraj.* Interestingly, he had also played Tilak in his first film, the Marathi historical *22 June 1897* (1979).

Another role close to his heart was that of Jyotirao Phule in Shyam Benegal's 53-episode historical drama series, *Bharat Ek Khoj.* It was based on Jawaharlal Nehru's 1946 book, *The Discovery of India.* Phule and his wife Savitribai were pioneers of Maharashtra's social reform movement, campaigning for the eradication of untouchability and the education of women and those from oppressed castes. Rima remembers that while shooting for the Doordarshan series, her father would have long, animated discussions with his friends on the language and culture of the time, even as he perfected Phule's look with his make-up man and tried valiantly to erase the Marathi accent from his diction with his director's help.

'Shyam Babu [Benegal] is an encyclopedia, and Baba followed him blindly. But he also did his own research. I remember him wearing my late grandfather's dhoti–kurta to get into the character of Phule. For *Sadak*, he would drape himself in my grandmother's *nauvari* [traditional nine-yard Maharashtrian sari] and walk around the house, asking her how he should carry the *palla*,' his daughter relays.

Sadashiv Amrapurkar also lives the character of Malhar Rao Holkar in Jayoo and Nachiket Patwardhan's historical drama, *Devi Ahilya Bai* (2002), which stars Shabana Azmi as Khaanda Rani, with Sadashiv as the first Maratha subedar of Malwa, who, after the death of his son, Khanderao, stops his wife Ahilya (Mallika Prasad) from committing sati and trains her in administrative duties and military warfare instead, so she can take over as queen of Malwa and protect the kingdom from invaders.

Rima's favourite performance of his is in *Vaastupurush: The Guardian Spirit of the House* (2002), a Marathi film directed by Sumitra Bhave and Sunil Sukthankar. It chronicles the life of a famous philanthropic doctor, Dr Bhaskar Deshpande, through a series of flashbacks after he returns to his native village. Sadashiv Amrapurkar plays Dr Bhaskar's father, a weak-willed freedom fighter who does little to support his family, and being a high-caste Brahmin, won't even allow his elder son to marry Krishna, the girl he loves, because she is a Dalit. It is Bhaskar's mother who supports his dream of becoming a doctor, and Krishna, who works as a nurse in the village's primary health centre, helps him live it by giving him her meagre savings. *Vaastupurush*, with a strong feminist message, bagged eight state awards, as well as the National Film Award for Best Feature Film in Marathi.

Despite all the awards and accolades, Sadashiv Amrapurkar remained a simple man with few needs. He was happy as long as he had enough to feed his family and eternally grateful to God for all the abundance he was showered with. 'Baba had never planned on becoming a star and when he did, along with his shoes, he would leave stardom outside the door before he entered. Within the walls of our home, he was simply a husband, father, friend and neighbour,' shares Rima.

He rarely went for film parties and only attended the Filmfare Awards after he was reminded that he was getting the best villain award for *Sadak*. However, Rima insists that he was not an introvert and his college friends would often drop by. Since Sunanda knew them well, both having studied together, there was always a lot of laughter and animated conversations in the house.

Prod her about his hobbies and she shares that her baba was a voracious reader, something he passed on to all three daughters. 'On the sets, between shots, he was usually reading. He never went to a library to borrow a book. If he wanted to read one, he would buy it because he wanted to support the publishing industry. We have a collection of over 10,000 books at home,' she informs, remembering how her father would be in touch with small booksellers who would procure rare books for him.

Her sister Sayali, who is settled in the US, once sent him the book *Tuesdays with Morrie: An Old Man, a Young Man, and Life's Greatest Lesson* (1997), the memoir of American author Mitch Albom, which details a series of his visits to his former sociology professor, Morrie Schwartz, who was dying of a neurodegenerative disease. The book topped *The New York Times* Non-Fiction Best Sellers List in 2000 and quickly became a family favourite. 'My mother translated it into Marathi, and that book was a bestseller too,' Rima says proudly.

Sadashiv Amrapurkar himself penned an 86-page paperback in Marathi, *Kimayagar*, based on a 225-minute Marathi play that he wrote with littérateur Vishnu Shirwadkar, better known by his pen name Kusumagraj. An adaptation of William Gibson's 1959 play *The Miracle Worker*, it is the story of Helen Keller's tumultuous life and focuses primarily on the 14-day challenge her teacher Anne Sullivan undertook to calm down the eight-year-old deaf and blind girl. Staged in 1993, the play was directed by Deepa Lagoo and the screenplay was published as a book.

He published another book, *Abhinayache Prathamik Saha Path*, a Marathi adaptation of Richard Boleslavski's *Acting: The First Six Lessons*. A must-read for all aspiring actors, students of cinema and working professionals, it sketches out six essential lessons for the reader and distils the challenges every actor invariably faces in his journey. 'Having grown up in rural Maharashtra, Baba knew that there were many young and talented actors out there who didn't have access to acting schools and training courses. He translated this book hoping that it would become a handy guide to the stage and screen for them,' Rima explains.

By 1995, the actor, who had always been a philanthropist and a Gandhian activist, believed he had earned enough for his family to live comfortably. He told them that it was time now for him to follow his heart and dedicate his life to social service. It was no longer important to be a top-ranking villain in Hindi cinema; what mattered was making the world a better place.

He was involved with a number of social organizations, such as Maharashtra Andhashraddha Nirmoolan Samiti, a committee for the eradication of blind faith. The man who had molested and murdered without remorse on screen was the trustee of Snehalaya, an NGO in Ahmednagar that aims to improve the lives of women, children and members of the LGBTQ+ community afflicted with HIV and AIDS, and victims of trafficking, sexual violence and poverty. He also quietly supported his writer-friend and activist Anil Awachat, who ran Muktangan, a rehabilitation centre for drug addicts, and raised ₹50 lakh with Narendra Dabholkar, Baba Adhav and Shriram Lagoo by staging the play *Lagnachi Bedi* in Goa and Maharashtra, the money going into a fund to support social workers.

Sadashiv Amrapurkar also spoke against wastage of water and noise pollution during Holi celebrations. His words angered a few lumpen right-wing individuals, who even beat him up, but he was not to be silenced. He went on morchas and dharnas as part of the Narmada Bachao Andolan. Even when he was ill and his feet hurt, he would march with Medha Patkar and other activists, his heart full of empathy for those who had been displaced from their homes due to the construction of Sardar Sarovar Dam. In 2011, he supported the Anna Hazare movement and created awareness about voting rights and democracy.

His love for social service has rubbed off on his daughters. Sayali, who graduated in Psychology, did her master's in Human Development. She is helping students and families from India, Pakistan, Bangladesh, Sri Lanka, Bhutan, Tibet and Nepal navigate the education system. With Kamala Puram, Sayali also runs an NGO, AshaUSA, to eliminate the stigma around mental health issues in the South Asian community. Her father, who himself supported non-profit organizations like the Institute for Psychological Health and the Muktangan Rehabilitation Center through fundraising and mental health awareness campaigns, was very proud of her achievements.

After working in over 300 films, not just in Hindi and Marathi, but Bengali, Oriya and Haryanvi too, Sadashiv Amrapurkar succumbed to a lung infection he had developed in October 2014. He passed away a month later, on 3 November, at the age of 64, bringing the curtains down on an illustrious career. Prime Minister Narendra Modi condoled his demise, describing him as a versatile actor, popular across generations.

His last performance was in *Bombay Talkies* (2013), and ranks among his best. In 'Star', Dibakar Banerjee's short film from the anthology movie, Sadashiv Amrapurkar plays a *natya samrat*, the cynical mentor of a struggling stage actor enacted by Nawazuddin Siddiqui. 'It was a difficult film for me to watch personally because Baba was very ill then and passed away soon after. But as a filmmaker, it amazed me to see how he was able to project so many different emotions in just a few scenes. His performance is an acting lesson for young aspirants,' Rima asserts.

'Star' brings to mind a Marathi film, *Painjan* (1995), in which the actor plays the lead role of a star performer with a tamasha troupe, Pilajirao Khanjire, who suddenly goes missing. This leads to a police investigation, which reveals him to be a drunkard, a womanizer and an insanely possessive lover. 'What a performance that was! He wrote the film as well,' his daughter raves.

In 2019, his wife Sunanda presented a Marathi film, *Purushottam*, which opened on 10 May, a day before what would have been Sadashiv Amrapurkar's sixty-ninth birthday. Produced under their own banner, Samvedana Film Foundation and Adarsh Group, it revolves around an honest officer who is committed to social work. His daughter Ketaki made her acting debut in the film, which Rima directed.

She admits that losing her husband so prematurely was really hard on her mother. 'They were together for so many years, and after Baba left, my mother would ask me poignantly, "Rima, whom do I fight with now?" Fortunately, a few months after his untimely demise, I discovered that I was pregnant and she found a new companion in my daughter,' she says sentimentally. Almost a decade has gone by, but the presence of Sadashiv Amrapurkar has not faded from their lives. 'At times I still feel that Baba has gone for a shoot for a couple of months and will return home soon,' Rima sighs.

GULSHAN GROVER

BAD MAN

'Aaj ke iss kalyug mein tumhara bhagwan
bhi iss shaitan se darta hai.'

—*Maidan-E-Jung* (1995)

Tri Nagar is unlikely to ring any bells, except with those who have been living in Delhi for decades. It is a largely agricultural locality on the outskirts of India's capital. That's where Bollywood's 'bad man' Gulshan Grover, the youngest of seven children, was born, in a shanty set in the middle of paddy fields, with no electricity for six miles. Life was a struggle for Bishamber Nath Grover and his wife Ramrakhi, their daughters Raj, Urmila, Rita, Ramana and Akanksha, and sons Ramesh Chandra and Gulshan. The high point of their lives was the annual Dussehra celebrations. This was the only time the children were allowed to stay up late and watch the local Ramleela, which was organized by their father and his friends. Sitting in the front row, little Gulshan watched enraptured as Lord Rama's journey came alive on the makeshift stage. At the age of five, he even got to be a part of Lord Hanuman's *vanar sena* (monkey army), making his debut as an actor, sitting atop one of the tree props.

'I still remember the fun and the excitement of having make-up smeared on my face and eating the bananas given to the "actors" for free. I was too young then to analyse my feelings, but it felt good to be on stage and have others looking up at me instead of sitting with my friends and watching others perform. My first experience in the spotlight brought with it a sense of importance,' Gulshan Grover muses.

Among the first students from his small government school to get a first class and pass high school with distinction in five subjects, he got admission to one of Delhi's oldest and most prestigious educational institutions, Shri Ram College of Commerce (SRCC). Of course, this meant that he had to walk nine kilometres to the nearest bus stop, change three buses and travel three hours everyday to reach his college in the North Campus of the University of Delhi, but it opened up a whole new world for him. As part of SRCC's Fine Arts Society, of which he was later voted president and secretary, he started doing plays, winning prizes in intercollegiate competitions, was invited to all-girls colleges like Miranda House to play male roles, and even dabbled in professional theatre with the Little Theatre Group. He graduated with honours, then took his family by surprise, confessing that he wanted to try his luck in films.

Explaining his reasons for wanting to make a career in acting, Gulshan Grover points out that at SRCC, he saw the children of big industrialists come to study commerce so they could take over the businesses their fathers had set up for them. 'I had no empire to inherit. I knew I would have to start from scratch and even then it would take a lifetime to build a corporate house of my own. But, at the same time, I wanted to make a name for myself, and the only way a boy from my background could make it big was by getting into show business, where you didn't need capital or family connections, where your talent could take you to the top,' he reasons.

His father gave him six months to make a place in the film industry, or return home to complete his master's and get a steady job. Once he reached Bombay, Gulshan Grover evaluated the market. As a student of Commerce, he understood demand and supply and quickly figured out that as an outsider to Bollywood, with no film background or godfather, he stood a better chance of making it as a villain rather than joining the crowd of aspiring heroes. 'Also, the khalnayak has no age bar. He enjoys a longer innings as his popularity and longevity is not dependent on good looks, youth or personal vanity. What works for him is the force of his personality and the strength of his performances,' says the actor, who didn't want to be around for five to six years, win accolades, then fade away into oblivion. For him, it was imperative to have a long shelf life because his parents and siblings had made a lot of sacrifices to send him to Bombay to live out his dream, and he had come carrying the aspirations of his entire neighbourhood.

However, despite his determination, Gulshan Grover didn't last even six months. The competition was cut-throat and the chances of success bleak. He quickly understood that there was little likelihood of him catching the eye of a producer swishing by in a flashy car, if he simply stood waiting in a studio car park or outside a restaurant on Bombay's Linking Road. After just three months, with no roles forthcoming, and losing even the ₹300 he had to a fraudulent actor, he returned home, gaunt from skipping meals and haunted by his life's first failure. Another man would have simply accepted a steady bank job or the professorial post his college was offering him, and settled down into a secure, middle-class existence. But Gulshan Grover was not ready to give up on his starry dreams.

He returned to the city of dreams, this time with a plan to train himself as an actor first before courting stardom. He enrolled for a one-year course at the Roshan Taneja School of Acting. He was adjudged the best actor of his batch by producer Surinder Kapoor, who had developed a liking for the quietly respectful, sincere boy who would drop by their Chembur home on weekends to rehearse his lessons with his son Anil Kapoor, who was studying with him. Even Tarachand Barjatya, the founder of Rajshri Productions and Sooraj Barjatya's producer grandfather, the other guest from the film industry invited to judge the final performances, was impressed with Gulshan Grover. However, he could not find a role for the actor whose eyes spit fire and whose deep baritone sparked a fear that would feel out of place in their soft family dramas.

Struggling to sustain himself in Bombay, Gulshan Grover accepted a teaching job at Roshan Taneja's acting school. 'This time, there was no despair or feeling of defeat as I saw others streak ahead of me in the race. Now, I was a well-trained actor and that gave me confidence. Being hard-working and dedicated to my craft, I knew I would break into the race soon; I just had to figure out how to get started,' he reminisces.

The break came out of the blue. One of his students was Sanjay Dutt, and he would go to the Ajanta Arts office as a private instructor to train Dutt, who was gearing up to be launched as an actor. Noticing the growing camaraderie between the youngsters, producer-director Sunil Dutt offered

Gulshan a role in his son's debut film *Rocky* (1981). He plays Jagga, a friend of Sanjay's Rocky, who rides around with him, singing songs, and is also a kind of comic love guru to him. 'Dutt-sahab not only gave me a role, Nargis Dutt-ji and he treated me like family. I was invited to every function at their Pali Hill bungalow and introduced to industry bigwigs and legendary stars like Dilip Kumar-sahab with dignity as Sanjay's friend and teacher who was working in the film with him. Thanks to them, I could see this world from up close and I will be forever indebted to them,' he recounts emotionally.

Soon after *Rocky*, Gulshan Grover landed another much-hyped film, *Ek Jaan Hain Hum* (1983), which was launching another star kid, Raj Kapoor's younger son Rajiv, who was fondly called Chimpu. They also bonded, and Gulshan found himself being welcomed into another prominent filmmaking family. '*Ek Jaan Hain Hum* was produced by F.C. Mehra and Parvesh C. Mehra, and directed by Rajiv Mehra. I went on to do 22–23 films with the Mehras, including *Sohni Mahiwal* [1984], *Kasam* [1988], *Ram Jaane* [1995] and *Khiladiyon Ka Khiladi* [1996],' he recalls.

However, it was Mohan Kumar's *Avtaar* (1983) that put him on the 'bad' path and made him a star. The film came at a time when his career had hit a roadblock. One evening, hungry and miserable, Gulshan Grover dropped by Vinay Shukla's home, hoping the writer-filmmaker and his wife would invite him to join them for dinner, and ran into Shabana Azmi. As was his usual custom, he had slipped out of his shoes, leaving them by the door, and walked into the living room in his stockings to find the actress seated there. Shabana knew him from his visits to her home, Janki Kutir, with Anil Kapoor, and immediately spotted the holes in his socks. Embarrassed, Gulshan mumbled that they mirrored his plight. 'No work, no money,' he sighed despondently.

His words struck a chord, and she strongly recommended him to producer-director Mohan Kumar for the role of Chandan in *Avtaar*. With the actress playing his mother on screen and his godmother off it, Gulshan sailed through with a fine performance. 'It helped that my character came from a middle-class Punjabi family not unlike my own. The only real surprise was that when we were filming the scene where Chandan tells his parents that he is leaving home and throws them some notes as repayment for what they had spent on his education, Shabana-ji suddenly started crying hysterically and slapping me. Once, twice, six, eight, 10 times, the slaps were unscripted, spontaneous and painful. But I did not wince even once, knowing that they were making the scene more convincing,' he recounts.

Avtaar released with a lot of fanfare because it featured two superstars, Rajesh Khanna and Shabana Azmi. It was a critically acclaimed film and a huge commercial success. Gulshan Grover's neighbours in Tri Nagar, simple, naive folk, flocked in droves to the theatres to see the film. They returned shocked, shaking their heads in disbelief and dismay over his new avatar. 'Your once sanskari beta who would come with you to the gurdwara every morning, respectfully touch our feet and do *seva* (social service), has changed irrevocably. Now he is an ungrateful brat, and the day is not far when he will disown his own parents for monetary gains,' they told his mother. Gulshan admits that while his father, a learned, enlightened man, understood from his experience with the Ramleela that his son was play-acting on screen, his chaiji, a simple housewife, would cry bitterly, hurt and upset with the neighbours for running down her child.

That year is memorable for another film, *Sadma* (1983).

Starring superstars from the South, Kamal Haasan and Sridevi, it revolves around a young girl who develops retrograde amnesia following an accident and regresses to being a six-year-old child. A remake of director Balu Mahendra's Tamil hit *Moondram Pirai* (1982), the film stars Gulshan Grover in the small role of a lecherous woodcutter, Balua, who lusts after and almost assaults Sridevi's child-woman, Reshmi, aka Nehalata. Even though he had studied acting, even taught it, his first rape scene was a mortifying experience.

As instructed by his director, he had not shaved in days. He hadn't even washed and was dressed in clothes that smelled foul. To ensure the stench did not scare away his leading lady, producer Romu N. Sippy insisted the actor at least spray on some cologne. On the set, Balu Mahendra explained the scene to Sridevi and Gulshan. For the actress, who had been working since she was four, it was all in the day's work. The actor, however, was a bundle of nerves as he tentatively circled Reshmi, then tried to pounce on her. Before he knew it, he was flying through the air and landed 10 feet away with an undignified thud after an unexpected push from the baby-faced heroine.

While Sippy, Kamal Haasan and Balu Mahendra hooted with laughter at their Humpty Dumpty villain's big fall, a sympathetic Sridevi, realizing how inexperienced and jittery Gulshan was, took him aside and gave him a few tips on how he should navigate a rape scene. Her words have stayed with him. 'One of the first things Sridevi explained was that I should never be disrespectful towards any actress. That was easy because since I was a child, I have been around women, my mother and five sisters, for whom I always had great respect. Not only will I never ill-treat a woman, I get violently aggressive towards any man who does so. The only time I would misbehave with a lady is if the role demands it,' he asserts.

Meanwhile, continuing with her lesson, Sridevi pointed out that even when shooting, he should be careful never to make his female co-star feel uncomfortable or awkward. He should remember that it was his character and not him misbehaving with the woman in the scene.

Following her advice, Gulshan not only pulled off the scene in *Sadma* with a perfect second take, but similar scenes in other films as well. The actor was also careful never to offend his mother in any way. 'For a very long time, whenever any of my films was released, one of my siblings would go and watch it first, before escorting Chaiji to the theatre. Just before I tore off a woman's clothes on screen or was beaten black and blue by the hero, she would be whisked out of the auditorium on some pretext or the other. After this happened a few times, she wised up to their ploy and would insist on sitting through the entire film,' he laughs at the memory.

Usually, in our country, the hero not only walks away into the sunset with the heroine at the end of the film, he also walks away with the admiration and adoration of all the women watching the film in the theatre. Gulshan Grover reversed the trend in Russia with the Indo-Russia co-production, *Sohni Mahiwal* (1984), in which he plays the antagonist, Noor, who tries to keep Sunny Deol's Mirza Izzat Beg and Poonam Dhillon's Sohni apart so he can marry her himself. He had grown out his beard and hair for the role. His skin was burnished from sitting in the sun for long hours and he had lined his eyes with kohl. On his first day in Tashkent, he caught the eye of a local woman who wooed him openly. It was awkward for him in the company of the film's cast, but flattering as well.

'Back home in India, however, the young girls who crowded the set in Chandigarh ran after Sunny for autographs and photographs while I went unrecognized. Even when they were made aware of my presence, they ran not towards me, but away from me,' he guffaws without rancour.

Over the past five decades, the actor has played the bad man in over 400 films. 'It's not as if I became a villain because I did not get hero roles,' he points out, sharing that he had turned down T. Rama Rao's *Mujhe Insaaf Chahiye* (1983) because he didn't want to play the hero, even one who left the heroine pregnant. The role was eventually played by Mithun Chakraborty. He also gave up on the opportunity to romance Hema Malini in an unconventional love story, *Ek Nai Paheli* (1984), this one directed by another South supremo, K. Balachander, who then opted for his *Ek Duuje Ke Liye* (1981) hero Kamal Haasan for the role. 'I also turned down T. Rama Rao-*garu's Nache Mayuri* [1986], another hero's role, but I went out of my way to convince him to sign me as the baddie Pratap in his *Yeh Desh* [1984] who, following his older brother, Shakti Kapoor's Dharamdas, instigates riots and assaults a girl in college, driving her to commit suicide. So you see, I became a villain by choice,' he reiterates.

Some of the characters Gulshan Grover has brought to life have become a part of movie lore today, as have their catchphrases. Who can forget *Khiladiyon Ka Khiladi*'s (1996) King Don? Despite missing a part of his hand, he is suave in fashionably long coats, all pumped up as he plots to put WWF's (now WWE's) giant wrestlers, 'Crush' (Brian Keith Adams) and 'The Undertaker' (Brian Lee Harris), in the ring to beat the competition posed by Rekha's queen don, Maya, who runs an illegal wrestling racket in New York. His one-liner in the film, '*Maya, teri to main palat doonga kaya* [Maya, I will turn the tables on you],' is often quoted.

In Umesh Mehra's *International Khiladi* (1999), he plays another don, Thakral, this one stylishly desi in dhotis and brocade kurtas, with women wrestlers to do his bidding. Kali Baba, the gangster of *Shola Aur Shabnam* (1992), is not as colourfully attired, but his boast, '*Hum jurm ki duniya ka colonel hoon* [I am the colonel of this world of crime],' is a war cry that still resonates. One of my favourite characters from his repertoire is *Sir*'s (1993) Chhapan 'Jimmy' Tikle. This one is not remembered for his exaggerated theatrics or his funky wardrobe, but the quiet menace he exudes on screen.

Sadashiv Amrapurkar, riding high after the critical and commercial adulation that the *Sadak* (1991) villain Maharani had received, was initially pencilled in to play the role, while Gulshan Grover was cast as his demented and dangerous younger brother. But three days before the film was to roll, director Mahesh Bhatt suddenly sprang it on him that he was playing the main antagonist.

While he was elated to land this challenging role, Gulshan, a method actor who believes in meticulous prep, asked the director for four days to get into the skin of this character. He also watched Bhatt's expressions and mannerisms when he was angry and agitated, and used him as a role model.

After a two-hour briefing from Bhatt, he called up an old photographer friend, Pradeep Chandra. 'I used to do a lot of work for Hindi Pocket Books, who brought out classics and romantic novels for as little as ₹1 a book to encourage the reading habit. I had shot Gulshan Grover and cinematographer Ashok Mehta for the cover of some of these books and we knew each other well,' recounts Chandra. He recalls how the actor had come knocking on his door on the day of his wedding and whisked him away for a shoot in Delhi's Lodhi Garden. It went on till late afternoon, making his aunt worry that Chandra, suffering an attack of pre-wedding jitters, had run off.

For the *Sir* shoot, Gulshan Grover wanted to wear a white suit he had brought along and instructed his make-up man, Suresh Dada, to cover his face cosmetically with pockmarks. 'This time we went to a bungalow in Juhu in Mumbai because I wanted a lot of empty space, and I made him stand against a white wall, zooming in on his face. He loved the pictures and took them to Mahesh Bhatt. That became the "look" of Chhapan Tikle,' reminisces the photographer, adding that they did about three to four changes, and some of the other 'looks' were also incorporated in other Mahesh Bhatt films.

The first time Gulshan Grover stepped on the set in full make-up and costume, a real-life gangster who was playing a role in the film exclaimed, '*Yeh to Chhapan Tikle hai* [He is Chhapan Tikle],' and the name stuck. 'I was to be called Jimmy earlier, but Chhapan Tikle sounded so much better. I discovered only later that it is a desi slang for a person with a face pitted with pockmarks,' he says.

Then, of course, there is the unforgettable Kesariya Vilayati in producer-director Subhash Ghai's *Ram Lakhan* (1989), which was not just a career-defining role, but a life-changing one, too. 'Today, everyone knows me as "Bad Man". Even my biography is titled *Bad Man*,' Gulshan smiles.

It seems impossible to believe that the character was an afterthought. With two A-list actors, Anil Kapoor and Jackie Shroff, a trio of popular actresses—Rakhee, Dimple Kapadia and Madhuri Dixit—along with several top-ranking villains, including Amrish Puri, Paresh Rawal, Anupam Kher, Satish Kaushik, Annu Kapoor, Anand Balraj and Raza Murad, the director did not need to add another name in his impressive ensemble cast. But Gulshan Grover was really keen to be a part of his much-talked-about multi-starrer. 'He was dressed in a pathani suit and a waistcoat with gold buttons,' remembers the showman. Today, the get-up, particularly with a *kambal* (blanket shawl) thrown over his shoulder, is iconic and familiar; but back then, with the wig, beard and moustache he was sporting, the actor was virtually unrecognizable. 'It was only when he piped up, saying, "Hello sir, I'm Gulshan Grover," that I knew it was him,' the filmmaker admits.

Once he got over his initial surprise, Subhash Ghai laughed appreciatively at the actor's earnest efforts to woo him, but had to regretfully tell him that he did not have a role for him. 'He went away disappointed. However, I could not get his "look" out of my mind. It showed the passion of a man for whom acting wasn't just a profession, but a matter of life and death. That couldn't go unrewarded,' the *Ram Lakhan* producer-director asserts.

Being one of the writers himself, he could tweak the plot and introduce a new character. After a couple of days, he called Gulshan Grover home for breakfast. This was a broad hint to the actor that he had something for him, but it wasn't until he was leaving that Subhash Ghai broached the subject. 'It's a brief role, but you get to keep your get-up,' he told the elated actor.

After they started shooting, the actor came to him one day, in his costume and make-up, wondering what he was supposed to say since he had not been given any scenes or dialogue. '*Kuchh nahin* [nothing],' the filmmaker retorted, and as Gulshan Grover gawked, told him he only had to introduce himself as 'Bad Man' every time he turned up on screen. 'Like Coca Cola, but in a more menacing way,' he instructed. The actor surrendered to the movie moghul's vision and reaped a rich harvest. 'Kesariya Vilayati was the smallest role in the film, yet it made the biggest impact!' Subhash Ghai marvels.

Even though he was still relatively new to the industry then, Gulshan Grover had the successful *Avtaar* behind him, had impressed in Yash Chopra's *Mashaal* (1984) where he was pitted against the legendary Dilip Kumar, and had a huge following in Russia after *Sohni Mahiwal*. Even the Ramsay horror film *Veerana* (1988) was a surprise hit, going on to acquire cult status. But it was *Ram Lakhan*'s 'bad man' who made him forever famous. He admits that to stand out in a crowd of big names with just one phrase is nothing short of a miracle. 'I give full credit to Subhash-ji for not just creating the character of Kesariya Vilayati for me, but also for his phenomenal success. Also, a big thank you to the late Ashok Mehta [the film's director of photography], who had been one of the permanent residents at Marina Guest House when I lived there during my first trip to Mumbai. He lit me up so well and made me look so powerful on screen,' the actor says gratefully.

He remembers how, on the day of the film's premiere, he had joined the team in the minibus Subhash Ghai had hired for the evening so they could go theatre-hopping together. To everyone's surprise, as they entered the first theatre, they were greeted by cries of 'bad man', which followed them all the way out. The same scene played out in the second and third theatres. By the end of the evening, Gulshan Grover had a new identity.

Two years later, he wowed Subhash Ghai again with his prep when he was signed to play Baliram in the filmmaker's ambitious *Saudagar* (1991). 'I worked out two distinct looks for my character—one young, one old,' Gulshan shares. In this film, he got to share the screen with two legends, Dilip Kumar and Raaj Kumar, who were reuniting 22 years after *Paigham*

(1959). 'My Bali drives a wedge between them, turning the childhood friends into foes for a while,' he reminds me.

While Gulshan Grover enjoyed playing the villain, he reveals that every time he was thrashed on screen, his mother would get agitated and abuse his tormentors loudly. 'This would disturb the others in the auditorium and they would try and hush her up, saying, "*Mataji, chhup ho jayiye* [Mother, please be quiet], we want to watch the film." As a doting mother, it was difficult for her to understand the difference between reel and real,' he laughs.

Gulshan's villains have occasionally brought on some laughs too. In Rajiv Rai's star-studded, action-packed thriller *Vishwatma* (1992), with his flashy suits, flute and old-world Hindi, Tapasvi Gunjal stands out in a crowd of villains, including Amrish Puri, Mahesh Anand, Kiran Kumar, Tej Sapru, Dan Dhanoa, Anand Balraj, Raza Murad, Rajesh Vivek, Amit Bhalla and Salim Khan. Lines like '*Pujya pitaji, yeh woh apraadhi hai jisne meri kanya pe daali kudrishti* [Father, this is the criminal whose evil eye fell on my girl]' gave a comic slant to his bad-man avatar. Surprisingly, this blend of terror and humour is not something he enjoys. 'I resisted the trend for a long time because I have always believed that the villain should ignite terror and fear. If he makes you laugh too, it will only dilute the primary emotion,' confides the actor.

Another interesting villain is Dost Khan, a terrorist who smuggles a Russian-made nuclear bomb into India, in Mani Shankar's *16 December* (2002). The title of the film refers to the end of the 1971 India–Pakistan War with the signing of the Pakistani Instrument of Surrender. In the film, to avenge this humiliation, Dost Khan comes up with the plan to wipe out India from the face of the earth. 'I had as many as 10 disguises in the film,' reminds the master of get-ups, admitting that he kept the director waiting for 10 days, till Danny Denzongpa, his *Lajja* (2001) co-star who was shooting with him in Hyderabad, admitted to him that while he had been signed to play Major General Vir Vijay Singh, an Indian Revenue Service intelligence officer and the film's hero, he would happily trade it for the villain's role. That sparked Gulshan Grover's interest immediately and he accepted the role of Dost Khan, which today ranks among his three top performances.

Interestingly, Gulshan Grover was among the first Indian actors to try his luck in Hollywood without relocating to the US or quitting Hindi films. His 'West Side Story' began in the '90s, during a Bollywood concert tour with Shah Rukh Khan, Juhi Chawla, Akshay Kumar and Kajol. During a stopover in Los Angeles, his NRI friends fixed a meeting for him with Dee McLachlan, the director of *The Second Jungle Book: Mowgli & Baloo* (1997), who was looking for an actor to play Buldeo in the American adventure film.

However, the American producers did not want an unknown Indian actor to play the important role of Mowgli's uncle who wants him dead, and replaced him with an American star. 'They even shot with this actor for a few days, but then, their unhappy director threatened to quit the project without the actor with the shifty, hypnotic eyes,' reminisces Gulshan Grover, admitting that his *Yes Boss* (1997) co-star Shah Rukh Khan convinced the film's producer, Ratan Jain, who had his dates, to let him fly off to Sri Lanka to pursue his Hollywood dream.

It wasn't easy making a place for himself in a different film industry. While he was a star back home, in the US, he was just another newbie actor who had to audition for roles that were usually nothing to crow about. However, he managed to meet the right people, promoting his debut film at the same event in Las Vegas as *Desperado* (1995) star Salma Hayek. 'Salma and I were to do a film together, *The Driver*, with her playing my wife, but the film did not take off,' Gulshan rues.

He lost the role of Captain Nemo to Naseeruddin Shah in Sean Connery's last film, *The League of Extraordinary Gentlemen* (2003), because his agents were holding out for a higher remuneration, but he got invited to dinner by Goldie Hawn. 'I chatted with Hollywood's golden girl and her beau, Kurt Russell, as well as Oscar-winning actress Susan Sarandon, over butter chicken and kebabs,' he reminisces.

Bruce Willis, Gulshan admits, was cold at the premiere of *Bandits* (2001), but another action hero, Steven Seagal, was wonderfully warm. However, as pictures of him with these stars appeared in newspapers and magazines, the roles back home dried up because Hindi film producers were afraid he would migrate one day, leaving them high and dry, despite his assurances to the contrary.

'What I did get were weird requests—like one from the son of a legendary actor who wanted me to ask Pierce Brosnan, who had just announced he would not be playing Bond again, if he would be interested in venturing into Bollywood,' he remembers with a chuckle. Interestingly, Gulshan Grover himself was signed to play Le Chiffre, the chess-whiz banker, mathematician and genius who is hired by international terrorists, in *Casino Royale* (2006). Unfortunately, a reporter-friend leaked the news before the official announcement and he lost one of the biggest roles of his career to Mads Mikkelsen.

He doesn't have regrets, however. Carrying DVDs in his suitcase on trips abroad, Gulshan Grover introduced mainstream Hindi cinema and its stars to Hollywood, paving the way for Aishwarya Rai, Priyanka Chopra, Irrfan Khan and Deepika Padukone to conquer the West. 'Do you know I was offered the policeman's role in Danny Boyle's *Slumdog Millionaire* [2008]? But I had another commitment, and the role went to Irrfan Khan,' he shares.

The satisfaction is that his son, Sanjay Grover, got to work with the Hollywood studio MGM for 15 years on *The Hobbit* and *Creed* series, the Bond franchise and the comedy-fantasy *Zookeeper* (2011), among others. Meanwhile, Gulshan Grover explored the world, working in French, German, Polish, Malaysian, Iranian and Nepalese cinema. Today, Sanjay, who was emotionally blackmailed into returning to their duplex in Mumbai, is brainstorming with his Hollywood counterparts on projects he can creatively produce with crossover talent, while Gulshan returned to playing the baddie in films like *Sadak 2* (2020), *Mumbai Saga* (2021), *Sooryavanshi* (2021) and *Indian 2* (2024).

'It's been over four decades and over 400 films; and the journey continues. As my mentor Mahesh Bhatt says every time he sees me, "Gulshan Grover, never over!"'

ASHUTOSH RANA
THE PLAYER OF MIND GAMES

'Inn aankhon mein dekhiye, dekhiye inn aankhon mein,
yeh to devdoot ki aankhen hai, darpan hai yeh aankhen,
jinme jhank ke nanhe munhe bachche devlok ke darshan
kar sakte hain...'

—*Sangharsh* (1999)

I f you are a Hindi film buff from the '90s, this dialogue will immediately bring back dark memories of Lajja Shankar Pandey from *Sangharsh* (1999). A quarter of a century later, Ashutosh Rana, who played a religious fanatic in the psychological thriller, willing to sacrifice young lives on the altar in his quest for immortality, reminds you that even Kamsa and Ravana from Hindu mythology, and Adolf Hitler from modern times, wanted to be not only invincible, but also immortal. '*Amar banna chahte the woh*, they wanted to live forever. Fortunately, none of them did,' says the actor.

Lajja Shankar Pandey is impaled before he can make the last human sacrifice, but Ashutosh Rana, who brought him to life so terrifyingly, will be remembered for posterity for a performance which is all fire and brimstone. The memory of the delusional god-man, a wet sari clinging to his body, his hair plastered to his head by the torrential downpour, his mouth wide open and emitting a bizarre sound, still sends a chill down the spine.

The film's presenter and writer Mahesh Bhatt shares that having grown up on a lot of westerns, he recalled depictions of Native Americans putting their finger in their mouth and rolling their tongues in a spine-chilling war cry. 'Our war cry was such a hit that even to this day, airport security guards remind me of it and imitate it,' the filmmaker chuckles.

Ashutosh points out that traditionally, the war cry is used to ward off evil spirits, and for Lajja Shankar Pandey, Akshay Kumar's unjustly implicated genius Professor Aman Varma and Preity Zinta's trainee CBI officer Reet Oberoi are evil spirits as they are stopping him from reaching his goal. Lauding him for the crazy edge he brought to the character, Mahesh Bhatt recalls the scene towards the end of the film when the Professor stops the god-man from beheading the child as the last sacrifice on the day of the solar eclipse, believing that it will make him immortal.

'I pointed out to Ashutosh before he faced the camera that I didn't want him to do this scene like a regular villain, but like a passionate believer. He nodded and asked me to stand next to the camera while he was doing it. Looking into my eyes, he gave the shot. There was such conviction in his eyes and his voice that he sounded and behaved as if he actually believed every word he was saying. That performance is unforgettable!' exclaims a still-awed Bhatt.

An equally impressed Tanuja Chandra, the director of *Sangarsh*, remembers that the actor had invited his family to one of the early screenings. 'After seeing the film, Ashutosh's sister refused to speak to him, telling him brusquely to stay away from her. I guess that too was a huge compliment for him as an actor,' she laughs.

Surprisingly, the actor was not the director's first choice for the all-important role, despite him having given an unforgettable performance in her directorial debut *Dushman* (1998) as the rapist and serial killer Gokul Pandit. Chandra reasons that with *Sangharsh* closely following *Dushman*, she thought he would seem repetitive in two consecutive crazy villainous turns. She admits Ashutosh Rana wasn't happy with her decision, but since she could not be persuaded to change her mind, they did not touch upon the subject for several weeks even as the director pondered who could play this chilling antagonist best.

'Then, one day, I was surprised by a call from a woman I had never met. She introduced herself as an actress and said she had loved *Dushman* and wanted to work with me. We spoke for about 10 minutes; I had absolutely no clue it was Ashutosh at the other end till he revealed it himself,' reminisces Chandra, adding that he reminded her that her tantrik in *Sangharsh* liked to impersonate women, so he had hit upon this idea to impress her. When she told him he had fooled her completely, he laughingly replied that now she would have to cast him as Lajja Shankar Pandey. 'After that flawless performance on the phone, how could I say no to him!' quips Chandra.

She acknowledges today that had she bypassed Ashutosh Rana then and opted for another actor, she would have regretted the decision all her life. In retrospect, she realizes that while Lajja Shankar Pandey is another psychotic villain in another psychological thriller, he is nothing like Gokul Pandit. The actor agrees, pointing out that not just their persona, even the way he portrays the two characters is dramatically different.

Blood-spattered Lajja Shankar Pandey looms large

on screen. He is exaggeratedly loud, almost theatrical, a high-pitched act that is impossible to miss. 'There's no *sur* [pitch] in Indian cinema higher than this,' asserts Ashutosh. Gokul Pandit, on the other hand, is under-played to the extent that he becomes almost invisible. Even though Gokul is always knocking on people's doors, they remember him only for the letters he delivers, with very few having a clear recollection of his face. 'Amitabh Bachchan made the common man a hero with films like *Deewaar* [1975] and *Sholay* [1975]. *Dushman* made the omnipotent villain the common man,' the actor says with satisfaction.

Ashutosh reminds you that before Gokul Pandit gate-crashed our world, the villain in Hindi cinema was either a scheming zamindar or a manipulative business tycoon, a smuggler or a don, a corrupt politician or a dreaded dacoit. 'But this khalnayak is an ordinary postman in a khaki uniform. He doesn't have a fleet of fast cars or a dozen horses galloping behind him; his only wealth is his bicycle, which he loses. Even the gun he gets hold of towards the end is not his own. Yet, he is dangerous,' he asserts.

Dushman is not an easy film to watch. And once you watch it, it's hard to forget—particularly Sonia's rape scene, which is raw and brutal. Chandra, who had issues with the way rape was depicted on screen—as a titillating sexual act rather than a traumatic assault—portrays it as the heinous crime that it is. Terrifying, not only for the woman being savaged on screen, but also for everyone seeing it happen before their eyes and being helpless to prevent it.

Delving into the etymology of the word *balatkar* (rape), Ashutosh Rana, an extremely well-read and knowledgeable man, shares that it means '*bal purvak kissi cheez ko apne adhikar mein kar lena* [using brute strength to forcibly possess something or someone]'. Possession, he asserts, does not always have to be physical. It can refer to possession of land, knowledge, even power. So, despite being a sadistic rapist, Gokul Pandit doesn't come on strongly, in a way that would repulse a woman or even alert her to be careful of this seemingly innocuous postman. There's only one scene to the contrary; the scene in which he arrives at the door of Kajol's Naina with a telegram and asks for a signature. She accepts his proffered pen, but it doesn't work. Even as she is shaking it ineffectually, his hand clamps down on hers. Guiding pen to paper, he says in a raspy whisper, '*Zara daba ke* [Press a little harder]'. The gesture is not overtly objectionable, nor are the words offensive on the surface, but there's something in his eyes that makes her squirm, pull away and go inside to get her own pen. By the time she signs and turns to give him the paper, he has disappeared, heading straight for a bar, where over two glasses of cheap alcohol, he decides which of the twins to take. 'Rape is as much physical torture as mental trauma. The wounds on the body will heal, but the scars on the mind never will,' the actor points out.

On *Dushman*'s silver jubilee, Kajol wrote on social media, '#25years to Dushman. One of the scariest films I have ever said yes to or even watched for that matter. #AshutoshRana scared the crap out of me on screen and I'm sure out of all of you guys as well.'* She is exceptional in a double role, playing identical twins Sonia and Naina, one of whom is raped by Gokul Pandit, putting the other on the path of revenge. But it is Ashutosh Rana as the creepy antagonist who makes your skin crawl even when you are

---

*@itsKajolD, *X* (formerly Twitter), 29 May 2023, 11.59 a.m., https://tinyurl.com/zch89hru. Accessed on 16 May 2024.

sitting in a packed auditorium or in the safety of your home.

Tanuja Chandra surprises you with another admission. She wasn't entirely convinced Ashutosh Rana was the right guy to play her *dushman*, not having seen much of his previous work. What tilted the scales in his favour was that when they met, the debutant director sensed a mad passion in the actor that matched hers. 'It was like something inside him was waiting to explode. I felt that if Ashutosh didn't get this role, he would die. And for me, this thirst is far more important than mere talent,' she asserts.

Once they started shooting, the director wanted everyone to hate Gokul Pandit as much as she did. She was gratified that Ashutosh was able to find the character's core so easily. 'Most villainous turns only scratch the surface, with the result that the character remains superficial. It's only when an actor plumbs the depths of the darkness, bringing something that is terrifyingly real and human to the fore, that it becomes a nightmare that we carry with us forever,' Chandra explains.

For Ashutosh Rana, there are two ways of playing a character. The first is to focus on the physicality—shaving one's head, wearing a wig, sticking on a moustache or a beard. The character then becomes memorable for his unusual get-up or look. The second is more cerebral, where one tries to figure out the way the character thinks. 'Your *vichar* [thoughts] influences your *vyavahar* [behaviour], determines your body language, shapes your personality and decides your goals,' the actor explains. It goes without saying that he adheres to the second approach. He doesn't care for costumes, but digs deep within himself to create the aura of menace around a negative character.

'It is important to not only grasp the character, but understand his psyche too. I had to get into the mind of not just Gokul, who does not believe he has done anything wrong and so feels no remorse, but also into the minds of all those in the auditorium watching him. I had to make them hate him, want to kill him, because such people should not exist,' the actor elucidates.

For Tanuja Chandra, it is a source of continued amazement that such a refined and cultured gentleman can play such characters with so much conviction. Raving about the animal vitality Ashutosh Rana brought to the screen in *Dushman* that made Gokul Pandit so compelling, Mahesh Bhatt says, 'Ashutosh is a man of the soil and he brings that earthiness and essence to his roles. It would not be possible to have such a long career in this business if the roots were not dug deep.'

∞

Ashutosh Neekhra was born on 10 November 1967 in Gadarwara, Narsinghpur, Madhya Pradesh. '*Thaat dehati hoon main,* I'm a true son of the soil,' he says proudly, endorsing Mahesh Bhatt's observation. What's interesting is that from an early age, this simple, soft-spoken, well-brought-up boy was fascinated by the khalnayak. Quiz him today on what draws him to negative characters and he points out that the antagonist is always self-assured, while the hero will deliberate long and hard on whether he should or should not do something. 'The villain has no such confusion, he is supremely confident and never conflicted in his decisions and actions,' explains the actor with the same self-assurance, which tells you that this man is a master of both his mind and his craft.

Every year, during the annual Dussehra festival, the Ramleela would be staged in his hometown. Ashutosh loved being on stage, and as he grew older, he yearned to play

Ravana. But to his disappointment, since the King of Lanka was a much older man, the role remained out of his reach. 'I landed the role of Meghanada, Ravana and Mandodari's son, but it was the father who fascinated me because he is neither completely black nor white, but is in an interesting grey zone,' he shares.

When he was 16, Ashutosh enrolled in Dr. Harisingh Gour Vishwavidyalya Sagar, a university in Madhya Pradesh. He continued to dabble in theatre and was also active in student politics. Then, encouraged by his spiritual guru, he moved to Delhi and joined the NSD, where he honed his skills before heading to Bombay, every aspiring actor's Mecca.

With no godfather and only his talent to back him, life was a struggle. But Ashutosh Rana was rooted in his resolve to follow his passion and make it as an actor. He flagged off his acting career with small roles on television, in shows like *Shikast*, *Tehkikaat*, *Aahat*, and *Farz*. He caught the eye as Tyagi in *Swabhimaan*, the first Indian soap to complete 500 episodes, which aired on Doordarshan. Mahesh Bhatt, who was the series' director, remembers walking into the editing room one day and being transfixed by a scene he saw playing out.

'It was a brilliant performance by a young actor I had not seen on the entertainment landscape till then,' he remembers, adding, 'What was even more impressive was that daily soaps were just emerging then—you could say we were the pioneers—so I knew that the actor did not have the luxury of several cuts and retakes, and yet I was mesmerized,' says Bhatt.

Scripted by Shobhaa De and Vinod Ranganathan, *Swabhimaan* is about inheritance and succession wars, and emotional turbulence, that threaten to sweep away its protagonist, Kitu Gidwani's Svetlana Bannerjee, after her business magnate lover dies suddenly. Ashutosh Rana plays Tyagi, a gangster with a heart of gold, who refuses to leave his roots, despite being in love with a city girl. The connection was immediate, but the actor admitted later that he was unsure about accepting what was then only a 10-episode role. It was his spiritual guru who urged him to do it, pointing out that at the start of his career, he should take up everything that came his way, small or big.

The advice paid off. Thanks to the audience's overwhelming response to the character and his own personal charisma, Tyagi was an integral part of *Swabhimaan* for two years, from 1995 to 1997.

After *Swabhimaan* came the shows *Waaris*, *Dhundh* and *Apradhi Kaun*, to name a few. Vikram Bhatt, who directed the actor in *Dhundh*, exclaims, 'Ashutosh is such a brilliant actor!' He remembers a scene in the TV serial in which the actor had to speak three to four lines, then laugh uncontrollably. 'He nailed it perfectly. The ability to laugh and cry without it seeming forced or fake is a rare talent and sets him apart,' the filmmaker says appreciatively.

I remember Ashutosh Rana as Keshav Thakral, the Bahubali of Ghaziabad, who terrorizes and traumatizes a young girl, Rachana, in *Kaali – Ek Agnipariksha*. What made his character even more terrifying was the television serial's striking similarity with the real-life story of Haryana's promising tennis player, Ruchika Girhotra, who was molested by SPS Rathore, disgraced top cop of Haryana, when she was just 14. When Ruchika refused to succumb to his advances or take back her case against him, her brother and father were harassed, following which she committed suicide.

More recently, he has acted in some amazing web series,

each very different from the other because Ashutosh Rana is loath to repeat himself. From Mughal Emperor Aurangzeb in the historical drama *Chhatrasal* to Mahadev Dogra, a former cop who carries the guilt of an unsolved case in *Aranyak*, from Jagganath Rai in Tigmanshu Dhulia's crime mystery drama *The Great Indian Murder* to IG Mukteshwar Chaubey, IPS, in Neeraj Pandey's *Khakee: The Bihar Chapter*, he has made his presence felt across the country.

On the big screen, he first caught the eye in Vikram Bhatt's *Ghulam* (1998). It was only a one-scene appearance, but a powerful scene and important to the narrative. The director had Paresh Rawal in mind for the role, but for some reason, it wasn't working out with him. 'That's when Boss [Mahesh Bhatt], who was directing *Swabhimaan*, suggested the name of a new actor, Ashutosh Rana. He was excited to play the part and I was more than happy,' shares the director. Mahesh Bhatt adds, 'The length of the role doesn't matter to Ashutosh. It's about what he brings to the role. He has an amazing ability to learn and relearn, and in the process, he always leaves his mark.'

In *Ghulam*, the actor appears in a black-and-white flashback and looms large in a pristine white kurta–pyjama. Siddhu (Siddharth Marathe, who grows up to be Aamir Khan) stops playing to gaze up at the stranger curiously. He is delighted when on the way up to their *barsati* (terrace apartment), the visitor introduces himself as Agrawal. Shyamsundar Agrawal is a name Siddhu has heard often, a fellow comrade of his father from the freedom-struggle days. Their reunion after 30 years, though, is not a happy one. Agrawal confronts Dalip Tahil's Mr Marathe and berates him for betraying five lives to save his own. He makes a mockery of his former comrade's patriotism, and his last roar, '*Bhagaudda, saale kaayar* [Absconder, bloody coward],' triggers a guilt so overwhelming that the other man self-immolates—a life-changing moment for Siddhu as he watches his father go up in flames. In just two minutes and 16 seconds, Ashutosh Rana had proved that he was meant for bigger things.

Vikram Bhatt went on to cast him in other films, including *Kasoor* (2001) and *Raaz* (2002), and admits that he soon became the quintessential must-have actor for Vishesh Films. When Pooja Bhatt, who was scouting for an actor to play Gokul Pandit in *Dushman*, saw his one scene in *Ghulam*, she told Vikram, 'I want this guy in my film.' Ashutosh Rana screamed with delight when he was offered the role, promising Mahesh Bhatt that he would make him proud by winning the Filmfare Award for Best Performance in a Negative Role. He kept his word. In fact, he set a record by picking up the award for a second consecutive year for his performance as Lajja Shankar Pandey.

I remember him walking up to the stage to receive the much-coveted Black Lady. His acceptance speeches, delivered in elegant, grandiloquent Hindi, had everyone in the audience turning to each other in wide-eyed bemusement because they had never heard some of the words he spoke, forget knowing what they meant. 'He is a boy from the heartland of India and he has always spoken amazing Hindi,' says Mahesh Bhatt, admitting that he has seen many actors come to Bollywood and try to fit into its hybrid culture, and had warned Ashutosh Rana against doing so. 'I told him to insist on speaking to journalists in Hindi instead of English, as is usual. In fact, he was among the first from his generation to spearhead this movement of popularizing Hindi in our film industry. Over time, his command over Hindi has become his trademark,' the filmmaker points out.

The actor has since authored a collection of poems, *Maun Muskaan Ki Maar* (2020). Another book, *Ramrajya*, based on the Ramayana, was released on Ram Navami, 2 April 2020. In May 2023, he was honoured with the Akhil Bharatiya Sanman Jeevan Gaurav Puraskar for his significant contribution to the Hindi language. The actor, in his quiet, gracious way, expressed his gratitude, stating on his social media, '*Kuch vyakti Hindi bol kar Hindi ko garima pradaan karte hain, main un saubhagyashali vyaktiyon mein se hoon jisse Hindi ne garima pradaan ki* [Some people enhance the dignity of Hindi by speaking it. I am one of those fortunate few whom Hindi has given dignity].*'

Ashutosh Rana has been happily married to actress Renuka Shahane for over two decades and is a doting father to sons Shauryaman and Satyendra. The always smiling couple are so compatible that they seem like two halves that complete each other. When they started dating, Renuka admitted she dropped in on the set of *Sangharsh* and heard him scream his now-iconic dialogue, '*Main insaan nahi hoon, ye jeevan maran tujh jaise tuchh prani ke zindagi ka hissa hai* [I am not human, this cycle of life and death is a part of the life of a despicable creature like you].' She was startled, more so when she saw Ashutosh Rana in his terrifying Lajja Shankar Pandey get-up. Fortunately, by then she knew the man behind the vicious character. Ashutosh is proud of the fact that he has always been able to keep the actor and the character, the person and the performer, distinct and apart.

After being married to a Maharashtrian for over a dozen years, Ashutosh debuted in Marathi cinema with Kishor

---

*@ranaashutosh10, *X* (formerly Twitter), 24 March 2023, 10.54 a.m., https://tinyurl.com/bdc73n6x. Accessed on 20 May 2024.

Pandurang Belekar's *Yeda* (2013). In the psychological thriller, set in a small town, he plays another diabolical character, a psychotic priest, Appa Kulkarni (Yeda), who terrorizes his family. 'If you let your emotions control you, you put yourself on the path of self-destruction. On the other hand, if you are able to control your emotions, you can do something constructive with your life. And there lies the distinction between the hero and the villain,' the actor explains. He adds that the villain is motivated by self-interest while the hero harnesses his energy to create a better society. '*Nayak samaaj ke saath chalta hai, khalnayak samaaj ke aage chalta hai. Nayak naman ki neeti mein vishwas karta hai, khalnayak daman ki neeti mein vishwas karta hai* [The hero moves with society while the villain tries to go ahead of it; the hero believes in submission and creation, the villain in repression and destruction],' he elucidates.

Working in a language that he hadn't mastered added to the lure of *Yeda*. 'Marathi is my children's mother tongue, not mine. And in this film, since Appa Kulkarni is an upper-caste Brahmin, his language is always refined and cultured even when he is ranting,' informs the actor, who has also experimented with Tamil, Telugu, Malayalam, Kannada, Bengali and Haryanvi cinema. One remembers him as the wanted gangster Jothi in the Tamil action thriller *Meagamann* (2014) whom the undercover cop played by Arya has to smoke out. Ashutosh is also brilliant as Narsappa in the Telugu film *Kalki* (2019). His motivation behind doing films in different languages is that he wants to be known as a pan-India and not a Hindi film actor.

He recalls his role model Dilip Kumar saying that all actors are toy sellers. Some empty their baskets in five years; some, like him, have stayed in the business for half a century.

Ashutosh Rana, too, is here to stay. While a lesser actor might have played a rapist in half a dozen films by now or rooted himself in the world of tantras and mantras after Lajja Shankar Pandey, Ashutosh Rana has refused to limit himself to a particular role or genre. Even his transgender character in *Shabnam Mausi* (2005), modelled on India's first transgender MLA, is a one-off act. 'I hate monotony, I need to surprise myself as an actor', he asserts, joking that this is why mimicry artists find it so hard to imitate him. '*Adakari* [performance] can be copied, not *kalakari* [art]', he states. Mahesh Bhatt adds, 'He is as versatile as Irrfan Khan and places no limits on himself. And if you set limitations, he will go beyond them.'

In 2019, the actor played rogue agent Hrithik Roshan's former boss, joint secretary of RAW, Colonel Sunil Luthra, in *War*. The character returned four years later in the blockbuster spy thriller *Pathaan* (2023), and had actor-producer Shah Rukh Khan describing Ashutosh Rana as a '*gyaani* [knowledgable]' and an '*antaryami* [omniscient]' apart from a 'very very fine artiste'. Mahesh Bhatt is equally laudatory, 'To see him hold his own when in the same space as a charismatic star like Shah Rukh makes me so proud. I really liked Ashutosh in *Pathaan*, as also in Alia's [daughter Alia Bhatt] film *Humpty Sharma Ki Dulhania* [2014], in which he plays her father.' The filmmaker also admits that he is often reminded of 'the extraordinary boy's brilliance' in two of his own home productions, the Vikram Bhatt-directed *Raaz* (2002) and earlier, in his own directorial *Zakhm* (1998).

In the first film of the hit horror franchise, *Raaz*, Ashutosh Rana plays Professor Agni Swaroop, a paranormal investigator, who is the first to sense the presence of a ghost, and in the end, is possessed by the vengeful spirit of Malini, going up in flames with her. In *Zakhm*, he is a right-wing fundamentalist leader, Subodh Malgaonkar, who fans communal hatred and tries to prevent Ajay Devgn's Ajay Desai from giving his mother, who was fatally burnt while coming out of a temple, a burial according to Islamic rites as per her last wish, insisting that she be cremated as a Hindu. Mahesh Bhatt admits that the religious angle in the film was complicated and he was heartened by Ashutosh Rana's innate understanding. 'It's not possible to survive for so long in the film industry unless your roots run deep,' he asserts.

In the early 2000s, Tanuja Chandra had directed a short film in which her 'dushman' surprised her by playing a compassionate character who inspires admiration and respect. 'In our films, the distinction between positive and negative characters is very definite, but when the writing is nuanced, an actor like Ashutosh can bring something original and wonderful to the table,' she asserts.

Chandra admits that while she would like to cast him as a bad man again, it might also be interesting to explore the space between good and evil, with the actor playing a character that is a mix of both, making him all the more dangerous. As her imagination takes wings, the filmmaker also toys with the idea of directing one of her favourite actors in a mature love story that is contemporary yet has that old-world charm. 'He could play a character who falls in love for the first time at 50 plus and through the film, navigates this strangely unfamiliar world of romance,' she says dreamily.

Even Mahesh Bhatt admits he would like to cast him as a 'hero' in a film, which raises the question: what is Ashutosh Rana like as a person? According to Chandra, he is a hardworking, respectful man with a delightful sense of humour, who reads a lot and has an insatiable hunger to learn new things.

'He always wants to learn,' the director says, remembering how delighted the actor used to be when told he had done a wonderful take. At the same time, he would not complain if asked to do another, happy to be given the chance to better his performance. 'And then there is his impressive command over Hindi. If you speak the language well, interacting with him can help you brush up on it. If you don't, it might help you learn it,' she laughs.

Ashutosh Rana, who is currently playing Ravana in Gaurav Bhardwaj's epic play *Humare Ram*, which portrays unseen stories from the Ramayana on stage, wants to play everything, from the King of Lanka to Vivekananda, from Krishna to Kamsa, from Duryodhana to Chanakya. 'Some of these people may no longer be alive, but *vyakti nahin rahe to kya hua* [so what if a person is not around], their *vyaktitva* [personality] will make these characters memorable,' he asserts.

One remembers his gang lord in *Awarapan* (2007) saying, '*Kissi insaan ka kadd jaanna ho, to pata lagao ke uske dushman kaun hain... Jitna bada dushman, utna bada woh* [To know the stature of a man, find out who his enemies are. The bigger the foe, the more powerful he is].' Well, this 'dushman' will always stand tall, no matter what he plays; and Rana-ji's fans will always look up to him with respect.

PUNEET ISSAR
REACHING EPIC HEIGHTS

'Bhratashri, lagate hain Draupadi ko dau par?'

—*Mahabharat* (1988–90)

24 July 1982.* It was Puneet Issar's first day on the set of Manmohan Desai's action comedy *Coolie* (1983). The son of director Sudesh Issar, he had landed the role of Bob when he accompanied filmmaker Yash Johar to Desai's set and impressed Man-ji, as the filmmaker was fondly called within the film fraternity, with his Atlas build, deep voice and martial arts moves. The debutant villain, who stood tall at six feet three inches, flexed his muscles, ready to take on the country's biggest superstar in the first shot of his life. All eyes were on the duo as they faced the camera for a scene they had rehearsed half a dozen times already, with Amitabh Bachchan, in the titular role of Iqbal Aslam Khan, easily dodging the younger actor's mock killer punches during their practice runs. 'Lights, camera, action!' the director hollered, and Puneet Issar's fists flashed. The senior actor, mistiming his jump, landed heavily on the table, its sharp edge ramming

---

*Bobb, Dilip, Chander Uday Singh, and Gita Abraham, 'From the India Today Archives (1982) | Coolie Mishap: When Amitabh Bachchan Had a Brush with Death', *India Today*, 6 March 2023, https://tinyurl.com/fbkdyuew. Accessed on 16 May 2024.

into his gut as he rolled off. He lay on the ground, motionless.

At this point, not many realized that the shot had gone wrong. In fact, there was a smattering of applause from the bystanders as, with a grimace of pain, Amitabh Bachchan slowly rose to his feet, clutching his stomach. Almost immediately, he crumpled to the ground, and Manmohan Desai rushed to his side. In response to his concerned queries, the 40-year-old actor admitted that he was hurt. A tense silence suddenly descended over the unit parked on the Jnana Bharathi campus of Bangalore University. The star was sent to his hotel to rest. Shooting continued, but the initial anticipation and elation had evaporated.

A doctor attended to Amitabh Bachchan in his hotel suite, prescribed a few sedatives and left, assuring him that it was a minor injury and there was no cause for concern. He advised the actor to sleep off the pain, but Bachchan spent the night in excruciating agony. The next morning, his family physician, K.M. Shah, was urgently summoned from Bombay. By now, it was beginning to dawn on Desai and his unit that all was not well with their leading man.

His family doctor wanted an X-ray done immediately, but it didn't reveal anything serious. However, the pain did not abate, and on the third day, another X-ray was done. There were signs of internal bleeding in this one. It was now obvious to everyone that something was seriously wrong with the superstar. A leading urologist, Dr H.S. Bhatt, joined the medical team, and a rupture in the intestine that had resulted in septicaemia was detected. The situation was grave as the star was wheeled in for an emergency splenectomy. For three days, he hovered between life and death in Bangalore. Then, on 31 July, following a slight improvement in his condition, he was flown home to Bombay.

He underwent a second surgery at Breach Candy Hospital and was declared clinically dead for some time before being put on a ventilator. It was the breaking news of the day. His family was devastated and his legion of fans distraught. However, the fighter that he was, Amitabh Bachchan battled on valiantly like he had so many times on screen, and was sitting up three days after the surgery. It would take another fortnight before he was off the critical list. Meanwhile, public anger against Puneet Issar was swelling with each passing day that their beloved 'angry young man' spent on a hospital bed. From a budding khalnayak on screen, he had become a real-life villain.

Thinking back to that dark period in his life 40 years later, Puneet Issar admits that he would get lots of blank, abusive and even threatening calls. Not surprising, given that Amitabh Bachchan was not just a much-loved Bollywood star but also a national icon. 'He had been my hero too for years, and I was guilt-stricken that he was in so much pain because of me,' laments the actor, who would visit the hospital frequently to check on the ailing superstar. His wife, Deepali, who shares a blood group with Bachchan, even donated blood for his treatment.

'One day, as I was leaving Breach Candy Hospital, a group of ladies sitting in the waiting room stopped me to ask how their hero was doing. I was overcome with emotion and simply nodded to indicate that he was slightly better. As I was walking away, I heard one of them say that someone had tried to kill Amit-ji and if she ever came face to face with the person, she would slap him hard. As I made a quick getaway, I thanked God that they hadn't recognized me, but all the way home, the guilt weighed heavily on me,' the actor reminisces.

When Amitabh Bachchan learnt that Puneet Issar had been branded a villain by an unforgiving *janta* (public), he sent a message across that he wanted to meet the young actor. 'Deepali and I drove to the hospital immediately. Amit-ji was still in the ICU, surrounded by a maze of machines. He had undergone a tracheostomy and a life-saving tracheal tube was sticking out of a cut in his neck. There were other tubes attached to him while several monitors kept constant vigil over his vitals,' he recounts.

The superstar assured them that he was feeling much better, but the famous baritone was a raspy, scratchy whisper. Guilt seared through Puneet Issar and tears welled up in his eyes. Amitabh Bachchan insisted that what had happened was just an accident and he should not blame himself for it. The words didn't reassure the young actor, and understanding this, the ailing superstar narrated how when they were shooting for a Prakash Mehra film, a glass he had aimed at Vinod Khanna had caught his co-star straight in the chin. 'Vinod was supposed to duck so it would sail past him harmlessly before crashing into the wall, but perhaps I moved too fast or he reacted a fraction of a second too late, he ended up with a deep cut in his chin which required six to seven stitches,' recounted Bachchan, realizing that the guilt he had felt then was what the younger actor was experiencing now. He told him what Vinod Khanna had told him back then, 'Relax, it was just an accident!'

As Puneet Issar got up to leave, he got out of bed, too, and throwing a friendly arm around his shoulder, laboriously walked the 10–15 steps to the door so that those strolling down the hospital's corridor or those seated in the waiting room could see them. 'It was his way of telling everyone that all was well between us to put the rumours to rest,' the younger actor surmises. To this day, he is eternally grateful to the superstar for his show of support. 'Amit-ji is not just one of our finest actors, but also a magnanimous man,' he asserts.

Amitabh Bachchan resumed shooting for *Coolie* on 7 January 1983. The location had changed; the same set had now been erected at Bombay's Chandivali Studio. It was the same shot, and the two actors picked up from where they had left off. Aware of the media scrutiny, the superstar treated his comeback like just another day at work. Puneet Issar admits that during the rehearsals, his heart was in his mouth as a montage of the accident flashed before his eyes. 'I was even more cautious during the shot, which thankfully, was okayed in one take. As those around us started clapping, I began to breathe again,' he narrates, the relief apparent even after four decades.

Coolie opened in the theatres on 2 December 1983. Manmohan Desai had rewritten the original ending, allowing his coolie to live after being shot by Kader Khan's Zafar Khan several times. In the original script, Iqbal had breathed his last shortly afterwards, but in the rewrite, bolstered by the prayers of coolies of all faiths, he makes a miraculous recovery. The action scene during which Amitabh Bachchan got injured was frozen for a few seconds, with a message appearing on screen to mark the moment. It struck an emotional note with the audience who packed the theatres. *Coolie* was a blockbuster!

It was just the kind of launch Puneet Issar had always dreamt of. But following the accident, while Amitabh Bachchan became a bigger superstar, Puneet continued to be perceived as a monster and ostracized by all. The senior actor may have forgiven him, but his fans hadn't. The blank calls, the abuse and threats continued; so did the hate mail. The younger actor didn't feature in Bachchan and Desai's next film, *Mard* (1985). In fact, the superstar and he haven't worked in another film since the accident. The film fraternity immediately jumped to the conclusion that he had been dumped by the duo, and many who had signed him replaced him in their films.

'I lost seven to eight films, and after that, the offers just dried up. From mid-1982 to almost 1986, maybe even 1987, I went through a really bad phase. But the struggle has only made me a stronger person,' Puneet Issar states, with no trace of bitterness, rancour or regret in his voice. To keep the kitchen fires burning, he started accepting minor roles, like that of Inspector Vijay in *Raja Aur Rana* (1984) and Rocky in Feroz Khan's *Janbaaz* (1986). In Tulsi and Shyam Ramsay's horror film, *Purana Mandir* (1984), he plays the hero's friend Anand. The film is a cult classic; but back then, a Ramsay film was not a feather in an actor's cap, so despite its phenomenal success, Puneet was still unable to find much work.

In Ashim Samanta's *Palay Khan* (1986), he plays Amar Singh, the loyal associate of the freedom fighter who rebels against British tyranny, but the film flopped. Ravi Chopra's critically acclaimed *Dahleez* (1986); another Ramsay horror film, *Tahkhana* (1986); the unofficial Bollywood remake *Superman* (1987), with him as the legendary superhero; T. Rama Rao's multi-starrer *Watan Ke Rakhwale* (1987); and J.P. Dutta's action-packed *Hathyar* (1989) showcased his versatility, but Puneet Issar's career refused to take off.

It was Avtar Bhogal's revenge drama, *Zakhmi Aurat* (1988), which finally turned the tide for him. He plays the rapist, Sukhdev, who is castrated in a gruesome form of revenge. '*Zakhmi Aurat* was my first substantial role after *Coolie* and it gave me a chance to prove myself as an actor. Till then, I had been dismissed as a fighter because I am an eighth-degree black belt in martial arts, and the validation felt good,' admits the actor, who was finally back in the race after a six-year struggle.

The same year, B.R. Chopra's television series, *Mahabharat*, started airing from 2 October 1988. Two years earlier, impressed by his physique, the producer and director had wanted to cast him as Bhima in his epic extravaganza; but to his surprise, Puneet Issar requested to be considered for the role of Duryodhana, wowing Chopra and his writer Dr Rahi Masoom Raza during the audition, not just with his performance and voice but also with his familiarity with literary works on the subject. 'I know Ramdhari Singh Dinkar's epic poem *Rashmirathi* by heart and can recite verses from Maithili Sharan Gupt's *maha kavya* [epic], *Jayadrath Vadh*, verbatim,' he says with understandable pride.

The director told Puneet that he could play Duryodhana if he could find another actor who was taller and bigger than him for playing Bhima. He did, in the Asian Games gold-medalist and Commonwealth Games silver-medalist discus thrower Praveen Kumar Sobti who, at six feet seven inches, topped him by four inches. It took two years for the shooting of *Mahabharat* to start, so Puneet had plenty of time to prepare for what would become the defining role of his career.

The eldest of the Kauravas starts out as a wilful, hot-headed and obdurate crown prince of the Kuru dynasty who, despite Bhishma Pitama's well-meaning advice, refuses to give even an inch of land to his Pandava cousins; instead, he is easily led down the garden path by his uncle Shakuni. Acknowledging this, the actor says, 'Even in the television series, till the thirty-eighth episode, Duryodhana is a shallow 20-year-old boy, but by the time we reached the forty-sixth episode, both he and I had grown in confidence and stature. The audience too was responding well to my character, and through long discussions with Chopra-sahab and his duo of writers, Dr Rahi Masoom Raza and Pandit Narendra Sharma, Duryodhana evolved to hold his own.'

By then, he knew not just his own lines by heart, but the dialogues of his co-stars as well. When in front of the camera, Puneet Issar did not need a single retake. He also put on an extra 22 kilograms to tilt the scales at 108 kilograms for the battle royale in the climax, shot over 18 days without any stunt doubles or cables. 'Praveen Kumar beat me black and blue with a real mace in the finale,' he remembers with a laugh. But the final victory was his. Like Amitabh Bachchan became the invincible Vijay after *Zanjeer* (1973) and *Deewaar* (1975), like Amjad Khan is still remembered as *Sholay*'s (1975) Gabbar Singh, and like Amrish Puri will always be *Mr. India*'s (1987) Mogambo, Puneet Issar, to this day, is instantly identified with *Mahabharat*'s Duryodhana despite the fact that many other actors have played the role before him and since.

Interestingly, Mukesh Khanna, popular as the superhero Shaktimaan, was the first choice for Duryodhana. 'But after 15 films as a hero, I didn't think I could play a villain convincingly. *Main andar se villain nahin hoon* [I am not a villain deep down], which is why I turned down the opportunity,' shares the actor. He went on to play Bhishma Pitama, able to empathize with the man who takes a vow of celibacy to remain a *brahmachari* (bachelor) all his life so his father, Shantanu, can marry the woman he loves, Satyavati, and their son can ascend the throne. Vijayendra Ghatge had been signed for the role initially, but dropped out because he did not want to sport a long, white beard.

Thinking back to his *Mahabharat* experience, Mukesh Khanna admits that initially they were all nervous because unlike the Ramayana, people weren't too familiar with this epic. 'To make matters worse, my wig did not fit properly. Only after we got one custom-made was I able to get into my stride,' informs the actor, remembering that Puneet Issar too had been a relative newcomer when he made his entry. 'But he used his physique and voice to his advantage, evolving as an actor. There have been many *Mahabharat*s since, but everyone is unanimous in their opinion that he is the best Duryodhana,' he applauds. Puneet recalls Mukesh Khanna as a senior actor who gave him a *chavvani* (25-paisa coin) for every good performance. 'I ended up with a pile of chavvanis,' he guffaws.

While Gajendra Chauhan as Yudhishthira, Praveen Kumar Sobti as Bhima, Arjun Firoz Khan as Arjuna and Mukesh Khanna as Bhishma Pitama were revered, Duryodhana quickly became the most hated man in the country. More so after Draupadi's attempted *vastraharan* (disrobing), without which, as Puneet Issar points out, there would have been no Mahabharata. Having gone through it earlier with *Coolie*, the toxicity did not bother him. 'I knew I had passed the test when, during a shoot in Jaipur, towards the end of the '80s or early '90s, Chopra-sahab and his *Mahabharat* team were invited to dinner at the palatial bungalow of one of the city's prominent Marwari families,' he reminisces.

By then, Puneet Issar was a household name, so he was somewhat surprised when the ladies of the house, who were serving the celebrity guests themselves, their faces decorously covered, studiously avoided him, leaving the servants to attend to him. 'It was even more baffling when Roopa Ganguly, who played Draupadi and was seated next to me, was suddenly whisked away from the table and taken inside. When she returned, she took a chair across the table from me, between Arjun [Arjun Firoz Khan] and Krishna

[Nitish Bharadwaj]. When our eyes met, she smirked,' he recounts.

Bemused by this strange behaviour, the actor finally reached out and grabbed the hand of the family matriarch as she was passing by, walking purposefully towards Bharadwaj with a bowl, and asked politely, '*Mataji*, won't you serve me too?' Even more miffed, she stalked away imperiously without bothering to answer him. The mystery was solved only after they got back to their hotel, with Roopa Ganguly explaining that so repulsed were they by his on-screen avatar, the ladies had begun to dislike Puneet Issar in real life. In fact, the elderly lady he had stopped, who was their host's grandmother, had even reprimanded her for sitting next to the wicked Duryodhana and insisted she switch places.

'Rather than upsetting me, this incident filled me with delight. Since I didn't get too many compliments, it was proof that I was doing my job convincingly,' exults the actor who, for two-and-a-half years, ruled in living rooms across the country every Sunday morning. Success was heady, but it took its toll. Every shot was preceded by intense mental conditioning and arduous physical prep, and as Duryodhana's importance in the narrative grew, his workload increased.

'For 12 hours a day, from 9.00 a.m. to 9.00 p.m., I would be shooting for *Mahabharat*. Then I would hurry back home, grab a quick bite and take a shower, and return to BR Recording Studio for two to three hours of dubbing every day. My voice grew gruff and my eyes turned red from exhaustion. I became increasingly short-tempered despite regular yoga *pranayama*s and *shavasana*s, snapping at everyone,' he admits, quick to add that he never threw temper tantrums in public.

The show aired every Sunday at 9.00 a.m., and life across

the country seemed to come to a standstill during that one hour as everyone, young and old, gathered in front of the television sets. One morning, at around 11.00 a.m., Puneet Issar got a call. The voice was familiar, but unexpected. Manmohan Desai raved, '*Kya kaam kiya hai Puneet, mazaa aa gaya* [What a performance Puneet, I loved it]!' The praise continued for a good 20 minutes. The duo reunited for Ketan Desai's *Anmol* (1993), a Cinderella-like love story with Rishi Kapoor and Manisha Koirala in the lead. It was the last film Manmohan Desai produced before his untimely death on 1 March 1994.

Mahabharat put Puneet Issar back on track and he continued with villainy in other films. In J.P. Dutta's crime drama *Hathyar* (1989), he is one of Paresh Rawal's henchmen who snatches Sangeeta Bijlani's baby from her arms and runs down the street. 'We were shooting in a marketplace and as soon as J.P.-sahab shouted "action", I dived into the milling crowd, grabbed the baby and sprinted away. For about 200 metres, I was chased by an irate mob who had no clue we were shooting a film. It was only after J.P.-sahab shouted "cut" that they realized I was not a kidnapper for real and walked away,' he laughs, relieved that he had not been beaten up. But he could not shake off the strange sense of unease brought on by the expression in the six-month-old baby's eyes. 'He had stared into my eyes for a moment before he started bawling and I realized at that moment that I didn't feel good about playing such roles,' Puneet confides, recalling how much he had also hated playing the mafia don Rana in Keshu Ramsay's *Ashaant* (1993) who prints fake currency notes and poses a threat to the country's security.

However, there were moments of pure pleasure as well. The same year, when he was shooting for another J.P. Dutta film, *Kshatriya* (1993), in Rajasthan, Puneet, who played Shakti Singh, the son of the scheming diwan of Mirtagarh, would have long conversations with Dharmendra, who religiously watched *Mahabharat* every Sunday and would discuss certain scenes with him in great detail. 'It felt wonderful!' he recalls.

Vijay Anand's 'Puneet, you are fantastic!' is another compliment he will always cherish as it came from one of the greatest directors of Hindi cinema. The legendary writer-producer-director Kamal Amrohi was also a huge fan of *Mahabharat* and never missed a single episode. His son, Tajdar Amrohi, reveals that his father, who had written classics like *Jailor* (1938), *Pukar* (1939), *Mahal* (1949), *Mughal-E-Azam* (1960), *Pakeezah* (1972) and *Razia Sultan* (1983), would often compliment his friend, Dr Rahi Masoom Raza, on his erudite and ornamental dialogue in the television series. 'Rahi-sahab would tell Baba that he was his role model and sometimes would even ask him to translate an Urdu word into Hindi. So, *takhliya*, used to good effect in *Mughal-E-Azam* as a plea for privacy or solitude, became "*ekant*" in *Mahabharat*,' he smiles.

He remembers that B.R. Chopra was extremely particular about the written word and would not move to the next episode unless he was completely satisfied with the dialogue, even if this meant that they shot only one episode a week. Tajdar Amrohi went to college with Puneet Issar's wife Deepali and remembers the actor as an amiable, smiling man with the voice of a villain. 'I would sometimes ask Deepali jokingly if Puneet used the same tone with her and she would burst out laughing,' he chuckles.

Mahabharat brought along a surprise offer from South India for Puneet. 'Bapu-garu wants to speak to you,' he was told one day as he took a call. The soft-spoken director, who had helmed Anil Kapoor and Vijayata Pandit's superhit love story *Mohabbat* (1985), wanted him to take a flight out to Hyderabad. The actor didn't think twice. 'I had loved Bapu-garu's Telugu mythological film *Seeta Kalyanam* [1976] and it was an honour to be introduced to his unit as *Mahabharat*'s Duryodhana, the "Godfather of Indian cinema" insisting that no one could have performed the role better,' he reminisces proudly.

The actor landed a role in Bapu's Telugu ETV devotional serial *Sri Bhagavatam*. That was the beginning of a successful innings in the South. He went on to feature in three Telugu Chiranjeevi starrers, *Master* (1997), *Indra: The Tiger* (2002) and *Tagore* (2003), and teamed up with Mohanlal in Sangeeth Sivan's *Yoddha* (1992), playing the black magician Vishaka in the sword and sorcery film. The following year, the actors reunited for another Malayalam film, the murder mystery *Pingami* (1994).

Puneet Issar also forayed into Tamil cinema with *I Love India* (1993) and *Uzhaippaali* (1993), and worked in Kannada films like *Samrat* (1994), *Rasika* (1994) and *Time Bomb* (1994). 'I experimented with Bengali cinema as well, films like *Bhagya Debata* [1995], *Josh* [2010] and *Besh Korechi Prem Korechi* [2015], and did a few Punjabi films like *Best of Luck* [2013] and *Fateh* [2014],' informs the actor, who wrote and directed a Punjabi film, *I Am Singh* (2011), on the plight of Sikh and Asian immigrants targeted by neo-Nazis and bigoted police in the US after the 9/11 attacks.

Before this, he had directed the TV action serial, *Hindustani*, and the small-screen mythological show, *Jai Mata Ki*. The latter features Hema Malini as Adi Shakti, Mahakali, Saraswati, Lakshmi and all other forms of Durga. Puneet owes his directorial debut in Bollywood to Salman Khan, whom he had crossed swords with in several Hindi films, including *Sanam Bewafa* (1991), *Jaagruti* (1993), *Suryavanshi* (1992), *Chandra Mukhi* (1993), *Partner* (2007), *God Tussi Great Ho* (2008) and *Ready* (2011).

'My father knew Salman's scriptwriter father, Salim Khan-sahab. Since I had a perfect 10 physique and was the only one at the time who was a martial arts expert, Salman looked up to me as an elder brother. When I was 22 and he was a wide-eyed boy of 14 or 15, he would hang around me while I trained. I would give him workout tips and he even accompanied me on a month-long schedule of *Purana Mandir* (1984) to Murud-Janjira,' Puneet informs.

By the time they got to working together in *Sanam Bewafa*, Salman Khan was a superstar, but their equation did not change. In 2002, the star promised to cast Puneet Issar in one of his films, but after that he didn't hear from him for around nine months. 'Then one day, he called my home and asked for the "big man" to come over. When I went across, Salman narrated the script of *Garv: Pride and Honour* [2004], and told me that I would be directing the film.' The surprise is still apparent in his voice. The action drama stars Salman in the lead, along with his brother Arbaaz.

A decade later, from 2014–15, Puneet participated in the eighth season of television reality show, *Bigg Boss*, hosted by Salman Khan. At 56, he was one of the oldest participants and one of the seven finalists. Gautam Gulati took the trophy, but the actor considers it an achievement that he lasted in the *Bigg Boss* house for 105 days.

In 2015, he made his stage debut. Rahul Bhuchar, who runs a theatre group in Delhi, approached him with a two-and-a-half-hour play, written in verse by Atul Satya

Koushik. *Raavan Ki Ramayan* interpreted the familiar epic from the point of view of its antagonist and premiered in Delhi on 6 August 2016. He cast Puneet Issar in the titular role of the King of Lanka, a wise sage and a devout Brahmin, a Shiva *bhakt* and a fearless warrior. The actor shed 15 kilograms, doing an hour of cardio, along with three hours of weight-training, running and martial arts daily, while following a stringent diet.

'Language has never been a problem. I had taught Sunny Deol and Sanjay Dutt Hindi and Urdu as their diction teacher, when they were being groomed for their launch during a short tenure at Roshan Taneja's acting academy,' the actor says proudly. But this time, it was different because if he changed even one word, the metre would change. He rehearsed for eight long months, memorizing every word before taking the stage. He made an impressive Ravana, flooring chief guest L.K. Advani and his daughter Pratibha with his power-packed histrionics and his command over the language at the play's premiere. 'After that, at the end of every show, on popular demand, I had to recite Duryodhana's dialogue from the *Mahabharat.* Even one word like "*mamashri*" had the audience clapping and cheering loudly,' he smiles.

He returned to the battleground with StarPlus's 2013 tele-epic *Mahabharat*, this time as Parashurama, with Arpit Ranka playing Duryodhana. In 2018, he brought a spin-off to the stage—*Mahabharata: The Epic Tale*, which he acted in, directed, and co-wrote with his son Siddhant in verse, reinterpreting the epic from the perspective of Karna and Duryodhana, drawing from Bhasa's Sanskrit play *Urubhangam.* He plays the older Duryodhana and Siddhant the younger version of the Kaurava, with Rahul Bhuchar as Karna.

Puneet Issar cast some of his former colleagues from B.R. Chopra's *Mahabharat,* like the late Gufi Paintal and Surendra Pal, in their familiar roles as Shakuni and Dronacharya. There were a few new faces too, like Urvashi Dholakia as Draupadi, Yashodhan Rana as Krishna, and Karan Sharma as Arjuna. Giant LED screens showing birds flying, deer flitting and pyres burning played behind the actors, with props in front, to give the impression of a 3D film. 'It took Siddhant and me two years to write the script with the idea that no character in Mahabharata, not even Yudhisthira, is completely white. Nor for that matter is Duryodhana totally black. Our play underlines that amidst all the greed, politicking and betrayals, the friendship between Duryodhana and Karna is as pure as the driven snow. The Mahabharata doesn't tell us what to do; if anything, it shows us what not to do, and that makes it interesting for me as an actor, writer and director to come up with different adaptations,' he explains.

After seeing this Mahabharata on stage, Mukesh Khanna presented Puneet with a ₹500 note, telling him to count how many chavvanis it amounted to. The play's run was cut short by the Covid-19 pandemic, but it returned a year-and-a-half later, in November 2021, with the 60-member troupe in a bio-bubble and security guards to keep the crowds at bay.

In 2022, he unveiled a four-year labour of love, *Jai Shri Ram: Ramayana,* in Mumbai. Co-written in verse with his son again, this stage adaptation of the Ramayana has him as Ravana, Siddhant as Rama, and Vindu Dara Singh as Hanuman. 'It is embellished with *chaupai*s and *doha*s [couplets], a dozen songs and four dances performed live. The technical team of the Broadway musicals *Aladdin* and *Beauty and the Beast* designed our LED backdrops,' informs Puneet Issar, whose association with the epics continues.

'Where there is Rama, there's Ravana. Where there is Krishna and Arjuna, there's Duryodhana and Karna too. Like every hero, every villain also has his own story. It is for us to bring that story to the world,' he concludes.

ACKNOWLEDGEMENTS

The idea for this book came from my commissioning editor, Rudra Narayan Sharma. I was working with him on another book, *Matinee Men: My Journey through Bollywood*, when he called me one evening and wondered if I would be interested in doing a book on Bollywood's bad men. I agreed immediately, simply for the pleasure of working with Rudra again, then wondered what I had got myself into because the gallery of rogues is so diverse and exhaustive. Whom do I include? Whom do I leave out? After much deliberation, I settled on these 13 (a good number for baddies) iconic villains simply because, with the exception of Jeevan and Amjad Khan, I had interacted personally with all of them.

I remain grateful to Pran-sahab for taking me through his life's journey at a time when talking was difficult. And to his son, Sunil Sikand, for a quick fact check on the chapter when he was no more.

Ajit-sahab was always just a call away. Till the 'Lion' fell silent.

Today, when actors rarely respond to WhatsApp texts, Danny Sir, who had spoken to me on the phone during the Covid-19 lockdown, apologized for not being prompt due to erratic network in Sikkim when going over his chapter. I ended up telling him about my childhood in Darjeeling and Shillong; how I can still taste the fresh air, smell the pines and touch the conifers. 'These memories will remain with you throughout your life,' he assured me.

I also caught Shakti Kapoor during the pandemic while he was on an evening walk on the beach alone. We spoke till an unexpected shower sent him rushing home, and continued our discussion the next evening. When I sent him the final chapter, he responded with a 'v nice' and a 'God Bless' sticker.

While Prem Chopra did not introduce himself saying *'Prem naam hai mera, Prem Chopra,'* he did give me the story behind his now iconic dialogue. Again, I have to thank Alexander Graham Bell's invention, the telephone, for staying connected to him.

Contrary to their screen image, 'Bad Man' Gulshan Grover and *Mahabharat's* Duryodhana Puneet Issar are courteous, articulate and affable gentlemen. It is always easy to chat with them.

I had resigned myself to going without a chapter on Ranjeet Sir when he finally called, in response to my numerous messages, and invited me to his home. I was thrilled to see an earlier book of mine, *Bad Man*, the memoir of Gulshan Grover, in his study and promised to add another one to the collection soon.

I was quite disappointed with the first draft of the chapter on Amjad Khan; it lacked emotion since I had never met him. A journalist friend, Farhana Farook, and late producer N.N. Sippy's daughter, Shabnam Pillai, suggested I speak to his wife. Shehla Ma'am turned 'Gabbar Singh' into a man of flesh and blood.

Many thanks to Renuka Shahane who put me in touch with her Rana-ji. As always, Ashutosh Rana floored me with his thoughts, and his high-flowing Hindi.

I had spoken with an ailing Sadashiv Amrapurkar-sahab about *Sadak*. After his untimely demise, his daughter, filmmaker Rima Amrapurkar, carried his story forward by sending me precise voice notes in her lovely voice.

Srishti Kumar coordinated a telephonic interview with her father, Kiran Kumar, and he brought his own father, Jeevan-sahab, alive during our conversation, while sharing his own story of stardom. Later, Srishti went out of her way to get the okay on the final edit within our deadline despite her phone crashing during those tense few days.

My meeting with Amrish Puri-ji had been too brief, but speaking with his grandson, actor Vardhan Puri, I learnt that his collection of hats, watches and shoes made Mogambo *khush* (happy).

I would also like to acknowledge Subhash Ghai, Mahesh Bhatt, Manoj Kumar, Biswajit Chatterjee, Prem Sagar, Boney Kapoor and the late Satish Kaushik for their inputs. I am also grateful to Dharmesh Darshan, Pankaj Parashar, Tanuja Chandra, Chandra Barot, Tajdar Amrohi and Nilesh Sahay. This book belongs to all of you.

Rudra has been an empathetic commissioning editor who, whenever I have turned to him with a problem, says, '*Main hoon na* [I am there],' borrowing the title of the Shah Rukh Khan blockbuster. My editors, Anshuman Yadav and Gauri Chopra, have also been extremely patient, wonderfully considerate and amazingly meticulous. This was Anshuman's last book with Rupa; he extended his last working day to finish it.

Thank you all.

Lastly, thanks to my husband, Pallab, my mother-in-law, Pushpa, and my daughter, Ranjika, who have lived through so many of my bad moods. Dolly Parton famously said, 'I think all creative people are a little bit nuts.' I have to agree.

✕